The Apocalypse Commentary of Tyconius

To Joe with best wishes,

Ken

European University Studies

Europäische Hochschulschriften
Publications Universitaires Européennes

Series XXIII

Theology

Reihe XXIII Série XXIII

Theologie
Théologie

Vol./Bd. 301

PETER LANG
Frankfurt am Main · Bern · New York

Kenneth B. Steinhauser

The Apocalypse Commentary of Tyconius

A History of Its Reception and Influence

PETER LANG
Frankfurt am Main · Bern · New York

CIP-Kurztitelaufnahme der Deutschen Bibliothek

Steinhauser, Kenneth B.:

The apocalypse commentary of Tyconius : a history of its reception and influence / Kenneth B. Steinhauser. – Frankfurt am Main ; Bern ; New York : Lang, 1987.
(European university studies ; Ser. 23; Theology ; Vol. 301)
ISBN 3-8204-9582-7
NE: Europäische Hochschulschriften / 23

Library of Congress Cataloging-in-Publication Data

Steinhauser, Kenneth B., 1946-
The Apocalypse commentary of Tyconius.

(European university studies. Series XXIII, Theology ; vol. 301 = Europäische Hochschulschriften. Reihe XIII, Theologie, ISSN 0721-3409 ; Bd. 301)
Thesis (doctoral)--Albert-Ludwigs-Univeristät, Freiburg im Breisgau, 1986.
Bibliography: p.
1. Ticonius, 4th cent. Commentarius in Apocalypsin. 2. Bible. N.T. Revelation–Criticism, interpretation, etc.--History. I. Title. II. Series: Europäische Hochschulschriften. Reihe XXIII, Theologie ; Bd. 301.
BS2825.S74 1987 228'.07 86-28728
ISBN 3-8204-9582-7

D 25

ISSN 0721-3409
ISBN 3-8204-9582-7

Printed in Germany

TABLE OF CONTENTS

Abbreviations

Standard English abbreviations, including the abbreviations of biblical books, have been taken from Joseph Gibaldi and Walter S. Achtert, MLA Handbook for Writers of Research Papers, Theses, and Dissertations (New York: Modern Language Association, 1980). The abbreviations of theological journals, dictionaries, lexica, series, etc. have been taken from Siegfried Schwertner, Theologische Realenzyklopädie: Abkürzungsverzeichnis (Berlin: Walter de Gruyter, 1976).

Preface

The present work was accepted as a doctoral dissertation by the Theological Faculty of the University of Freiburg im Breisgau in the Summer Semester of 1986. I would like to thank my mentor and teacher, Prof. Dr. Karl Suso Frank, for his help and advice -- and I might add for his patience -- in guiding the progress of my research. In addition, I also wish to thank Prof. Dr. Helmut Riedlinger for his evaluation of the work.

Certainly I owe a debt of thanks to my ordinary, the Most Reverend Francis J. Mugavero, Bishop of Brooklyn, for his encouragement and support of my scholarly work. The Diocese of Brooklyn generously provided the scholarship for my studies in Tübingen and Freiburg.

I would also like to thank my colleagues who sit on the Faculty Development Committee of Belmont Abbey College for providing the publication grant.

Finally, I dedicate this work to my mother and to the memory of my late father. To them I say a special word of thanks.

Belmont, North Carolina — Kenneth B. Steinhauser

September 27, 1986

Chapter I

Introduction to the lost commentary

A. The problem

Without a doubt the greatest obstacle to the progress of Tyconian research has been the loss of his Apocalypse Commentary. This loss not only limits our access to the thought of a controversial churchman and independent theologian but also deprives us of the first attempt in the western Church to apply a system of exegetical rules to the interpretation of a single biblical book. The unique character and importance of Tyconius' Apocalypse Commentary is confirmed by its tremendous influence on subsequent writers in late antiquity and the early Middle Ages. Indeed we can be thankful that later generations acknowledged the importance of Tyconius' commentary by borrowing from it extensively; otherwise we would have no significant knowledge of its contents. Nine authors have had immediate[1] access to the Apocalypse Commentary of Tyconius, which is reflected in their writings. Proceeding chronologically, we have Jerome's revision of the commentary of Victorinus of Pettau,[2] the so-called pseudo-Augustinian homilies written by Caesarius of Arles,[3] the commentary of Primasius of Hadrumetum,[4] the <u>Complexiones</u> of Cassiodore,[5] the <u>Commemoratorium</u> of pseudo-Jerome,[6] an anonymous capitulary contained in the Codex Oratorii B6,[7] the commentary of Bede the Venerable,[8] the lengthy commentary of Ambrosius Autpertus,[9] and finally the commentary of Beatus of Liébana.[10] In varying degrees these authors have passed on the contents of the lost Apocalypse Commentary of Tyconius in some cases quoting his words verbatim. In addition, there are two manuscript fragments, both of which have been published: Turin F. IV. 1. 18[11] and Budapest S. Fr. 1. m. 1.[12] Although the monastery at Saint Gall listed a manuscript of the work in a catalogue of the ninth century, no manuscript is to be found there.[13] The problem, with which we are confronted may be stated rather simply: To what extent, if at all, is a reconstruction of the text of the lost commentary of Tyconius possible using the data which standing at our disposal?

B. History of the research

1. The first approach -- a preference for Beatus
2. The second approach -- from Beatus to the Turin Fragment
3. The third approach -- looking elsewhere

Fortunately, we are not forced to start from scratch in attempting to answer this question. Past research has borne fruit on two accounts. First, previous studies, though incomplete, have brought the problem into sharp focus, delineating clearly the task which lies before us. Second, a great number of passages influenced by Tyconius have been identified and occasionally the exact text of the lost commentary has been retrieved. A brief survey of the research will provide an excellent point of departure in approaching this question. One may identify three distinct approaches, or perhaps three schools of thought, among scholars who have researched the Apocalypse Commentary of Tyconius. The first approach was characterized above all by a preference for using the commentary of Beatus in attempting to arrive at Tyconius. In the second approach there was a definite shift away from Beatus toward the Turin Fragment as the more faithful transmitter of Tyconius' lost work. The third approach has been marked by a greater desire to consider the other commentaries, which have been somewhat neglected in earlier studies, while the question of choosing between Beatus and the Turin Fragment has fallen into the background.

1. The first approach -- a preference for Beatus

In 1886 J. Haußleiter[14] proposed the possibility of reconstructing the lost commentary of Tyconius on the basis of comparisons among the commentaries of Primasius and Bede taken together, the pseudo-Augustinian homilies, and above all the commentary of Beatus of Liébana. His concrete text examples come from the commentaries of Primasius and Beatus, both of whom copied from Tyconius. Since Beatus did not use Primasius' commentary in composing his work, any agreement between them may be traced back to Tyconius as a common source. Haußleiter believed further that Beatus was extremely faithful to his sources and copied from them accurately. Nevertheless, from the very beginning he conceded that the Tyconian commentary could be only partially reconstructed. In the same year W. Bousset[15] described how to go about reconstructing Tyconius' lost commentary. One must search out the passages where Beatus has parallels either in Primasius' commentary or in the pseudo-Augustinian homilies. However, since Beatus, Primasius, and pseudo-Augustine also share the Hieronymian recension of Victorinus' commentary as a common source, the passages in which they agree with Jerome may be eliminated from consideration; where the commentaries otherwise correspond, one may be certain of a Tyconian influence. Since Primasius and pseudo-Augustine made their own revisions in the text, the less creative Beatus remains the most faithful witness to the lost commentary. Where Beatus transmits passages which Primasius and pseudo-Augustine omit, the Turin Fragment serves as a valuable check on their accuracy. Bousset's work suffers from two serious deficiencies. First, he grossly misjudged the commentary of Beatus by proposing the simplistic formula that once all known sources have been eliminated from Beatus' commentary, only Tyconius will remain.[16]

Second, he asserted that Tyconius' exegesis is so original that one may readily identify his thought without great effort simply be reading those authors who copied from him.[17] Such a method must be regarded as capricious and arbitrary.

At the turn of the century T. Hahn published his Tyconius-Studien, which remains the only monograph and the standard work on Tyconius research.[18] Following in Bousset's footsteps, Hahn embarked upon a more thorough study of the texts of the Tyconian family. His findings have served as the foundation for all subsequent scholarship, which unfortunately reflects not only the accomplishments but also the inadequacies of his work. First and foremost, Hahn asserted that Beatus offers us the best chance to recover the original text of Tyconius.[19] Since Beatus was not talented enough to make revisions in his sources, he simply copied without attempting to assimilate them into his commentary. For example, we find in his work specific references to Africa of the fourth century and to issues totally foreign to the theological debates of his own time.[20] Publishing the results of the research of his colleague Bousset, Hahn identified all those passages where Beatus names his sources.[21] Furthermore, he identified the passages in Beatus' commentary which he believed to be Tyconian because of their parallels in the commentaries of Primasius, Bede, and the pseudo-Augustinian homilies.[22] Finally, he asserted that the lengthy introduction to Beatus' commentary was written by Tyconius.[23] Second, as a corollary to his preference for Beatus, Hahn rejected the Turin Fragment as unreliable in regard to both the wording and the thought of Tyconius' commentary.[24] The intentional omission of references to Africa, clear instances of changes in the text, and stylistic characteristics which show Beatus to be more understandable and less abbreviated, were for him decisive. However, Hahn did maintain that the Turin Fragment is indeed based on a Tyconian prototype although the fragment does reflect the revisions of a later writer, who wished to bring Tyconius' commentary up to date for his contemporaries. Therefore, the Turin Fragment does remain a valuable document, especially in helping to sift the Tyconian passages out of Beatus' commentary. Third, in spite of the extensive literature influenced by Tyconius, Hahn came to the rather pessimistic overall conclusion that a word for word reconstruction of the Tyconian commentary is impossible. How then does one arrive at the lost commentary? Hahn's solution was an extremely practical one. He simply cited Beatus, whose commentary does afford some insight into the thought of Tyconius. In this respect Hahn considered the <u>recapitulationes</u> especially reliable.[25]

Since Hahn's study remains fundamental to any investigation of the lost commentary, I will occasionally be focusing attention on it in the course of this research. At the present time I wish to limit my observations to two items. Prescinding for the moment from the more detailed study of Beatus and the Turin Fragment which will follow,[26] I state my first criticism in a general way: Hahn found too much Tyconius in Beatus and not enough Tyconius in the Turin Fragment. Of course, this does not invalidate any of Hahn's legitimate findings, for example the correct observations that Beatus copied extensively and accurately from his sources and that the Turin Fragment suffered later editorial revisions. The objection could best be termed one of degree. Hahn's dependence upon Beatus is too great and his rejection of the Turin Fragment too severe. Second, Hahn's practical solution of simply citing Beatus in his study of Tyconius leaves much to be desired. Given the facts that the original text of Tyconius is in some cases irretrievably lost and that Beatus is the best witness to this lost text, one might consider the practical dependence upon Beatus a rather logical and necessary conclusion. Unfortunately, this excessive confidence in Beatus as the faithful transmitter of Tyconius' thought has led to great confusion. Not only Hahn but also subsequent authors seem to quote Beatus as if they were quoting Tyconius.[27] One must be more precise. When citing a Tyconian passage in Beatus' commentary, one must keep in mind that, although the passage might have been greatly influenced by Tyconius, nevertheless Beatus is its author. In certain specific cases, after a detailed comparison with the other commentaries in the Tyconian family, one might be able to determine the exact words of Tyconius. However, when a comparison shows the text to be ambiguous, one may not presume that Beatus has recorded the original words of Tyconius. Perhaps this objection will be made clear in the light of two examples from scholars who based their work on Hahn's conclusions. F. D. Moorrees[28] writes that Tyconius differentiates four classes of pseudo-prophets: heretics, schismatics, superstitious people, and hypocrites. He adds that Tyconius places the _circumcelliones_ in the third class. Moorrees' statements are based upon Hahn's understanding of Beatus' praefatio, 5, 48-62. However, the passage has no parallels in the other commentaries of the Tyconian tradition. Furthermore, large sections of the passage mentioned were copied from Isidore of Seville.[29] As we will see in the following investigations,[30] this fourfold division does not find its origin in Tyconius but in the _Etymologiae_ of Isidore. A second example is the article of L. J. van der Lof,[31] who wrote that according to Tyconius the bishop has disciplinary authority in the community, including the power of making specific regulations. The basis for his assertion is Beatus 2, 4, 9-10, where the word _episcopus_ appears twice. However, if one looks to the parallel passages in the Turin Fragment and the commentary of Primasius, one finds no reference to a bishop. A far more likely explanation is that the word _episcopus_ originates from Beatus, who was concerned with the adoptionist tendencies of his contemporary Elipando, Bishop of Toledo.[32] It is not necessary to belabor the point. Citing Beatus alone in the study of Tyconius is simply inadequate. Furthermore, this practice has retarded the progress of research by leading, as we have seen, to drastic misunderstandings. Unfortunately, as late as 1976 S. Alvarez Campos in his investigation of the sources of Beatus' commentary identifies extensive passages as Tyconian on the exclusive basis of Tyconian content, style, and vocabulary, Donatist theology, and particular historical and geographic characteristics where no concrete parallels exist in the Tyconian literature.[33]

In his study of the Latin translations of the Apocalypse H. J. Vogels[34] has provided us with much valuable information in regard to the commentary of Tyconius. His goal was, of course, entirely different from that of the previously mentioned researchers. Vogels wished to present a history of the Latin translations of the Apocalypse. To achieve this end, he dealt with the problem of a possible reconstruction of the Apocalypse text which Tyconius used.

Although he was not primarily concerned with a reconstruction of the commentary itself, nevertheless of necessity he had to turn to the very same sources which researchers of Tyconius use. Therefore, his work may be of great assistance in dealing with the question of a possible reconstruction of the Tyconian commentary. In fact, his different point of view, limited to the Apocalypse text alone, is extremely advantageous because of its independence from the normal Tyconian problematic. The results of Vogels' complex research may be summarized in the following six statements. First, Beatus offers an almost complete text of the Apocalypse translation used by Tyconius.[35] Second, the biblical text of the Turin Fragment does occasionally depart from the biblical text used by Tyconius.[36] Third, the pseudo-Augustinian homilies also give an accurate Tyconian biblical text but often in shortened form.[37] Vogels also proposed the possibility that the text was already abbreviated in pseudo-Augustine's sources. Fourth, the biblical text of the pseudo-Augustinian homilies shows more influence from the Vulgate than the biblical text of the Turin Fragment shows.[38] Nevertheless, Vogels concedes the possibility that an occasional reading found in pseudo-Augustine may be preferred to the Turin Fragment. Fifth, both Bede and Primasius offer many biblical passages which are expressly stated as coming from Tyconius as well as other passages, identified as an _alia editio_ or _alia translatio,_ which often come from Tyconius.[39] Sixth, although the biblical texts of both Primasius and Tyconius manifest characteristics peculiar to the _vetus latina,_ they used different translations.[40]

Vogels did not attempt a word for word reconstruction of the

Tyconian Apocalypse text but rather presented varying witnesses separately.[41] The value of this information is quite apparent. Of course, it would false to immediately conclude that the commentary of Tyconius in every case shared the same fate as the biblical text contained therein. Vogels himself pointed out that a biblical text is more likely to suffer revisions at the hands of subsequent authors or copyists. Nevertheless, Vogels' research, though restricted for the most part to the biblical text of Tyconius, may be applied to the problem of reconstructing the commentary itself. First, he confirmed the superiority of Beatus in transmitting the text of Tyconius. Second, he has presented much detailed and helpful information in regard to other commentaries of the Tyconian tradition. Third, having concluded that a word for word reconstruction of Tyconius' Apocalypse text was not possible, Vogels did not limit himself to the biblical text of one commentary alone but presented the biblical text of all commentaries in the Tyconian tradition. The problem Vogels faced in regard to the biblical text is similar to the problem Hahn faced in regard to the whole commentary. Vogels' solution appears to be much more satisfactory since various important commentaries have not been neglected and thus subsequent research has not been shunted off in one direction through an excessive dependence upon one commentary alone.

Finally, three other authors play secondary roles in this first phase of Tyconian research. P. Monceaux[42] presented a good description of the problem in his literary history of Christian Africa. He has followed Hahn rather closely and has brought no new results. H. A. Sanders,[43] editor of the only critical edition of Beatus' commentary, advanced in his introduction the theory that

Beatus wrote three editions of his work with the earliest edition being most faithful to his sources. If we accept Sander's hypothesis, we would then have to prefer Beatus' first edition in attempting to reconstruct the commentary of Tyconius. W. Neuss[44] totally rejected Sanders' hypothesis, basing his conclusion on a precise textual analysis confirmed by a study of the illuminations in extant manuscripts of Beatus' commentary. I will deal with the problems raised by Sanders and Neuss in greater detail when treating Beatus individually.[45]

2. The second approach -- from Beatus to the Turin Fragment

In 1902 the English Benedictine H. L. Ramsay published two articles concerning Beatus' Apocalypse commentary, the one[46] being a study of the commentary itself and the other[47] a study of its manuscripts. In his treatment of the commentary Ramsay addressed himself to two issues which are pertinent to our research, namely the structure and content of Beatus' commentary and its sources. First, he described the commentary of Beatus as a chain of quotations taken from various authors. In demonstrating this point, he analyzed the structure of the commentary's introduction and, contrary to the assertion of Bousset and Hahn, who believed that the introduction was written by Tyconius himself, Ramsay showed that it had been copied from various books, especially the works of Isidore of Seville.[48] Second, besides composing a list[49] of those passages which come from Gregory, Isidore, Jerome, Augustine, Ambrose, and Fulgentius, he considered in detail the chief sources of Beatus, namely Victorinus, Apringius,[50] and Tyconius. In regard to a possible reconstruction of the commentary of Tyconius, Ramsay drew two conclusions. First, the Turin Fragment contains the most exclusive, though not the most adequate, presentation of Tyconius' commentary. It offers a precise tool both for identifying analogous pieces in Beatus and for deciding at what point Primasius and pseudo-Augustine depend upon Augustine.[51] Second, pointing out that Hahn had also attributed to Tyconius several passages of Beatus' commentary actually written by Gregory the Great, Ramsay insisted that one exercise extreme caution in attempting to restore the text of Tyconius with the help of Beatus alone.[52] Although we can hardly assert that he preferred the Turin Fragment to Beatus as the more faithful witness to the original text of Tyconius, Ramsay did introduce limitations to the use of Beatus' commentary in attempting a reconstruction while at the same time more seriously considering the application of the Turin Fragment to this task.

Objecting to the traditional opinion favoring Beatus, A. Pincherle[53] presented two further arguments in support of Ramsay's position. First, he questioned the use of the Hieronymian recension of Victorinus' commentary in attempting to reconstruct the commentary of Tyconius.[54] Here Pincherle hit a sore spot in Tyconian research. The relationship of Victorinus and Jerome-Victorinus to the other commentaries of the Tyconian family has been a constant source of confusion. Due to the absence of extrinsic criteria, Monceaux considered the mixture of Victorinus, Jerome, and Tyconius inextricably entangled.[55] Vogels wondered if perhaps Tyconius had been familiar with the commentary of Victorinus.[56] Nevertheless Haußleiter was able to produce an excellent critical edition of both the edition of Victorinus and the recension of Jerome.[57] Furthermore he identified seven passages from Tyconius which Jerome had introduced into the text.[58] These findings of Haußleiter were contrary to those of Bousset, who maintained a partial dependence of Beatus, Primasius, and pseudo-Augustine upon Victorinus of Pettau.[59] In regard to the disagreement between Bousset and Haußleiter, Pincherle indicated how infrequently Beatus, pseudo-Augustine, and Jerome-Victorinus agree with one another while at the same time diverging from the recension of Victorinus. Only under these circumstances is it possible to affirm the dependence of all three upon Tyconius rather than the dependence of Beatus and pseudo-Augustine upon Victorinus. Pincherle limited to three the passages where he considered the use of Tyconius by Jerome certain, including one passage not indicated by Haußleiter.[60] According to Pincherle more often than not agreement between Beatus, pseudo-Augustine, and Jerome-Victorinus indicates a dependence upon the earlier commentary of Victorinus. Second, Pincherle asserted that with the aid of the other witnesses it is often possible to correct the text of Beatus in the deficient edition of Florez.[61] He presented a random example from the comments on Rev. 9:13ff. in the Turin Fragment and its parallels. In addition, according to Pincherle, Beatus was not the faithful copyist as was once believed; he did not hesitate to insert his own observations into the text. On the basis of these two objections Pincherle came to the conclusion that we must turn to the Turin Fragment: "Among the materials to be used for a reconstruction of the lost commentary of Tyconius, the Codex of Turin merits, therefore, to be collated in the first place."[62]

However, although Pincherle's arguments in both cases are based upon accurate observation and sound judgment, they do not entirely correspond to the conclusion at which he arrived. In regard to his first objection one must point out that Jerome-Victorinus plays a secondary role in reconstructing the commentary of Tyconius. Even after those passages which depend upon Jerome-Victorinus have been eliminated, there still remains a bulk of material which may be obtained from comparing Beatus with pseudo-Augustine and Primasius. Pincherle's second objection, as demonstrated by his textual example, allows one to draw a conclusion in regard to the Florez edition of Beatus' commentary. However, a judgment on the value of Beatus' commentary itself in reconstructing Tyconius would, of course, require further investigation. Finally, both of his arguments call the use of Beatus' commentary into question but do not shed more light on the possible use of the Turin Fragment. In this regard we must be attentive to certain limitations which Pincherle failed to consider. First, there are many instances where Beatus, pseudo-Augustine, and Primasius correspond, while no parallels exist in the Turin Fragment. As the name betrays, the Turin Fragment is extremely fragmentary containing only those sections which comment on Rev. 2:18-4:1 and 7:16-12:6. Second, we do have evidence already presented in the biblical work of Vogels[63] and, as we will see shortly, in the introduction of Lo Bue's edition[64] that the Turin Fragment did indeed suffer subsequent alteration. In other words, in at least some passages where Beatus is more reliable than the Turin Fragment. Although Pincherle is correct in arguing that the Turin Fragment merits proper recognition, nevertheless because of the above stated limitations, it should not be collated in the first place.

Although he was not concerned with the problem of reconstructing Tyconius' commentary, M. del Alamo[65] did present some further evidence which supports Pincherle's contention that Beatus was more creative than formerly believed. Alamo found in Beatus' commentary several veiled references against adoptionism, a heresy current in Mozarabic Spain during the eighth century. The content of Beatus' anti-adoptionist polemic is known through his letter to Elipando,[66] which he wrote some years after the commentary. A comparison between this letter and the commentary reveals many allusions to his anti-adoptionist preoccupation. With the help of this information, we can identify numerous passages in the commentary which were not omitted by the other witnesses of the Tyconian tradition but rather added by Beatus.[67]

In 1963 the posthumous publication of F. Lo Bue's edition of the Turin Codex filled a long standing lacuna in Tyconian research. He produced an excellent critical edition improving upon that of the Spicilegium Casinense in three aspects: he corrected errors, completed the deficient critical apparatus, and expanded the registration of parallel passages in the Tyconian literature to include Beatus. Besides presenting textual and paleographical background in his introductory essay, Lo Bue addressed himself to the problem of the relationship of the Turin Fragment to the original commentary of Tyconius. His presentation of this problem is quite balanced. On one hand, he recognized that the Turin Fragment has been transmitted independently of the commentaries of the Tyconian family.

On the other hand, he acknowledged that it is by no means a direct reproduction of the original work of Tyconius. In order to ascertain the value of the Turin Fragment, while neither depreciating nor overestimating the document, one must compare it to the original commentary of Tyconius. One may carry out this comparison because the Tyconian origin of certain passages in the commentaries of Primasius, Jerome, Bede, and Beatus is certain. By comparing the Turin Fragment to those passages whose Tyconian origin is certain, Lo Bue was able to advance three assertions. First, in some cases it is totally impossible to unravel the sources and establish the original text.[68] Second, the Turin Fragment "does not preserve the Tyconian text which other commentators had before them, but a text which at a certain period of its history underwent some degree of modification."[69] Third, the so-called African passages of Beatus' commentary appear to have been systematically eliminated from the Turin Codex.[70] Finally, Lo Bue attempted to judge the value of the Turin Fragment toward reconstructing the commentary of Tyconius. Actually, the chief problem arises from those passages which are without parallels in the other Tyconian literature.[71] Although we know that the Turin Fragment does occasionally depart from the Tyconian archetype, one may not immediately eliminate as non-Tyconian certain passages which are preserved only there. Lo Bue came to the following conclusions: First, certain passages were most likely derived from Tyconius while being omitted from the commentaries of the Tyconian tradition. The reason for the omissions might have been simply a lack of interest in the specific passage or perhaps a different goal on the part of the author or even the inability to read or understand the existing manuscript. One may judge the passages as

Tyconian on the basis of the Liber regularum [72] and the commentaries, where Tyconian principles of exegesis are presented. Second, another series of passages was probably interpolated. These passages possess a common phraseology and an ecclesiological content which departs greatly from the commentaries, especially from that of Beatus. We may thank Lo Bue for an excellent critical edition of the Turin Fragment and for a penetrating study, both of which have opened new paths for further research.

3. The third approach -- looking elsewhere

In his treatment of the lost commentary of Tyconius, I. M. Gómez[73] indicated that he wished to consider the principles of literary and textual criticism in regard to a possible reconstruction of the lost commentary. According to Gomez, this task leads one to an impossible situation. On one hand, we may judge the value and reliability of the texts only by comparing them to the lost commentary. On the other hand, we know the lost commentary only through these texts. In the face of this dilemma, Gómez has opted for a middle road. One can reconstruct some passages in which the Turin Fragment offers the possibility of controlling its own text through comparison to the commentaries. Gómez executed his study in three steps: the ideological-literary personality of Tyconius, the external structure and internal character of the commentary, and the literary history of the commentary or the sources of a reconstruction. Gómez placed great emphasis upon references of ancient authors, especially Gennadius[74] and Augustine,[75] to the commentary of Tyconius and upon those few passages which are directly quoted in

Bede, Primasius, Cassiodore, and Ambrosius Autpertus. On the basis of this evidence we have sufficient information to arrive at an idea of the contents of the lost commentary. In regard to the problem of reconstructing the text of the commentary, Gómez merely gave a brief description of the various documents influenced by Tyconius. Although it is necessary to consider all the Tyconian literature, Beatus and the Turin Fragment do remain the best witnesses to the lost commentary. They must be the heart of an attempt at a reconstruction. Unfortunately, Gómez's article also suffers from several deficiencies. His complete disregard of the work of Pincherle is inexcusable. Furthermore, he frequently adopted questionable conclusions of other researchers without further critical inquiry, for example Monceaux's remark that the commentary had a lengthy introduction[76] or A. C. Vega's assertion that Apringius copied from Primasius.[77] Finally, his treatment of the problem of a possible reconstruction is superficial because he did nothing more than list the texts which need to be studied.

Lest Tyconian research be considered a tug of war between the opposing camps of those who favor Beatus struggling against those who favor the Turin Fragment, we should focus our attention on the less significant but nevertheless important texts of the Tyconian family. These texts should not be neglected because frequently we have access to extensive and reliable witnesses to the lost commentary. In addition to Haußleiter's edition of Victorinus and its introduction[78] is his article regarding the editio princeps of Primasius' commentary.[79] G. Morin has made a thorough study of the pseudo-Augustinian homilies, advancing the hypothesis, which is generally accepted, that Caesarius of Arles is their author;[80] some years later he published a critical edition of the work.[81] Indicating Bede's familiarity with the exegesis of Tyconius, G. Bonner[82] reported on the place of Bede's Explanatio in the history of the Apocalypse commentaries. Furthermore he identified those Tyconian passages in Bede's commentary which could be discovered through comparison with the other texts. The capitulary of the codex Oratorii B6, mentioned in passing by Haußleiter,[83] has not been the subject of any investigation. Although certain textual problems regarding the Complexiones of Cassiodore have been addressed,[84] the work is also relatively unresearched. S. Bovo[85] investigated the sources of the commentary of Ambrosius Autpertus and indicated those passages which were dependent upon Tyconius and others. In investigating pseudo-Jerome's Commemoratorium I discovered a definite but minute dependence upon Tyconius.[86] Finally, in 1976 L. Mezey[87] published a brief fragment of the lost commentary, which he had discovered in the library of the Central Seminary in Budapest.

C. Toward a solution

1. Explanation of the method

2. The goal of the present study

After this brief survey of the research, it is quite evident that we are confronted with an extremely perplexing problem which shows little promise of being solved. Nevertheless, to avoid prejudicing the results of this investigation, a reasonably objective approach, which at the same time corresponds to the reality of the situation at hand, must be adopted. In this way I hope to arrive at the most satisfactory solution to the problem given the resources available. Previous research has uncovered some pitfalls which must be avoided. However, previous research has also in many respects given an example which deserves to be imitated. Perhaps the best suggestion on how to go about reconstructing the lost commentary comes from Lo Bue who proposed the following five step approach:

> The problem of the reconstruction of the text of the Commentary of Tyconius can be subdivided, as a matter of method, under five heads: the study one by one of the writings which depend more or less directly on the Tyconian archetype; establishing where possible their mutual relations; isolating those passages in which the thought of the Donatist writer seems apparent; determining which of these are preserved in the form of continued paraphrase and which as fragmentary extracts; and discovering the original text as far as possible by a careful synoptic procedure.[88]

On the whole Lo Bue's suggestion is sound. However, his approach should not be adopted without certain modifications. His third step is extremely weak. After having investigated the sources of Tyconius individually and collectively, he would search out the thought of

Tyconius. Actually, if we are to take this method seriously, at this point we do not yet know the thought of Tyconius. If his thought is the basis for determining the text and then the text latter becomes the basis for investigating his thought, we find ourselves caught in a vicious circle similar to the dilemma of which Gómez warned.[89] Unfortunately, Gómez retreated from the problem by abandoning the richest texts in favor of the most reliable where direct quotations are explicitly identified. Therefore, in order to retain the strengths of Lo Bue's suggested approach while avoiding Gómez's preoccupation with certainty, my method in this endeavor will encompass four steps:

1) The various commentaries and fragments which are immediately dependent upon Tyconius' lost commentary will be individually investigated.

2) I will determine the relationship of these texts to one another.

3) I will determine the relationship of these texts to the Tyconian archetype.

4) Through a systematic comparison of the texts, I will construct a Tyconian synopsis.

Actually, the original text of Tyconius could have undergone alteration at three different points along its route to us. First, already before the later commentators copied from him, various Tyconian manuscripts and even summaries of the original work may have been, and indeed probably were, in circulation. Second, as we already know, the later authors modified the text of Tyconius in writing their own commentaries. Third, each of these commentaries has in turn its own manuscript tradition and textual history. The text of Tyconius could have undergone modification after having been incorporated into one of these commentaries. Therefore, we have three stages at which changes could have been quite easily introduced into the original text of Tyconius. The stated method in four steps takes all these factors into consideration.

1. Explanation of the method

First, each text must be individually investigated in regard to the goals which the author wished to achieve, the historical circumstances under which he wrote, and the way in which he used his sources. Here and in the second step I am admittedly following the suggestion of Lo Bue. Quite clearly we cannot draw any significant conclusions in regard to the lost commentary until we have an understanding of the texts at our disposal. In other words, we are interested in all those aspects of the text which will assist us in arriving at the lost commentary of Tyconius.

Second, after having investigated each text individually, I will then examine them collectively to determine the relationship of these texts to one another, an absolutely necessary aspect of my research. A systematic comparison of the various commentaries with the goal of discovering the text of Tyconius will be most fruitful if we are certain of two facts: First, we must know that the author used the commentary of Tyconius as a source. Second, we must be certain that the author did not have access to the commentary of Tyconius through one of the other subsequent commentaries. In other words, the Tyconian passages will be most evident in those cases where the various texts are dependent upon Tyconius but independent of one another. It is astounding how frequently this basic principle has been violated in past investigations.

The third step, though absent from Lo Bue's suggested procedure, has been added here in order to determine the faithfulness of each text to the Tyconian archetype. Research will show that there is sufficient material to construct a partial genealogy of the Tyconian manuscripts circulated in antiquity. We may also judge the quality of the these manuscripts relative to the archetype. Varying degrees of dependence which the later commentaries manifest in regard to the lost commentary of Tyconius might have been due not only to choice but also to necessity. In many cases the various authors admittedly chose to edit or revise the text of Tyconius according to their own goals and needs. However, other divergencies might be the result of a complicated manuscript tradition.[90] When we consider that Tyconius wrote his commentary in the fourth century and that Primasius, Caesarius, and Cassiodore copied from this work in the sixth century and Beatus, Bede, and Ambrosius Autpertus as late as the eighth century, then we should not be surprised if these authors used quite different manuscripts which had undergone diverse and irregular modification during their transmission. In fact, Vogels explicitly indicated that pseudo-Augustine (Caesarius of Arles) probably used an Apocalypse text which was already abbreviated in his sources.[91]

The fourth and final step consists of a synoptic comparison. In this regard we may rely at least partially on the previous research. Hahn published in his study a catalogue of the Tyconian sections of Beatus' commentary, unfortunately without indicating the parallel passages.[92] In his edition of the Turin Fragment Lo Bue made a complete critical apparatus where he indicated the parallel passages in the Tyconian literature. Bonner also listed the Tyconian passages of Bede's commentary.[93] Alvarez Campos published a table of the various sources of Beatus.[94] Although each of these items will assist us greatly, we will have to compare all the texts which reflect Tyconius' lost commentary. Since my method is based above all upon comparing the texts, one might object that any passage of Tyconius which is not explicitly identified by the author and which appears in only one of these texts will not be uncovered. The difficulty here is especially acute in regard to those passages in the commentary of Beatus which might very well have come from Tyconius but have no parallels in the other Tyconian literature. To alleviate this problem somewhat I will also include the _Liber regularum_ in my comparisons. Here we have a Tyconian source of which we may be certain. However, contrary to the assertion of E. Romero Pose,[95] I hold the ancient sermon _In natali_ to be non-Tyconian and thus useless in this study.[96] Furthermore, when investigating the commentaries individually, I intend to examine those passages without parallels with the hope of determining their origin. However, in no case do I wish to fall into the trap of identifying a passage as Tyconian because it simply appears to contain the thought of Tyconius. Using the thought of Tyconius as a norm contains the inherent danger of self-deception. One need only to point to those words of Gregory the Great, which Hahn falsely identified as Tyconian because Tyconius' thought appeared to be so obviously present.[97] The _Liber regularum_ and the few direct quotations in Bede, Primasius,

Cassiodore, and Ambrosius Autpertus do not sufficiently present the thought of Tyconius in all its ramifications and to such a degree so as to enable us to extract it from the sources without external assistance. Of course, I must concede that I might overlook some Tyconian passages in the process. However, I have no other choice in the matter. A comparison of the texts is the only reasonable way to identify the Tyconian passages contained therein. Furthermore, I am avoiding or at least minimizing the danger of erroneously identifying a passage as Tyconian when it is not. The principles involved are apparent: we must first identify the passages which were influenced by the lost commentary, and then determine the text of Tyconius to the extent that is possible. After dealing with this initial problem, one is then free to investigate the thought of Tyconius in the lost commentary. Any attempt to accomplish both at once can only lead to confusion.

2. The goal of this study

My investigation has a single goal. Through my study of the commentaries which were influenced by Tyconius and the existing manuscript fragments, I wish to determine, to the degree that is possible, the text of the lost commentary. Since the exact wording of the original commentary may in some cases never be retrieved, this goal will be best accomplished through the construction of a Tyconian synopsis. My approach is analogous to that which Vogels used in investigating Tyconius' text of the Apocalypse. After studying each of the texts in detail and their relationship to one another, he listed the results in regard to each text separately. In other words, he did not attempt to combine all the Apocalypse texts of the various commentaries into one single smooth-flowing Apocalypse text of Tyconius. Nor did he limit himself to the most reliable text alone, as both Hahn and Alvarez Campos had limited themselves to Beatus, whose work they considered to reflect most accurately the original commentary of Tyconius.[98] Realizing that a reconstruction of the Apocalypse text was impossible, Vogels left all the texts intact and remained content to present each text separately, for example "the Tyconius text of the pseudo-Augustinian homilies," "the Tyconius text of Beatus," etc.[99] I propose to adopt a similar approach in regard to the commentary of Tyconius. Since the original wording of Tyconius will be in many if not most cases irretrievable even where parallels are available, I will identify the Tyconian passages in the various texts. In certain limited cases the exact wording of Tyconius' text may be apparent. However, since we possess rather unsatisfactory editions of Bede, Beatus, and Cassiodore, the editing of a critical text is at the present time impossible. The Tyconian synopsis grants us the broadest possible access to the lost commentary with the greatest amount of objectivity and reliability.

The contribution will be twofold. First, the lost commentary will be made as available as it possibly can be to anyone interested in studying the thought of Tyconius. Researchers will no longer have to limit themselves to Tyconius' <u>Liber regularum</u> nor will they have to grapple with chaos in their study of the lost Apocalypse Commentary. Second, with the synopsis complete, research on the textual questions will be open to further expansion as critical texts of the more important works become available.

Chapter II

Investigation of works influenced by Tyconius

A. Victorinus and Jerome-Victorinus

1. The life and writings of Victorinus

a. Some biographical notes

Victorinus, bishop of Pettau (ancient Poetovium in Pannonia Superior, modern Ptuj in Yugoslavia) suffered martyrdom in the persecution of Diocletian most probably in the year 304. He is the first biblical exegete of the Latin Church. Jerome's remark that his Greek was better than his Latin is usually taken to mean that Victorinus was Greek by birth and learned Latin as a second language.[1] According to the Roman martyrology, the commemoration of his martyrdom is celebrated November 2nd.

b. His works

In his <u>De viris inlustribus</u> Jerome gives a partial list of the works of Victorinus:

> commentarii in genesim, in exodum, in Leuiticum, in Esaiam, in Ezechiel, in Abacuc, in ecclesiasten, in canticum canticorum, in apocalysim Iohannis, adversum omnes hereses, et multa alia.[2]

Furthermore, in his translation of Origen's homilies on Luke as well as in his Matthew commentary, Jerome also makes mention of a commentary on Matthew's gospel which Victorinus wrote.[3] Of all these exegetical works only the Apocalypse commentary is extant. We also possess a short study of Victorinus with the title <u>De fabrica mundi</u>, which treats the days of creation; it does not appear to have been part of the lost Genesis commentary.[4] All other works attributed to Victorinus must be considered doubtful. A. Harnack asserted that Victorinus' <u>Adversum omnes hereses</u> is identical with a writing of pseudo-Tertullian bearing the same name.[5] G. Mercati found some fragments he believes a chiliastic leaning stemming from Victorinus' Matthew commentary.[6] A. Wilmart attributed to Victorinus the anonymous <u>De decem virginibus.</u> [7] Finally, J. Wöhrer argued that Victorinus of Pettau is the author of two brief fragments occasionally attributed to Marius Victorinus.[8]

The exegesis of Victorinus is based upon Greek authors, namely Papias, Irenaeus, Hippolytus, and especially Origen. In fact, Jerome explicitly mentions that Victorinus was an imitator of Origen.[9]

The reference by Cassiodore that Victorinus was a great orator is due to a confusion between the the martyred bishop of Pettau and C. Marius Victorinus, an African of the fourth century.[10] The Decretum Gelasianum de libris recipiendis et not recipiendis declared the works of Victorinus to be apocryphal,[11] most probably on account of the chiliastic tendencies.

2. The Apocalypse commentary of Victorinus

a. Edition and revisions

In 1916 Haußleiter first published the editio Victorini, namely the original commentary of Victorinus which had been preserved in the Codex Ottobonianus latinus 3288 A and two secondary manuscripts.[12] Before the discovery of the manuscript, the work was known only in Jerome's edition. Since Jerome had become one of the foremost scholars of the West, his advice was often sought especially in regard to exegetical questions.[13] One such seeker of wisdom was a certain unknown Anatolius, who had come into possession of the original commentary of Victorinus on the Apocalypse. Anatolius asked Jerome to judge the worth of the commentary. This request presented Jerome with an extremely difficult problem. First, Jerome was a staunch opponent of any literal interpretation of the Apocalypse and its chiliastic conclusions which he considered Jewish mythology. On the other hand, Jerome was confronted with the exegetical work of a bishop and martyr, and thus had to be extremely cautious in his criticism. His solution was simply to revise the commentary.[14] First, Jerome corrected the primitive Latin of

Victorinus. Second, he introduced in the text quotations from a later translation of the sacred scriptures. Third, he also occasionally changed the wording of the exposition of Victorinus. Fourth, he omitted what displeased him, above all the chiliastic sections toward the end of the commentary. Fifth, he also added his own comments and included several sections which he had taken from his contemporary Tyconius. Sixth, he transposed certain sections of the original commentary.[15] After this major revision of Jerome, the commentary underwent two further revisions. In the recensio posterior the scriptural quotations from the Apocalypse were augmented. Finally, the recensio postrema is a mixture of the previous recensions.

b. Method

At this point we must consider two aspects of the method of Victorinus. First, what is to be understood under the expression 'commentary'? Victorinus does not give a verse by verse commentary of the entire text of a biblical book. From his Apocalypse commentary it is evident that he selected certain critical passages and explained them to his readers. Cassiodore seems to have noticed this trait of Victorinus because he avoids applying the word 'commentary' to the work of Victorinus but simply states that Victorinus dealt briefly with some difficult places in the Apocalypse.[16]

The second and perhaps more important aspect of the method of Victorinus is his theory of recapitulatio. [17] He was the first to use this principle which later became incorporated as an independent rule in the Liber regularum of Tyconius.[18] Both Victorinus and

Tyconius seem to have been influenced by Tertullian who uses the term without the precision of the subsequent exegetes.[19] According to the theory of recapitulation, the Apocalypse does not present a continuous series of future events but rather repeats the same succession of events under different forms. Strange as it may seem, this theory, which enabled Victorinus to develop his chiliastic interpretation, is the same theory which Tyconius used to free himself from chiliasm. By refusing to see an historical unity in the apocalyptic visions, Victorinus was forced to construct a theological unity based on millenarianism. Tyconius, on the other hand, was much more literary in his approach and used the theory of recapitulation as an exegetical principle to free him from a literal interpretation of the Apocalypse. In any event, the theory is extremely productive toward developing a consistent and integral interpretation of the events recorded in the the Apocalypse.

c. Content

The next step is to consider the content of the original commentary of Victorinus under four main aspects -- soteriology, eschatology, Christology, and exegesis.[20]

In the explanation of Rev. 5:5 Victorinus writes that the slaughtered lamb as well as the lion has destroyed death and freed man.[21] Just as all men through one body have been subjected to death, so also through one body the faithful will be born again to life and will rise from the dead. Victorinus often repeats that Christ overcame death.

According to Victorinus the two prophets Eliah and Jeremiah will come again at the end of time.[22] They are the two witnesses who will preach against the antichrist. During this time the antichrist will establish his kingdom on earth, which will last for three years and six months. The two prophets will be killed by the antichrist. Nevertheless, they will rise again on the fourth day so that no one may be like God. An interesting aspect of Victorinus' interpretation is the identification of the antichrist with none other than the Emperor Nero, who will return to earth from hell during this time.[23] Victorinus mentions that the Apocalypse was written under the rule of the Emperor Domitian. Then came seven emperors so that Nero is the eighth, namely the one who will return from the underworld. In this way Victorinus combined the prophecy of the antichrist with the concrete historical person Nero. According to Rev. 12, there will be a great battle in heaven and the antichrist will be defeated by the angels.[24]

Victorinus also writes of the thousand year kingdom of Christ on earth.[25] The new song is an indication of a new expectation of a kingdom of untold promise. The time of the harvest points to the kingdom of Christ and the future appearance of the kingdom of the saints. When Christ rules, the kingdom of the world will be destroyed. Where the apostles first established the Church, namely in Judea, all the saints will come together and worship their Lord.

The Christology of Victorinus is above all a 'spirit Christology.'[26] That is to say that he does not clearly distinguish between the Son and the Holy Spirit. In his commentary on Rev. 12:1 he writes: coronam patrum significat secundum carnis natiuitatem, ex quibus erat spiritus carnem sumpturus.[27] Jerome replaced the word 'spiritus' with 'Christus' in his revision. Nevertheless, in spite of this inaccuracy, Victorinus was firm on the resurrection. Christ has overcome the underworld. He was the first to rise from the dead. Through him all men will be born again to new life and will rise from the dead.[28] The woman clothed with the sun is the Church of the fathers, the prophets, the saints, and the apostles,[29] Being clothed with the sun is an indication of the hope of the resurrection and the glory of the promise.

An important aspect of Victorinus' understanding of the Bible is based upon the unity of the Old and New Testaments. In his explanation of Rev. 5:1 the book with the seventh seal is the Old Testament, which was opened through the sufferings of Jesus Christ who conquered death.[30] According to Victorinus a testament remains sealed until the one who made the testament dies. Therefore, for him there are not two testaments but only the one testament which was established through Jesus Christ with Moses and remained sealed until the victory of Jesus over death. This constitutes a single time period.

d. Jerome's revision

As already mentioned, Jerome revised the commentary of Victorinus at the request of a certain Anatolius. The extent of this revision is contained in his prefatory letter to Anatolius where he states that from the beginning of the letter to the sign of the cross the work contains the word for word reproduction of the commentary of Victorinus. In this section he made only minor changes, mostly polishing the language of the author. According to Morin, the sign of the cross which Jerome mentions is the monogram of Christ, which the antichrist wished to change and adopt for himself.[31] It appears in the text after Rev. 13:18. Nevertheless, Haußleiter believes he has found the cross which Jerome mentioned at the beginning of the comments on Rev. 20:6.[32] In any event, the end of the commentary contains the most extensive revisions of Jerome. Above all, Jerome spiritualized the very concrete interpretation of Victorinus. This is most clear in his explanation of Rev. 20-22.[33] In the place of martyrdom, which was a concrete reality at the time of Victorinus, came virginity as the unbloody martyrdom. For Jerome the number ten meant the decalogue and the number 100 meant the crown of virginity. Jerome also removed those sections which mentioned the concrete kingdom of God on earth. In fact, the thousand year kingdom was condemned as a heresy like that of the heretic Cerinth. And so the cornerstone of Victorinus' theology, namely the thousand year kingdom, came to be condemned in his own work.

3. Tyconius and Victorinus

a. Jerome's use of Tyconius in his revision

In the text and index of his critical edition[34] Haußleiter indicated an allusion to Tyconius in the introduction of Jerome at 14,12 as well as six passages which were taken from the lost commentary of Tyconius and inserted in the commentary of Victorinus by Jerome: 71,15-17; 77,3-79,2; 81,6-9; 135,10; 137,4-8; 143,10. While acknowledging Haußleiter's insight, Bousset observed that Beatus, Primasius, and Caesarius have a minor dependency upon Victorinus.[35] As Pincherle correctly pointed out, this complicates the situation somewhat. Since Beatus had access to the commentary of Jerome-Victorinus, a mere coincidence between the two does not provide sufficient evidence to conclude that both used Tyconius.[36] Actually to prove the use of Tyconius on the part of Jerome, two circumstances must coincide. First, there must be agreement between Beatus, Caesarius, and Jerome-Victorinus. Second, none of these three may agree with the primitive text of Victorinus. When these two conditions exist simultaneously, we certainly have the text of the lost commentary of Tyconius. Therefore, Pincherle discounted all the passages indicated by Haußleiter except two, 77,3-79,2 and 81,6-9, while adding one which was overlooked by Haußleiter, namely 23,4-6.

Although the guidelines which Pincherle established for determining whether a passage is Tyconian or not are correct, a study of all the indicated passages reveals that Pincherle's concrete judgment in each case except one is absolutely false. I would also discount a Tyconian influence at 143,10-11 where Haußleiter asserts that both Augustine and Jerome copied from Tyconius as a common source. This can hardly be proven especially since an extensive dependence of Augustine upon Jerome-Victorinus is apparent.[37] However, all of the other passages were copied from Tyconius by Jerome as Haußleiter asserted. Each of the three passages must be considered individually.

The first passage deals with the black horse mentioned at Rev. 6:6:

Recensio Hieronymi, CSEL 49,71,15-17

Statera in manu: libra examinis, in qua singulorum merita ostenderet. ait dux: uinum et oleum ne laeseris, id est hominem spiritalem ne plagis percusseris. hic est equus niger.

Beatus, Caesarius, Primasius, and Bede all contain a similar passage. 38 However, in each case the black horse is mentioned first and the explanation follows. In Jerome-Victorinus the passage closes with the reference to the black horse: his est equus niger. For Beatus, Caesarius, Bede, and Primasius to be dependent upon Jerome-Victorinus, they would have each had to have inverted the word and its explanation acting independently of one another. This is hardly possible. A far more plausible explanation is that they all copied from Tyconius while Jerome introduced the change in sequence.

The second passage and its parallels also indicate a common dependence upon the lost commentary of Tyconius:

Recensio Hieronymi, CSEL 49,135,10-12

et exiet sanguis [de torculari] usque ad frenos equorum: exiet ultio usque ad principes populorum, id est rectores, siue diabolum siue angelos eius. nouissimo certamine exiet ultio sanguinis effusi...

Bede, PL 93,177,15-18

Exiit ultio usque ad rectores populorum. Usque enim ad diabolum et ejus angelos novissimo certamine exiit ultio sanguinis sanctorum effusi.

Beatus, 7,2,35-36

exiet damnationis ultio usque ad rectores populorum, usque enim ad diabolum et eius angelos, id est homines malos. in novissimo vero certamine in diem iudicii exiit ultio sanguinis effusi...

The underlined passages indicate quite clearly that Jerome, Bede, and Beatus copied from Tyconius. The wording of Bede and Beatus is exactly the same while that of Jerome is different.

The third passage deals with the comments at Rev. 15:1 concerning the last persecution, where Tyconius illustrates his point with a quotation from Leviticus:

Recensio Hieronymi, CSEL 49,137,4-8

Eandem repetens persecutionem dicit apocalypsis: angelos septem habentes plagas [septem nouissimas], quoniam in his finita est ira dei. semper enim ira dei percutit populum contumacem septem plagis -- id est perfecte, ut in Leuitico dicit --, quae in ultimio futurae sunt, cum ecclesia de medio exierit.

Both Caesarius and Beatus contain the phrase in Levitico frequenter repetit [39] where Jerome simply has in Leuitico dicit. Once again a common dependence of all three upon Tyconius is apparent.

b. Place of Victorinus and Jerome-Victorinus in the Tyconian tradition

For the purposes of our investigation we need also to determine the place of Victorinus and Jerome-Victorinus within the Tyconian tradition. Which editions were used by Caesarius and Beatus? The extensive agreement between Caesarius and Victorinus would indicate that Caesarius had access to the original commentary of Victorinus but not to Jerome-Victorinus. Beatus, on the other hand, had access to Jerome-Victorinus but not to Victorinus. Although Pincherle seems to strongly imply these relationships, he does not explicitly state which editions were used by Caesarius and Beatus.

Finally, I would like to completely present as far as possible the position of Jerome-Victorinus in the Tyconian tradition. The task of determining the relationship of Victorinus and Jerome-Victorinus to Primasius, Bede, and Ambrosius Autpertus remains. Since in his introduction Ambrosius Autpertus explicitly acknowledges the use of the commentary of Victorinus as revised by Jerome,[40] no further research is necessary in this regard. However, both Primasius and Bede will require some detailed investigation.

First, comparing the wording of Primasius to Jerome-Victorinus indicates that Primasius did have access to the Hieronymian revision. This may be demonstrated with one example from the comments on Rev. 1:13:

<u>Editio Victorini,</u> CSEL 49,20,1-5

<u>ambulans</u> inter medium candelabrorum aureorum, <u>id est</u> inter medium ecclesiarum, sicut <u>per Salomonem dixit:</u> inter semitas iustorum <u>ambulo.</u> cuius antiquitas et inmortalitas, maiestatis origo, 'in capite candor' ostenditur. caput autem Christi deus est.

<u>Recensio Hieronymi,</u> CSEL 49,21,1-5

<u>ambulantem</u> inter medium candelabrorum aureorum, inter medium <u>dicit</u> ecclesiarum, sicut <u>in Salomone dicit:</u> inter semitas iustorum <u>ambulabo.</u> cuius antiquitas et inmortalitas, maiestatis origo, in capite candor ostenditur. caput autem Christi deus est.

Primasius, CChr.SL 92, 16,204-17,208

<u>ambulantem</u> inter medium candelabrorum aureorum. Inter medium <u>dicit</u> ecclesiarum, sicut et <u>in Salomone dicit:</u> Inter semitam iustorum <u>ambulabo.</u> Cuius antiquitas et immortalitas maiestatis origo in capite candor ostenditur.

The underlined passages make it abundantly clear that Primasius must be dependent upon Jerome-Victorinus.

Second, although the influence appears to have been minor, Bede also had access to Jerome-Victorinus.[41] The existence of a non-Tyconian passage common to Bede and Jerome-Victorinus but absent from Victorinus and Primasius will demonstrate this point:

<u>Recensio Hieronymi</u>, CSEL 49,125,3-6

interpretatur enim 'Teitan', quem gentiles Solem Phoebumque appellant, computaturque grece sic: T tau trecenti, E e quinque, I iota decem, T tau trecenti, A alfa unum, N ni quinquaginta, qui simul ducti fiunt sexcenti sexaginta sex.

Bede, PL 93,172,25-28

Hic numerus apud Graecos in nomine Titanis, id est, gigantis, dicitur inveniri, hoc modo. T enim ccc, E v, I x, T ccc, A i, N l.

Bede then proceeds to cite Primasius while indicating the differences between the two interpretations. Although Bede does not mention the source of the first interpretation, the textual comparison above reveals Jerome-Victorinus as that source.

Therefore, the progress of the research may be summarized schematically as follows:

(1) Haußleiter

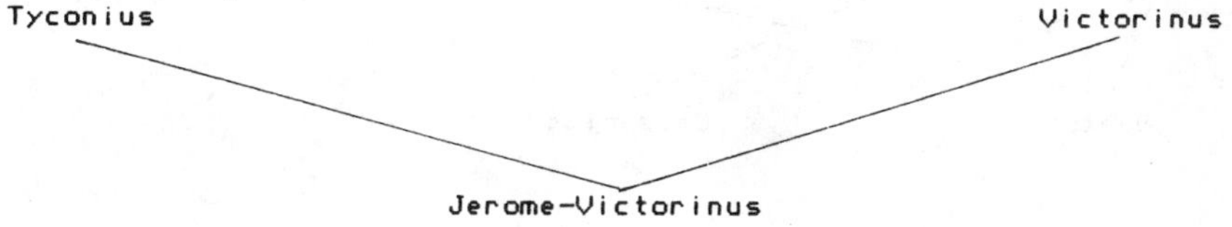

Tyconius   Victorinus

Jerome-Victorinus

(2) Bousset

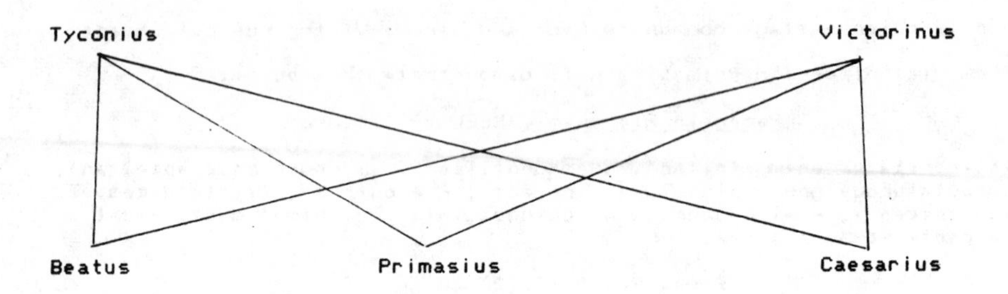

(3) Pincherle

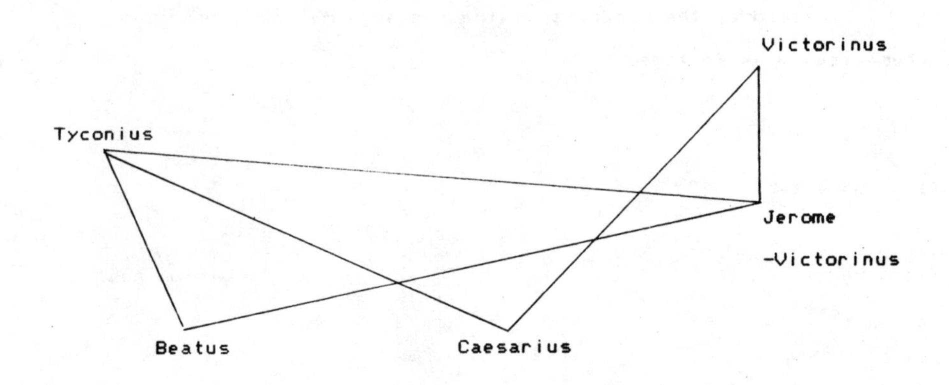

(4) Complete Tyconian tradition

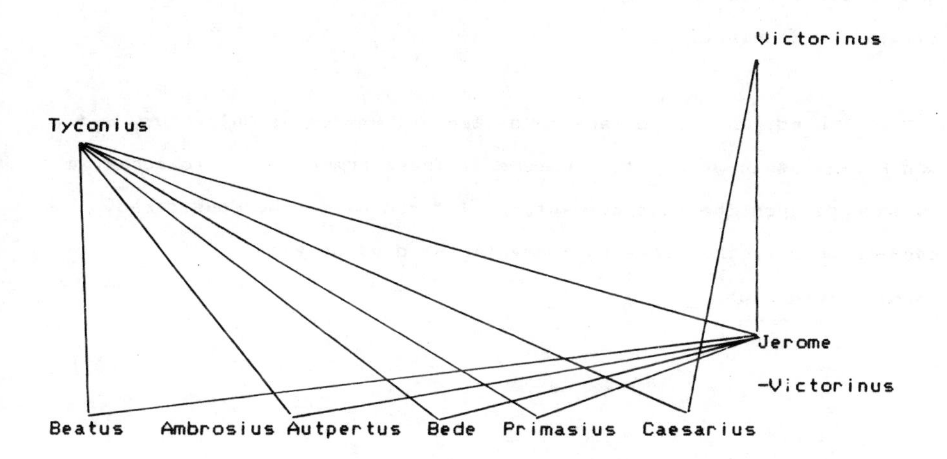

c. Role of Jerome-Victorinus in a possible reconstruction

First, thus far we have six definite Tyconian passages in the Hieronymian revision of the commentary of Victorinus:

(1) 23, 4-6

(2) 71, 15-17

(3) 77, 3 - 79, 2

(4) 81, 5-9

(5) 135, 10 - 137,2

(6) 137, 4-8.

It seems highly unlikely that any further passages will be discovered.

Second, the principles laid down by Pincherle must be

followed. We have a Tyconian passage only where Beatus, Caesarius, and Jerome-Victorinus coincide while simultaneously diverging from original Victorinus.

Third, when a comparison of Beatus, Ambrosius Autpertus, Bede, and Primasius shows any two or more of these commentaries to agree, a dependence upon the lost commentary of Tyconius may be considered certain only if the agreeing commentaries diverge from Jerome-Victorinus.

B. Caesarius

1. Life and writings of Caesarius
2. <u>Expositio de Apocalypsi sancti Iohannis</u> (the pseudo-Augustinian homilies)
    a. Authorship
    b. Form
    c. Date
    d. Structure
    e. Sources
    f. Results

1. Life and writings of Caesarius

The chief source of biographical information about Caesarius is a *Vita* written shortly after his death by Cyprian of Toulon and other friends and disciples. He was born of a Roman family in the area of Cabillonum (Chalon-sur-Saone). About the age of twenty he entered the monastery at Lerins on the island of Saint Honorat. There he dedicated himself to monastic life, especially the study of the fathers. Caesarius read broadly and became familiar with diverse theological traditions including the writings of Hilarius of Arles, Vincent of Lerins, Faustus of Riez, Irenaeus, Origen, Ambrose, John Chrysostom, and even Ephraem the Syrian in Latin translation. However, the young monk was most greatly influenced by Augustine. The rigorous life of the monastery injured his health forcing him to immigrate to Arles, which offered not only a more healthful climate but also the best medical care. There Caesarius visited the school of the rhetor Julianus Pomerius, whose ascetic lifestyle and preaching he admired greatly. Aeonius, bishop of Arles, ordained Caesarius deacon and then priest and entrusted him with the supervision of the monastery on the Rhone Island. Several years later Aeonius died and Caesarius succeeded him. In 502 Caesarius was ordained bishop and took control of the most important diocese in Gaul, Arles, which he was destined to rule for the next forty years. On two separate occasions, in 505 under the Visigoth King Alarich II and later in 512 under the Ostrogoth King Theoderich, Bishop Caesarius became embroiled in political controversy only to be both times vindicated. During his rule as bishop, he showed great personal interest in the day to day problems of the faithful; this is reflected above all in his frequent, often daily preaching. In addition, he encouraged the monastic movement, writing rules and establishing a cloister under the direction of his sister Caesarea. In the course of the years he managed to bring Arles closer to Rome becoming the first known bishop in the West to be awarded the pallium. He called no fewer than six synods -- Agde (506), Arles (524), Carpentras (527), Orange (529), Vaison (529), and Marseilles (533). His greatest theological concerns were the struggles against Arianism and Semipelagianism. On August 27, 542 Caesarius died at the age of 72.[42]

First and foremost among the writings of Caesarius are his sermons,[43] which have been passed down to us in various collections often under the name of Augustine. Caesarius preached prolifically, usually basing his homilies on scriptural texts. His preaching is directed toward the common folk and is thus extremely valuable for understanding the religious climate of his times. The homilies reveal a continuing struggle to prevent among the faithful lapses into pagan practices and superstition. His other writings[44] include two monastic rules, one for men and another for women, as well as several tractates against Arianism and Semipelagianism. Several letters and the Testamentum sancti Caesarii are also genuine. Finally, of primary interest to our study is an Apocalypse commentary also known as the pseudo-Augustinian homilies,[45] which will now be treated in greater detail.

2. Expositio de Apocalypsi de sancti Iohannis (the pseudo-Augustinian homilies)

a. Authorship

G. Morin has built an indisputable case for considering Caesarius author of the so-called pseudo-Augustinian homilies.[46] First, he refutes O. Bardenhewer's assertion that Gennadius of Marseilles is the author of the work in question.[47] The only manuscript that mentions Gennadius is codex H.6 of Saint John's College in Cambridge, which obviously received both its title and author from an industrious scribe who was familiar with the spurious last chapter of Gennadius' De viribus inlustribus.[48] Second, Morin found many stylistic similarities between the pseudo-Augustinian homilies and other known homilies of Caesarius. In this context he cites above all the Quinquaginta homiliarum, a collection of sermons clearly composed by Caesarius using Augustine as a source. Since Morin's arguments are based upon neither ambiguous Sprachgefühl nor general content, but rather upon specific, concrete words and expressions, Caesarian authorship of the pseudo-Augustinian collection cannot be questioned.

b. Form

Though certain that Caesarius wrote the pseudo-Augustinian homilies, we must also concede that the work is atypical. In no other instance do we possess a collection of scriptural homilies based upon a single biblical book. Morin speculates that the pseudo-Augustinian homilies were never actually preached by the bishop of Arles but rather represent a collection of material which he wished to use in writing a future series of homilies.[49] Apparently Caesarius never had the opportunity to revise his notes and the collection of raw material has been passed down to us as it now stands. According to Morin, there is sufficient reason to advance this hypothesis because we possess similar collections from Caesarius -- for example, the Vatican cod. lat. 9882, which contains six collections of homilies attributed to Isidore, Augustine, and Caesarius. Actually, this hypothesis is quite reasonable because it does solve two major problems with the text. First, the pseudo-Augustinian collection has obviously been formed out of a preexisting Apocalypse commentary which was converted into a series of homilies. Second, Caesarius' style as well as his pastoral and theological interests are most conspicuous. Morin's hypothesis reconciles both of these characteristics by taking into consideration the source or sources while at the same time accounting for Caesarius' work on the text.

c. Date

Unfortunately, that great scholar of Caesarius, Morin, never attempted to date the pseudo-Augustinian homilies and thus the task falls upon us. In any event we may be absolutely certain that the work was written during Caesarius' rule as bishop of Arles, namely between 502 and 542. G. Langgärtner has attempted to date the collection more accurately on the basis of its content.[50] In the tenth sermon there is a reference to the heretics' persecution of the Church, which has taken the place of the earlier pagan persecutions.[51] Caesarius writes that Arians are now in power.[52] Thus Langgärtner would date the collection possibly before the death of Alarich in 507 and in any case before the end of Ostrogoth rule roughly in the decade after the death of Theoderich the Great in 526. Langgärtner's observation concerning the text is accurate. We do have a direct historical reference to heretics and specifically to Arians, who are exercising political power at the time the text was written. Unfortunately, Langgärtner has managed to achieve nothing with this information. Using this and other references, we are capable of far greater precision.

Let us now investigate the matter more closely. First, in addition to the one explicit reference to the Arians there are many references to persecution. Of course, some of these references originate from Caesarius' sources. Nevertheless, in one case Caesarius himself supplements the text of Tyconius by drawing upon Hegesippus.[53] The reference is to the fall of Jerusalem which seems to be a veiled allusion to the siege of Arles. Second, we must consider the historical facts. When Caesarius ascended to the see of Arles in 502, the Visigoths were ruling. Although the Visigoths were

Arian Christians, it seems that the local Roman population and specifically the Catholics had fared well under their rule.[54] Between the years 508 and 510 the city of Arles was besieged by an alliance of Franks and Burgundians. The inhabitants of the city, although they would have been for the most part Romans and thus Catholic, did not attempt to come to the aid of the Catholic Franks but rather opposed them.[55] Nevertheless, the city would never have been able to hold out against the onslaught had not the Ostrogoths come to its aid. As a result of the war the effective rule of the city of Arles passed from the Visigoths to the Ostrogoths. Ostrogoth rules seems to have been much stricter. Reading Caesarius' Sermon 127, which he preached in the year 510 immediately after the unsuccessful siege of the city, we have the impression that its inhabitants were suffering greatly under their new rulers.[56]

Bringing the concrete textual references into synchronization with the historical events can help to determine the date of composition with the greatest possible accuracy. One may indeed consider the siege of Jerusalem a subtle reminder of the siege of Arles. Caesarius draws the same parallel between Jerusalem and Arles more explicitly in Sermon 127 also quoting Hegesippus in that instance. Therefore, the pseudo-Augustinian homilies should be dated after 510, namely after the unsuccessful siege of Arles. Ostrogoth rule after this date coincides very well with the references to the Arians who were then in power, especially since the Ostrogoths were stricter than the Visigoths. With 510 being the earliest possible date of composition, the latest would be after the decline of Ostrogoth rule over Arles. This is far more difficult to determine since Ostrogoth strength waned gradually.[57] The death of Theodorich the Great was followed by a series of palace intrigues, which left the dynasty internally unstable. The consolidation of the Byzantine empire under the emperor Justinian served only to highlight Ostrogoth weakness. As a result of the treaty of 537 Arles officially passed into the hands of Childebert I, the Merovingian King. Although the concrete effects of this treaty are questioned in some quarters,[58] its provisions do nevertheless indicate the decline of Ostrogoth power. Therefore, we may set the outer limit for the composition of the pseudo-Augustinian homilies at the year 537. However, an earlier date is more probable. Thus I propose that the collection was composed between the years 510 and 537, most likely, however, in the decade after the siege of Arles when those events would still have been fresh in mind and Ostrogoth rule would have been an evident and unpleasant reality.

d. Structure

In regard to the structure of the collection we may rely for the most part on the outline of Vogels, whose table indicates what chapters of the Apocalypse are treated in the various homilies.[59] The entire collection bears the title _Expositio de Apocalypse sancti Iohannis,_ while the various sections are identified not as homilies but as _sequentiae._ Often traces of a genuine homelitic style may be found especially either at the beginning or the end of some sections. However, for the most part the work is simply an Apocalypse commentary, which has been artificially divided into homilies. In several instances there is a _recapitulatio_ at the end of the homily, which is a Caesarian characteristic.

e. Sources

The two chief sources of Caesarius, the unrevised commentary of Victorinus and the lost commentary of Tyconius, are known. Victorinus plays a greater role in the first two homilies than in the rest of the collection. Sometimes Caesarius copies from Victorinus' commentary verbatim. Occasionally, he simply extracts the definition of a word or the explanation of an expression. In these cases the typical Caesarian expression, potest (possunt/possumus)...intellegi, assures us that Caesarius himself incorporated the quotations into the text.[60] Several times he introduces the words of Victorinus as a second opinion with the expression et aliter [61] or item aliter.[62] The expression sicut scriptum est is usually reserved for scriptural quotations.[63] On at least two occasions the words et aliter betray a quotation from an unknown source.[64] In each case the suspicion is confirmed by the lack of a parallel in the other Tyconian literature. Finally, there are several passages which seem to be merely influenced by Victorinus but were essentially written by Caesarius.[65]

The most unusual characteristic of the text is the use of Tyconius' commentary. Even a cursory glance over Vogels' table shows immediately that the Apocalypse commentary is not complete; while strangely enough at the same time many verses are commented upon twice. Since these duplicate passages are strikingly similar, the only logical explanation for such repetition within a single work is the use of two different manuscripts of the same source in making the compilation. Without a doubt Caesarius had two copies of Tyconius' commentary. Exactly how faithful these two copies are to the original commentary of Tyconius can only be determined through careful comparison to the other Tyconian literature. In any event the text of Tyconius did undergo some revision before reaching Caesarius, especially the recension which will be identified here as B. In addition, Caesarius himself occasionally changed the text of both Tyconian recensions, introducing his own comments. On one occasion Caesarius even distances himself from the opinion of Tyconius by writing: volunt aliqui...intellegi.[66] Recension B is an abbreviated version written in shorter sentences; it lets itself be identified through the constant repetition of the words quod autem dicit (dixit) dispersed throughout the text. The actual basis of the entire pseudo-Augustinian homilies is Tyconian recension A, which has been edited and partially revised by Caesarius. A is supplemented by Victorinus, especially in the first two homilies, and by Tyconian recension B throughout the work. Finally, some sections do come from Caesarius, who might on occasion also use another source.

In his work on the Latin Apocalypse text, Vogels attempted to identify the two Tyconian recensions[67] as well as the quotations from Victorinus.[68] Due to progress in the research, above all the availability of Morin's critical edition, Vogels' findings are now open to revision. First, in regard to the two Tyconian recensions Vogels did not attempt to analyze the first and second homilies. Quite clearly Caesarius had dedicated more time to these passages integrating the two Tyconian manuscripts with one another while drawing heavily upon Victorinus. Nevertheless, some sections can now be identified. In the subsequent homilies Vogels' work for the most part needs only occasional revision. Second, in regard to the identification of quotations from Victorinus, many corrections must be made. On the one hand, there are several passages from Victorinus which Vogels completely overlooked.[69] On the other hand, there are several passages identified by Vogels as coming from Victorinus which actually pertain to the Tyconian tradition.[70] Therefore, I have undertaken an analysis of the entire pseudo-Augustinian collection, indicating the source of each passage as far as possible. In this regard there are certain criteria to be followed. First, a simple comparison to the text of Victorinus will reveal if he is a source. Second, parallel passages in any of the other Tyconian literature indicates either A or B. Recension B can be identified by the telltale quod autem dicit (dixit) which customarily introduces the biblical phrase about to be explained. B is also usually more succinct. Third, passages from Caesarius himself must be identified through criteria of style or content.[71] In the subsequent schema the various sources will be identified by the following symbols:

V Victorinus

A Tyconius recension A

B Tyconius recension B

C Caesarius, where he does not rely on a source

X possible unknown source

? identification not possible

At the end of each homily a short explanation of the division and a description of the characteristics of the text will follow.

References to the book of the Apocalypse are also indicated; when the reference is in parenthesis, the Apocalypse text is not directly quoted. Scriptural texts other than the Apocalypse are not taken into consideration.

Expositio de Apocalypsi sancti Iohannis.

210,2-211,1 Ea...cognoscite	C	--
211,1-3 In...gratiae	? A or B	(1:4)
211,3-4 Quod...Pilato	B	1:5
211,4-7 Fecit...sacerdotium	V 18,9-11	1:6
211,7-10 Et...Christo	? A or B	1:12; 1:13
211,11-15 Quod...sanctorum	B	1:13
211,15-212,13 sicut...redditur	A	(1:13); 1:14; 1:15
212,13-17 In zona...protulit	V 22,3-7	(1:13); 1:16
212,17-20 et...dicitur	V 24,5-10	(1:16)
212,20-27 Vox...eius	V 24,18-26,6	1:15
213,1-3 Quod...reliqua	B	1:16
213,4-15 Septem...aeternam	V 26,9-30,5	(1:16)
213,16-19 Et...dicit	C	--
213,19-20 Testis...est	V	1:5
213,20-28 Septem...dignetur	C	1:13

Remarks on homily 1

Caesarius was quite free when quoting from the commentary of Victorinus. He omits sections and sometimes adds his own words. Often he merely paraphrases. One may safely assume that he was just as free in utilizing his other sources. Caesarius' revision of the text is apparent on at least two occasions: <u>et gratia baptismi nullis praecedentibus meritis venit</u> (211,22) and <u>in voce, praedicatio apostolorum. Quod autem supra dixit</u> (212,21-22). The <u>recapitulatio</u> (213,16-28) is essentially from Caesarius based on the previous text.

Incipit sequentia de expositione Apocalypsi

214,2-3 Fratres...intellegitur	C	--
214,3-4 quod...tuum	B	2:5
214,4 hoc...populum	V 34,7-8	(2:5)
214,4 pro peccatis	C	--
214,4-6 et...sua	A	2:16
214,6-10 Et..eorum	B	1:16
214,10-12 Stellam...est	V 38,16-19	2:28
214,12-14 peccatum...sequantur	C	--
214,14-15 Non...habere	V 40,8-10	(3:2)
214,16 Et ideo	C	--
214,16-18 dicit...impleas	V 42,18- 44,2	3:18

214,19-21 Ostium...est	V 44,8-11	4:1
214,21-215,3 Solium..saeculi	V 26,12-18	4:2; 4:3
215,3-5 potest...patiuntur	C	(4:3)
215,5-7 Mare...datur	V 48,5-8	4:6
215,7-216,19 Quod...christianum	A	1:18; (1:20); 2:1
216,19-217,8 Quod...boni	B	2:5; 2:7; 2:9; 2:10; 2:13
217,8-12 Vincenti...vitae	A	2:17
217,13 Possimus...accipere	V 38,4	(2:17)
217,13-18 Et...crucifixissent	A	2:17
217,18-21 Quod...imponunt	B	2:20
217,21-218,5 Potest...mali	A	2:20; 2:24; 2:25; 2:26; 2:27; 2:28

Remarks on homily 2

The expression <u>potest (possit, possunt)...intellegi</u> is typical of Caesarius (cf. 425,1; 474,23; 475,6; 475,22; 588,19); therefore, 215,3-5 has been attributed to Caesarius. Since both 215,3-5 and 214,12-14 lie in the midst of quotations from Victorinus, Caesarian authorship rather than the use of A or B is more probable. Vogels, whose opinion I have followed for the remainder for the sermon, begins his classification at 215,7. In the section 215,7-216,19 the words and phrasing as well as the ideas of Caesarius are most evident; cf. <u>Sermones</u> (ed. Morin; 1,1,256,12-22; 630,10). The section 217,21-218,5 is a greatly abbreviated <u>recapitulatio,</u> reflecting Caesarius' concern with heretics.

Item sequentia de Apocalypsi. III.

218,7-9 Modo..est	C	--
218,9-219,15 Novi...conveniunt	A	3:1; 3:2; 3:7; 3:8; 3:12; 3:16; 3:18; 4:1; 4:2; 4:3
219,15-18 Iaspis...ignem	V 46,14-18	(4:3)
219,18-220,27 In...aquilae	A	4:4; 4:5; 4:6; 4:7; 4:8
220,27 et aliter	C	--
220,27 -221,7 alae...animal	V 54,8-21	(4:8)
221,7 in caelum	probably C	--
221,7-9 Et...deum	A	4:8
221,9-10 Viginti...apostolos	V 56,3-5	(4:10 or 4:4)
221,11-12 fulgora...testamenti	V 56,14-17	(4:5)
221,12-20 Mittentes...Adam	A	4:11

Remarks on homily 3

The structure of this homily is much less complicated than that of the previous two. Caesarius basically used A, where Rev. 3 and 4 is treated, which he on several occasions supplemented with Victorinus.

IIII. Sequentia de Apocalypsi.

221,22 -223,4 Et...novum	A	5:1; 5:2; 5:3; 5:4; 5:6; 5:7; 5:8; 5:9

223,4-10 cantantes...testamenti	V 66,2-19	(5:9)
223,10-23 Et vidi...saeculorum	A	5:11; 5:12; 5:13
223,23 Amen	C	--

Remarks on homily 4

This homily is similar to the previous one, being limited to the text of A on Rev. 5, supplemented in one instance with Victorinus.

V. Item sequentia.

223,25-26 Sicut...Iohannes	C	--
223,26 --224,7 Et...sanctum	A	6:2
224,7-11 Postea...sunt	V 68,3-8	(6:2)
224,11-21 Et...habet	A	6:3; 6:4
224,21 Sicut...est	C	--
224,21-225,12 equum...mors	B	(6:2); (6:4); 6:5; 6:6
225,13-14 Tres...praedixit	V 68,8-10	(6:8)
225,14-15 quae...sunt	probably C	--
225,15-30 Quod...aeternum	B	6:9; 6:12; 6:13; 6:14; 6:15
225,30-32 auxiliante...Amen	C	--

Remarks on homily 5

Once again the structure is not at all complicated. The switch from A to B is evident and even introduced by Caesarius with the words: <u>Sicut ergo supra dictum est.</u>

VI. Item sequentia.

226,2-25 Et...congredi	A	7:2; 7:3; 6:5; 6:6; 6:8
226,25-26 Tres...praenuntiatur	V 68,8-9	(6:8)
226,26-228,4 Equus...abscondatur	A	(6:2); (6:4); (6:8); 6:8; 6:5; 6:12; 6:13; 6:14; 6:15; 6:16
228,4 et aliter	C	--
228,4-7 qui...puniantur	X	(6:16)
228,7-26 Donec...albis	A	7:3; 6:6; 7:4; 7:9
228,26-27 Stolas...intellegit	V 76,1-2	(7:9)
228,27-229,27 Et...motus	A	7:11; 7:13; 7:14; 7:15; 7:16; 7:17; 8:1; 8:2; 8:3; 8:5
229,27-28 Omnia...virtutes	V 56,16-17	(8:5)
229,28-231,6 Et...volat	A	8:6; 8:7; 8:8; 8:9; 8:10; 8:11; 8:12; 8:13
231,6-7 Sicut...est	C	--
231,7-17 alius...albis	B	(7:2); 7:3; 6:6; (7:4); (7:9)
231,16 in...sancti	V 76,1-2	(7:9)
231,16-232,26 Angelos...volat	B	(7:11); 7:13; 7:14; 7:15; 8:1; 8:2; 8:3; 8:5; 8:6; 8:7; 8:8; 8:10; 8:11; 8:12; 8:13
232,26-29 concedat...etc.	C	--

Remarks on homily 6

What appears to be a complicated collage of various texts

might be much more simple than first meets the eye. The A text begins with the comments on Rev. 7:2-3. Then, the sixth chapter of the Apocalypse is treated after which Rev. 7:3 is again taken up, followed by Rev. 6:6; 7:4 etc. Then A continues to Rev. 8:13. The B text beginning at 231,7 is similar except that chapter 6 is not treated at length. However, in B we also find Rev. 6:6 following 7:3. Interestingly enough the same order is to be found at Beatus 4,4,16-18, which leads one to believe that this order stands in the original text of Tyconius at this point. Therefore, we could hypothesize that the comments on chapter 6, which appear to be entirely out of place, were actually introduced into the text because the author or editor (either Caesarius or the editor of A) was misled by the original text of Tyconius. Basically in this sermon we have the A text on chapters 7 and 8 with chapter 6 being inserted into chapter 7. Then follows the B text on chapters 7 and 8 without the insertion. Also note that the references to baptism at 230,22-23 probably come from Caesarius.

VII. Item sequentia.

232,32-33 Modo...quia	C	--
232,33-235,13 quinto...sol	A	9:1; 9:2; 9:3; 9:4; 9:5; 9:6; 9:7; 9:8; 9:10; 9:11; 9:12; 9:13; 9:14;9:15; 9:16; 9:17; 9:19; 10:1
235,13 id...resurrectione	V 88,8	(10:1)
235,13-15 sicut...ignis	A	10:1
235,15 pedes...dicit	V 88,11-12	(10:1)

235,15-236,5 per...resurrectionem	A	10:2; 10:3; 10:4; 10:6; 10:7
236,6 Quod...est	C	--
236,6-238,3 quinto...signatum	B	9:1; 9:2; 9:5; 9:7; 9:11; 9:14; 9:17; 9:19; 10:1; 10:2; 10:3; 10:4
238,3-5 Quam... Amen	C	--

Remarks on homily 7

Here we have text A on Rev. 9 and 10 followed by text B on the same serving as a recapitulatio -- a pattern which will repeat itself with variations in many of the following sermons.

VIII. Item sequentia.

238,7-15 Vox...intellexeris	A	10:8; 10:9
238,15-16 sicut...aliter	C	--
238,16-21 Erit...asperum	X	10:9
238,21-241,6 Et...reddentibus	A	11:1; 11:2; 11:3; 11:4; 11:5; 11:6; 11:7; 11:8; 11:9; 11:10; 11:11; 11:12
241,6 Unde...dignetur	C	--

VIIII. Item sequentia.

241,8-9 Quod...quia	C	--
241,9-242,2 In...possunt	A	11:13; 11:19; 12:1
242,2-3 Sole...significat	V 106,4-5	(12:1)
242,3-9 propter...terram	A	12:3; 12:4

242,9-11 Clauda...mulieris	C	--
242,11-243,29 Multi...est	A	12:2; 12:4; 12:5; 12:6; 12:7; 12:8; 12:9; 12:10; 12:12
243,29-30 De...dignetus	C	--

Remarks on homily 9

Once again the comments on baptism at 242,9-11 are probably from Caesarius.

X. Item sequentia.

243,32 Modo...quia	C	--
243,32-244,18 cum...virtutis	A	12:13; 12:14; 12:15; 12:16
244,18 item aliter	C	--
244,18-22 mulierem...est	V 110, 10-112, 3	(12:14)
244,22-23 Aqua...vindictam	V 112,11-14	(12:16)
244,23-245,6 Et...commixtum	A	12:17; 12:18; 13:1; 13:2
246,6 pedes...eius	V 116,12-15	13:2
245,7-26 Et dedit...in vobis	C	13:2; 13:3; 13:4
245,26-246,8 Et data...signata	A	13:5; 13:6; 13:7; 13:8
246,8 Quod...prestare	C	--

Remarks on homily 10

In this sermon at 245,7-26 Caesarius turns his attention to

heretics, specifically the Arians. Caesarius does depend upon sources at this point and his own comments are inextricably woven into his sources.

XI. Item sequentia.

246,10-11 In...dicentem	C	--
246,11-248,8 Et...reliqua	A	13:11; 13:12; 13:13; 13:16; 13:15; 13:16; 13:17; 13:18; 14:1; 14:2; 14:4
248,8-15 Quod...conligatam	B	14:4
248,15-23 Addit...reliqua	A	14:5; 14:6: 14:7
248,23-25 Volunt...praedicabit	V 130,10-14	(14:6)
248,25-249,15 Et...ecclesia	A	14:8; 14:14
249,15-17 Forte...spiritalem	? C	--
249,17-27 falcem...sexcenti	A	14:19; 14:20

Remarks of homily 11

Caesarius' influence seems to be more evident in this sermon than in many of the others. For example, 246,21-25 as well as 248,12-15 deal with heresies and heretics, a concern of Caesarius. Section 249,15-17 has been singled out in the schema because it does not seem to fit at all.

XII. Item sequentia.

250,2-3 In...vidisse	C	--
250,3-252,10	A	15:1; 15:2; 15:3; 15:5; 15:6;

Aliud...Christo		15:7; (16:2); 16:3; 16:8; 16:9; 16:10; 16:11; 16:12

Item sequentia de Apocalypsi. XIII.

252,12-13 Sanctus...loqueretur	C	--
252,13-254,14 solito...nimis	A	16:13; 16:14; 16:18; 16:19; 16:20; 16:21
254,14-23 Recapitulat...luxuriae	B	17:1; 17:2; 17:3; 17:4
254,24-256,16 Nam...Amen	C	17:15; 16:16; 20:8; 17:3

Remarks on homily 13

One should not be confused by the threefold mention of a recapitulation (252,14; 253,20; 254,14); there is also such a reference at Beatus 8,6,3 and Primasius 897, 41. Caesarius' _recapitulatio,_ as Morin points out, begins at 254,24, being indicated by the words _sicut iam dictum est._ At 255,17-20 Caesarius was influenced by Hegesippus; cf. _Sermo_ 127 (ed. Morin; 1,1,501-504). Caesarius himself appears to have written 256,1-16 using the previous text; compare, for example, 256,4-5 with 254,21-22 and 256,5-9 with 254,27-30. The expression _quantum possumus_ is typical of Caesarius. Some Tyconian elements are present at 254,24-255,1 and 256,1-10 making this section extremely complex. This and the next homily comment upon Rev. 17:3 four times: 254,14-23; 254,24-255,1; 256,1-10; 256,19-24!

Item sequentia. XIIII.

256,18-19 viderit...ecclesiae	A	17:3; 17:4; 17:5; 17:6; 17:8
257,22-258,15 Quod...ecclesiae	B	17:8
258,15-20	C	--

De...Amen

Item sequentia. XV.

258,22-24 In...dei	C	--
258,24-260,9 qui...moratur 18:2	A	17:12; 17:13; 17:14; 17:15; 17:16; 17:17; 17:18; 18:1;
160,9-10 Reges...dei	C	--

Remarks on homily 15

Notice that the same words begin and end the sermon; Caesarius is referring here to the civil rulers, namely the Ostrogoth oppressors.

Item sequentia. XVI.

260,12-19 Quotiens...dicit	C	--
260,19-264,5 Quoniam...adimpletur	A	18:3; 18:4; 18:5; 18:6; 18:7; 18:8; 18:9; 18:10; 18:13; 18:15; 18:16; 18:17; 18:18; 19:19; 20:1; 20:2

Remarks on homily 16

Vogels[72] points out that the remarks on Rev. 18:18 (263,17) actually continue after interruption in the next sermon at 265,27 with the words <u>post haec ait.</u>

Item sequentia de Apocalypsi. XVII.

264,7-9 Ea...se	C	--
264,9-266,31 caelum...iniustitiis	A	19:11; 19:12; 19:13; 19:14; 19:15; 19:16; 19:17; 19:18; 20:3; 18:19;18:20; 18:21; 18:22; 18:23; 18:24

266,32-267,24 In...est	B	19:12; 19:15; 19:17; 19:18; 20:3
267,24-26 isti...sustinere	? C	(20:3)
267,26-268,8 Quod...posteritatem	B	18:10; 18:21; 18:23; 18:24
268,8-11 quia...saeculorum	C	--

Remarks on homily 17

The switch from A to B is once again signaled by Caesarius with the words de quo supra dictum est beginning the recapitulatio. The reference to sufficient grace, namely the inability of being tempted beyond one's strength (267,24-26), divided the comments on Rev. 19 (including 20:3) from those on Rev. 18. This inverse order is also present in the A text.

Item sequentia. XVIII.

268,13-14 In...ait	C	--
268,14-271,22 audivi...secunda	A	19:1; 19:2; 19:3; 19:6; 19:7; 19:8; 20:4; 20:5; 20:6; 20:7; 20:8; 20:9; 20:10; 20:12; 20:13; 20:14; 20:15; 21:1; 21:2; 21:3; 21:4; 21:5; 21:6 21:7; 21:8
271,23 Quod...est	C	--
271,23-273,1 indicavit...filius	B	19:2; 19:3; 19:7; (20:14); 20:5; 20:6; (20:7); (20:8); 20:9; 20:13; 20:14; 21:6; 21:7
272,2-3 quod...Amen	C	--

Item sequentia. XVIIII.

273,5-6 Sicut...dicens	C	--

273,6-276,20 veni...cito	A	21:9; 21:10; 21:11; 21:12; 21:13; 21:14; 21:15; 21:18; 21:19; 21:20; 21:21; 21:22; 21:23; 21:24; 21:25; 21:26; 21:27; 22:1; 22:2; 22:3; 22:4; 22:5; 22:10; 22:11; 22:12;22:13; 22:14; 22:15; 22:16; 22:17; 22:18; 22:19; 22:20
276,21-277,29 Mons...apertae	B	(21:10); (21:11); (21:12); (21:13); (21:15); (21:18); (21:19); (21:20); (21:21); (21:24) 21:22; 21:23; (21:24); (22:2); 22:5; 22:11; 22:10
277,29-34 Et...Amen	C	22:20

f. Results

Following is a summary of findings concerning the possible use of Caesarius' pseudo-Augustine homilies in reconstructing the lost Tyconius text:

1. The lost Tyconius commentary was used by Caesarius in two recensions, identified above as A and B.
2. Both recensions probably were incomplete and had undergone some revision before reaching Caesarius.
3. Caesarius himself further edited and revised both A and B while writing the homilies.
4. A will <u>usually</u> but not always be more reliable than B.
5. The passages which come from Victorinus, Caesarius and other unidentified sources are to be eliminated in the reconstruction.
6. There might still remain within the sections indicated above as A or B some brief and isolated passages from Caesarius or other sources which have not yet been identified.

C. Primasius

1. The life and writings of Primasius
2. The Apocalypse commentary of Primasius
    a. Manuscripts and printed editions
    b. Structure of Primasius' commentary
    c. Date of composition
    d. Prologue, conclusion, introduction, and <u>capitula</u>
    e. Sources of Primasius' commentary
    f. Primasius and Tyconius
    g. Results

1. The life and writings of Primasius

Biographical information about Primasius is sparse.[73] Despite some confusion we are certain that Primasius was bishop of Hadrumetum, the principal city of the province of Byzancena. We catch a brief glimpse into Primasius' life because of his involvement in the Three Chapters controversy, especially in regard to the power struggle between Emperor Justinian and Pope Vigilius.[74] During the controversy Primasius was closely aligned with Pope Vigilius, who seemed to be constantly changing his position. Primasius was among the African bishops who were summoned to Constantinople by imperial edict in 551.[75] In obeisance to the Pope he also refused to participate in the Second Council of Constantinople, explicitly informing Bishop Theodore of Limyra: <u>Papa non praesente non venio.</u>[76] Later he affixed his signature to the <u>Constitutum</u> of Pope Vigilius. Finally, after Vigilius had condemned the Three

Chapters, Primasius followed suit.[77] The chronicler, Victor of Tunnuna, who himself suffered exile to a monastery because of his views, vehemently condemned Primasius as an opportunist, who had taken advantage of the situation to become Primate of Byzancena. He informs us that Primasius died shortly after returning to Africa. Since Victor includes these remarks in his chronicle under the year 552, most scholars conclude that Primasius died during that year or shortly thereafter.[78] However, Haußleiter questions the accuracy of Victor's account, which is certainly prejudiced against Primasius, and opts instead for a later date closer to 558.[79] Indeed, it is difficult to explain how Primasius' signature could have appeared on the Constitutum of May 14, 553 after his death in 552.

In addition to the Apocalypse commentary, the existence of only one other writing of Primasius is documented. Although the work has been lost, Haußleiter[80] has been able to describe its characteristics on the basis of Cassiodore's testimony.[81] First, the work was written by Primasius as an appendix to his Apocalypse commentary, or the both pieces were at least connected with one another in the manuscript which Cassiodore possessed. Second, the work consisted of one book with the title, Quid faciat haereticum. Third, the book deals with the gifts which may be brought to the altar in the temple of the Lord. According to Haußleiter, this last statement can be understood only analogously in the light of Rev. 11:1 and 8:5. Therefore, he concluded that the lost work was less a polemical condemnation of heretics than an ethical instruction. Isidore later described the work as three books presenting a catalogue of heresies much in the style of Augustine's De haeresibus ad

Quodvultdeum, which Primasius supposedly wished to complete.[82] The separation of Quid faciat haereticum from Primasius' Apocalypse commentary and its subsequent association with Augustine's De haeresibus contributed to Isidore's misrepresentation of the work. Both the commentary on the epistle to the Hebrews and the commentary on the epistles of Saint Paul,[83] which unfortunately had given Primasius the reputation of being a bad exegete, are spurious.[84]

2. The Apocalypse commentary of Primasius

a. Manuscripts and printed editions

In editing the version of the Apocalypse used by the ancient African church on the basis of Primasius' commentary, Haußleiter undertook a thorough investigation of the four manuscripts at his disposal, dividing them into three families and constructing a genealogy.[85] Having discovered an Oxford manuscript from the Bodleian Library after his work was written, he treated it in an appendix and concluded that it constituted a separate tradition belonging to none of the three groups already identified;[86] variations in the Apocalypse text from this manuscript have been introduced into the critical apparatus of his edition. Later he identified three editiones principes of the commentary -- Cologne (1535), Paris (1544) and Basel (1544) -- and concluded that Cologne edition is the basis for all subsequent printings with the sole exception of the Basel edition.[87] In the supplement volume of Migne those longer passages which were entirely omitted from the Paris edition,[88] which was the parent of the Migne edition, were eventually supplied through the Basel edition.[89] However, Haußleiter's critical edition was limited exclusively to the Apocalypse text in Primasius' commentary.[90] Vogels evaluated Haußleiter's findings in his own study of the Latin Apocalypse text and stands for the most part in agreement with him.[91] According to Vogels, Haußleiter's major flaw was to presuppose the existence of a single commonly accepted Apocalypse version in the African church. Vogels rightly asserted that no such unity in regard to the biblical text existed before the Vulgate. In regard to the Apocalypse text he proposed only minor modifications.

A. W. Adams has recently produced the first critical edition of Primasius' commentary.[92] His minute description of the seven extant manuscripts and the three editiones principes has clarified the genealogy and affirmed Haußleiter's conclusions. The Paris edition and all subsequent printed editions were based on the Cologne edition of 1535 except the Basel edition of 1544 which was based on a now lost Murbach manuscript. However, Adams' unique contribution is his evaluation of the Codex Bodleianus MS. Douce 140 (21714) and its collation in the present edition. This is the same manuscript which had been initially overlooked by Haußleiter. The Bodleianus, which is the oldest witness to Primasius' commentary, stands at the head of the genealogy and provides approximately 147 lines of printed text found nowhere else. Unfortunately one must exercise due caution in using Adams' apparatus and tables since he does occasionally overlook some references. For example, 15,179-16,199 and 33,260-261 and 48,51-57 correspond to Beatus 1,4,28-31; 34-35; 41-42 and 2,4,38 and 3,2,28-29 respectively, while 82,490-493 corresponds to Caesarius

222,4-6.

b. The structure of Primasius' commentary

Primasius composed his commentary in five books with the first two having their own short introductions. At the beginning of the work there is a prologue and at the end a concluding summary. Each book begins with a list of chapter headings or capitula. The structure of the entire commentary is presented in the following outline:

Prologue (CChr.SL 92, 1-4)

Book I (CChr.SL 92, 5-58)

- introduction
- capitula I-VII
- commentary on Rev. 1-4

Book II (CChr.SL 92, 59-132)

- capitula I-X
- introduction
- commentary on Rev. 5-8:1

Book III (CChr.SL 92, 133-190)

- capitula I-XXII
- commentary on Rev. 8:2-12

Book IV (CChr.SL 92, 191-247)

- capitula I-XX
- commentary on Rev. 13-17

Book V (CChr.SL 92, 248-311)

- capitula I-XXXIX
- commentary on Rev. 18-22

Concluding summary (CChr.SL 92, 312-316)

c. Date of composition

Although there is no concrete reference to the date of Primasius' commentary, we do have both external and internal evidence at our disposal, which will enable us to arrive at a reasonable hypothesis. First, in his Institutiones Cassiodore (480-575) mentions Primasius' commentary and explicitly calls it a contemporary writing.[93] Although the reference is of little assistance in determining the exact date of composition, it prevents one both from doubting Primasius' authorship and from attempting to place the work in a later era. Second, Primasius in his comments on Rev. 12:1 mentions six heretical leaders, who according to him propound Christological errors: Valentinus, Bardesanes, Apollinaris, Nestorius, Eutyches, and Timotheus Aelurus.[94] Since Timotheus, Patriarch of Alexandria, was a monophysite and ardent opponent of Chalcedon,[95] Primasius most probably wrote this reference toward the beginning of the Three Chapters controversy. Therefore, I concur with the opinion of Haußleiter, who would set the date of composition as early as possible during the life of Primasius, about 540.[96]

d. Prologue, conclusion, introduction, and capitula

Now let us turn our attention to those parts of Primasius' work which do not belong specifically to the commentary on the Apocalypse as such -- (1) the prologue, (2) the concluding summary, (3) the introductions to Books I and II and (4) the chapter headings or _capitula._

(1) The prologue[97] is addressed to "an illustrious and religious man" named Castor, about whom no further information is available. Primasius then clearly and explicitly names Augustine and Tyconius as his sources. In regard to the latter, however, he is somewhat defensive, insisting that good and worthwhile teaching can even be found in the writings of a heretic. Primasius uses a quite vivid metaphor, that of collecting precious gems from a dungheap, to describe the task at hand in regard to the commentary of the Donatist theologian. Though distancing himself from Tyconius, Primasius relies on him from the very beginning of his work, explaining that one and the same thing may be described in the Apocalypse in many pictures. He also insists on the worth of the Apocalypse, quoting Epistle 58 of Saint Jerome,[98] whose statement occasionally reappears in introductions to Apocalypse commentaries.[99]

(2) The conclusion[100] to the commentary is in the words of Primasius a _recapitulatio,_ a summary of the contents of each of the five books. Haußleiter's edition divides the summary into twenty numbered chapters on the basis of the Basel _editio princeps._ [101] Adams' edition concurs.[102]

(3) The introduction to Book I[103] explains the meaning of the title 'apocalypse,' the authorship of Saint John, and the time and place of composition. The introduction of Book II presents some exegetical principles.[104] Although the law of God is a unity because of the one Spirit, it can be understood in three ways

corresponding to the multiple distribution of grace and the three ways sins can be forgiven by either baptism or penance or martyrdom.

Although Primasius relied upon sources, we may be certain that he himself wrote both the prologue and the conclusion to the commentary. The introductions to both Books I and II are filled with specific information, which indicates a somewhat greater reliance on sources. General information on the Apocalypse as found in the introduction to Book I is often contained in prefaces to the biblical book in various codices.[105] The exegetical principles expressed in the introduction to Book II, which speak of the threefold understanding of the law of God, seem to bear evidence of an Origenian influence.[106] Both introductions are, nevertheless, integral to the work and were obviously written by Primasius. The capitula, however, are essentially different from all the above mentioned sections of Primasius' commentary and demand our special attention.

(4) Haußleiter investigated the capitula and came to the conclusion that they were not written by Primasius but were taken from elsewhere and introduced by Primasius into the commentary.[107] Unfortunately, I cannot entirely agree with Haußleiter's assertion. One can readily see that Primasius himself did not write the capitula. However, that he himself introduced these chapter headings into the commentary is doubtful and highly improbable.

First, we are certain that Primasius did not write the capitula. Haußleiter points out that this would have been a useless repetition of the conclusion which essentially presents the reader with chapter headings in the form of a summary. Furthermore, many of the capitula do not correspond to the contents of the commentary. The most evident disparity between the commentary and the capitula is in regard to Rev. 20:1-21:5, where capitula XII to XXI of Book V in no way resemble the commentary's lengthy quotation from Augustine's De civitate Dei.[108] In addition, the chapter headings are not a unity in themselves since they refer both to the Apocalypse itself and to a commentary on the Apocalypse. The biblical translation used in the capitula is not that of Primasius; sometimes the Apocalypse text corresponds to Tyconius' translation, other times to the Vulgate. The evidence is overwhelming that Primasius did not write the capitula.

This leaves us with the second and more urgent question: where did the capitula come from? Haußleiter would have us believe that Primasius drew upon some source and tailored the already existing capitula to fit his commentary. This theory is supported by the unusually large number of chapter headings. The twenty-four elders multiplied by the four animals before the throne gives us the 96 capitula.[109] Haußleiter cites some parallels in the commentary of Andreas of Caesarea and in several manuscripts, all of which divide the Apocalypse either into twenty-four sections, or by multiples of twenty-four.

Haußleiter's theory, however, makes more sense if the capitula were introduced into the commentary not by Primasius but by someone else. This would have had to occur shortly after the composition of the work since the capitula or portions thereof are found in every manuscript. The extremely short length of the capitula does not offer much information in regard to either content or style. Nor does the literary form give a point of orientation; the capitula are simply 'little chapters,' which summarize the contents of a written work, usually a biblical book. The vocabulary of the capitula, for example the two non-biblical Greek words haeresiarces and gastrimargia or error gentilitatis as a technical term for paganism,[110] indicates a late date of composition; nevertheless, the capitula could have been written at the time of Primasius or even a century earlier. Therefore, the only indication that Primasius had nothing to do with the capitula lies in their total non-integration into the commentary. As Haußleiter himself points out, the chapter headings simply do not correspond to the contents of the commentary in many instances. Furthermore, the capitula libri primi are placed between the introduction to Book I and the beginning of the commentary, while the capitula libri secundi are placed before the introduction to Book II. The overall impression concerning the relationship of the capitula to the rest of the commentary is one of complete disparity and disharmony. This would be, however, most unusual for Primasius, whose acknowledged and unacknowledged sources are always well integrated into his work. Therefore, because of the lack of congruence between the capitula and the commentary, I conclude that Primasius is not their author and, furthermore, that he himself did not introduce them into his commentary.

e. Sources of Primasius' commentary

Primasius approaches his sources in two distinct ways. In eight instances he names his source and its author and quotes it directly. His other, more common, procedure is simply to copy from the source without any specific acknowledgement. Actually in his prologue Primasius does acknowledge the extensive use of both Augustine and Tyconius and, therefore, does not explicitly name them each time he copies from them. However, his obvious use of the Hieronymian recension of Victorinus' commentary is nowhere acknowledged.[111]

First are those passages where Primasius explicitly acknowledges his source. He directly quotes Augustine six times, Jerome once, and Cyprian once.[112] In each case the references are rather matter-of-factly cited. Primasius does not especially rely on the authority of the fathers, nor does he use them to support argumentation. All of the quotations are either instructional or inspirational. His use of Augustine's <u>De sancta virginitate</u> shows us how he deals with a source. He begins the quotation but repeatedly breaks off and continues elsewhere further on in Augustine's text. However, the passages which he does use are recorded verbatim. His use of <u>De civitate Dei</u> is similar. Primasius' longest single acknowledged quotation is from Augustine's letter <u>Ad Maximum,</u> which is recorded nowhere else and would have been otherwise lost.

Second, there are occasions when Primasius quotes his sources -- namely Augustine and Tyconius, both of whom he mentions in his prologue -- with no explicit acknowledgement in the text of the commentary. The most obvious case, which has already been mentioned, is the lengthy quotation from Book 20 of <u>De civitate Dei</u> in regard to Rev. 20:1-21:5. Once again what he does quote is in word for word correspondence with the original. However, as with his acknowledged quotations Primasius does not hesitate to interrupt the text of the cited work and to continue at a different point. Although both beginning and end of the quotation as well as the interruptions and omissions seem to be arbitrary, his approach is by no means confused. He does not haphazardly quote from various places but proceeds from a starting point directly through the text, departing from his source and using his own words where he deems necessary. Although more often than not the quotation is verbatim, Primasius does occasionally paraphrase, as in the following example:

Primasius, CChr.SL 92, 282,262-266

Illi itaque intelligentur noui et ueteris Testamenti, ut cum in eis ostenditur quid deus fieri praecepisset, in illo clareret quid horum quisque non fecisset siue fecisset. Qui liber non carnaliter cogitandus, nec tamquam scripto exaratus uitas continere putandus est singulorum iudicio recensendas.

<u>De civitate Dei</u> 20,14 (CChr.SL 48, 724,31-42)

Qui est, inquit, uitae uniuscuiusque. Ergo illi libri, quos priore loco posuit, intellegendi sunt sancti, et ueteres et noui, ut in illis ostenderetur, quae Deus fieri sua mandata iussisset; in illo autem, qui est uitae uniuscuiusque, quid horum quisque non fecisset siue fecisset. Qui liber si carnaliter cogitetur, quis eius magnitudinem aut longitudinem ualeat aestimare? Aut quanto tempore legi poterit liber, in quo scriptae sunt uniuersae uitae uniuersorum? An tantus angelorum numerus aderit, quantus hominum erit, et uitam suam quisque ab angelo sibi adhibito audiet recitari? Non ergo unus liber erit omnium, sed singuli singulorum. Scriptura uero ista unum uolens intellegi: Et alius, inquit, liber apertus est.

Since a running quotation from Augustine's work is interrupted at this point, we have below a passage which Primasius choose to omit and above his paraphrase of the omitted passage. Therefore, this is an ideal example to demonstrate how Primasius goes about paraphrasing a source. In order to abbreviate his source, Primasius is forced to become more explicit. There are two concrete examples of this in the text. First, he adds the single word testamenti in order to omit the longer and more ambiguous reference to the books which are to be understood as sacred. Second, he omits the conditional aspect of the rhetorical question in order to state the same sentence less verbosely as a simple fact.

On the basis of Primasius' quotations from works which are known to us, we may draw some conclusions as to his method of using sources. First, Primasius often copies verbatim from his sources. Second, when he chooses to omit a specific section from an ongoing quotation, the omitted section is sometimes paraphrased, sometimes replaced by his own comments, or sometimes totally ignored. Since external criteria will often be lacking in regard to quotations from Tyconius, being aware of Primasius' usual method of dealing with sources will prove to be quite helpful.

f. Primasius and Tyconius

In his entire commentary Primasius mentions Tyconius only twice. The first reference is contained in the prologue, where Primasius acknowledges his selective use of Tyconius' commentary.[113] The second reference is in regard to the translation of Rev. 9:16: Alia porro translatio quam Ticonius exposuit habet....[114] Nowhere is Tyconius mentioned as a commentator of the Apocalypse. Although Primasius certainly depended greatly upon Tyconius' commentary, he scarcely refers to his person, carefully maintaining a respectable distance between himself and the Donatist.

There are seventeen such references to an alia translatio or an equivalent expression,[115] but the above mentioned reference is the only occasion on which Primasius identifies the "other translation" with that of Tyconius. Two questions arise: First, does the "other translation" refer to the translation of Tyconius in each case? Second, does the Apocalypse text of Tyconius appear in the commentary of Primasius on other occasions without specific mention?

Before attempting to answer the first question, let us list the seventeen explicit references to the "other translation" in Primasius' commentary:[116]

Revelation	Primasius
2:17	CCh.SL 92, 31, 195
2:22	CCh.SL 92, 34, 272
4:6	CCh.SL 92, 50, 92
4:8	CCh.SL 92, 56, 225
4:11	CCh.SL 92, 58, 70
6:13	CCh.SL 92, 102, 242
8:9	CCh.SL 92, 140, 114
8:11	CCh.SL 92, 140, 121
9:6	CCh.SL 92, 149, 113
9:16	CCh.SL 92, 155, 246
10:1	CCh.SL 92, 159, 10
10:4	CCh.SL 92, 161, 54
11:8	CCh.SL 92, 169, 96
11:18	CCh.SL 92, 176, 249
13:12	CCh.SL 92, 198, 135

13:13 CCh.SL 92, 200, 179

22:11 CCh.SL 92, 305, 139

Haußleiter does not list the references to the "other translation" at Rev. 11:18 and 13:13; however, he does consider his list to reflect the Tyconian Apocalypse text in each case.[117] Vogels, on the other hand, would make one exception, attributing the alia editio at Rev. 4:6 to Victorinus' Apocalypse text.[118] Neither Haußleiter nor Vogels explains the aliae translationes at Rev. 9:6. The use of the plural in this case prevents us from treating the expression alia translatio or the like as synonymous with "the translation of Tyconius." Nevertheless, barring the one exception indicated by Vogels, we are dealing with a Tyconian Apocalypse text in every instance.

In answer to the second question one may certainly assert that Primasius' use of the Tyconian Apocalypse text is by no means limited to these seventeen references. Primasius is not as close to the exact wording of Tyconius' Apocalypse text as Beatus, Caesarius, or Bede. However, where variant readings are recorded, we are usually dealing with a Tyconian text. Nevertheless, it is often impossible to distinguish between the text of Primasius and that of Tyconius or between a biblical quotation and a paraphrase. In such instances the other witnesses are of great assistance.[119]

Of far greater significance in this investigation is, of course, Primasius' use of Tyconius' commentary. Unfortunately, in calling attention to an excursus in Primasius' commentary at Rev. 5:1,[120] Haußleiter selected a passage which may hardly be considered exemplary.[121] Insisting that the section originates from an unnamed common source, Haußleiter considered the parallel passage of Ambrosius Autpertus[122] to be more complete and more accurate. If indeed his assertion were true, this relatively lengthy passage would be an important find. However, there are several peculiar difficulties which cannot be ignored. First, the passage is admittedly an excursus, departing from the normal verse by verse treatment of the Apocalypse. Second, it is omitted from all Tyconian parallels except the above mentioned commentary of Ambrosius Autpertus, who, however, also knew and used the commentary of Primasius. Third, a spot check of several biblical quotations does not reveal the translation used by Tyconius. Autpertus at this point either used a Vulgate or copied his Apocalypse text from Primasius.[123] The wording of several quotations from Gal. 4:22-28[124] deviates from the wording of the same biblical passages contained in Tyconius' Liber regularum.[125] Fourth, the book of the seven seals is itself a popular theme. Apringius,[126] Isidore,[127] and Beatus[128] all consider the seven seals references to seven specific Christ-events. Autpertus associates the seven seals with the seven gifts of the Holy Spirit.[129] Both of these aspects are brought together in pseudo-Jerome's De septem sigillis.[130] Therefore, contrary to the assertion of Haußleiter I must conclude that Autpertus and Primasius did not have a common source but rather that Autpertus copied from Primasius.[131] For the present let us devote our attention to some typical and indisputable instances of Primasius' quoting from Tyconius, which will enable us to determine whether or not Primasius observed certain methods or patterns in his use of Tyconius' commentary. In the light of this research we will be better equipped to investigate the more unusual and difficult Tyconian passages of Primasius' commentary.

The first example is actually in regard to the comments on Rev. 1:19, but Primasius records the passage at Rev. 2:1. A parallel passage may be found only in the commentary of Beatus, who, of course, did not have Primasius' commentary:

Beatus 1,5,71-73

quem veniens Dominus ipse dividet et non totum servum sed partem eius cum hypocritis pone in finem bella intestina, id est, pugna intra ecclesiam, et septiformis ecclesiae membra, in praesentibus diversa opera, et quae oportet fieri post haec demonstrare futura. non dixit, scribe quae sunt aut quae fuerunt, sed quae oportet post haec fieri. ostendit usque in messis maturitatem zizania crescere, et laboratoribus praecipit bestias et aves abigere.

Primasius, CChr.SL 92, 23,17-24,24

quem veniens dominus ipse diuidet, et non totum seruum, sed partem, inquit, eius cum hypocritis ponet. Incipiens ergo bella intestina, et septiformis ecclesiae diuersa opera in praesentibus futura monstrare, non dixit scribe quae sunt sed quae fieri oportet, praedicans usque in finem saeculi malos cum bonis in ecclesia commisceri, quae sine dubio amplectenda pro bonis, non tamen est deserenda pro malis.

Both passages contain the expression <u>bella intestina,</u> which immediately signals the influence of Tyconius. According to Gennadius[132] Tyconius wrote a work entitled <u>De bello intestino,</u> which is believed to have been of a polemical nature.[133] In his <u>Liber regularum</u> Tyconius mentions the two-fold seed of Abraham, namely Esau and Jacob, "two peoples struggling in the one womb of mother Church."[134] Beatus' text specifically identifies the <u>bella intestina</u> as <u>pugna intra ecclesiam.</u>

Beatus' text also alludes to the parable of the weeds and the wheat.[135] Augustine used this image often in his anti-Donatist polemic in order to demonstrate that good and bad will exist side by side within the Church until the final harvest, the last judgment.[136] Actually, in this matter Tyconius' views were diametrically opposed tc common Donatist teaching, which excluded all sinners from the church. Augustine, of course, took maximum advantage of the rift within the Donatist church and cited Tyconius in his letter against Parmenian, Donatist bishop of Carthage.[137] In the Liber regularum we find not only the same ideas[138] but also the same image.[139]

The thought of Tyconius is apparent both in the passage from Primasius and in the parallel from Beatus. The question arises as to which passage is more faithful to the words of Tyconius. Primasius has quite clearly abbreviated the section. He omits the very important ecclesial reference to baptism; he omits also the further explanation of the bella intestina. The biblical imagery of the weeds growing until the harvest is replaced by a simple statement of fact that good and bad are mixed within the church until the end of the world. The reference from Beatus in this case better conveys the thought and words of the original.

A second example is in regard to Rev. 10:9; again we cite the parallel from Beatus:

Beatus 5,10,34

hic liber amaritudinem ventri tuo faciet, cum praedicare et operare coeperis, quod intellexeris.

Primasius, CChr.SL 92, 163,89-92

id est, cum perceperis, oblectaberis divini eloquii diuini dulcedine et spe salutis promissae, et divinae suauitate iustitiae, sed amaritudinem profecto senties cum hoc et deuotis et indeuotis coeperis praedicare.

One would be hard pressed to determine which passage is more faithful to Tyconius were it not for the abundance of parallel passages in the other Tyconian literature:

Turin Fragment 319

Id est, dum perceperis delectaberis eloquii diuini dulcedine, et amaritudinem senties cum operari et praedicare coeperis quod intellexeris.

Caesarius 238,13-15

id est, cum perceperis, oblectaberis eloquii divini dulcedine; sed amaritudinem senties, cum praedicare et operari coeperis quod intellexeris

It is obvious that Primasius in this case expanded upon the comments of Tyconius.

We may now draw some conclusions in regard to Primasius' use of Tyconius' commentary. First, Primasius acknowledged in his prologue the selective use of Tyconius. Second, he explicitly mentions Tyconius in his commentary only once as the representative of another Apocalypse translation but never as a commentator of the Apocalypse. Third, Primasius' quotations from Tyconius correspond to the description in his prologue. His use is selective -- he includes some passages from Tyconius and omits others; and finally, he alters his source as he sees fit.

g. Results

In summary my findings in regard to the use of the commentary of Primasius in a possible reconstruction of Tyconius' lost commentary suggest that:

1. Primasius used the lost commentary of Tyconius extensively in writing his own commentary on the Apocalypse. Indeed, Tyconius may rightly be considered his chief source.

2. Primasius' use of all sources is varied. He sometimes copies word for word, sometimes paraphrases, and sometimes adds his own comments.

3. We may expect greater sėlectivity in his use of Tyconius. Primasius admits this in his prologue and carries it out in his commentary.

D. Cassiodore

1. The life and writings of Cassiodore
2. Complexiones
    a. Date of composition
    b. History of the text
    c. Literary form
        (1) Breves -- divisa commonitio
        (2) Complexiones -- iuncta copulatio
    d. Structure
3. References to Tyconius' commentary
    a. Institutiones, 1,9,3
    b. Complexiones, prologus
    c. Complexiones, 14
    d. Complexiones, 16
4. Use of Cassiodore's Complexiones

1. The life and writings of Cassiodore

Flavius Magnus Aurelius Cassiodorus Senator was born in Scyllacium in Brutium (Squillace in Calabria).[140] Since his own writings are the only sources of biographical information, we cannot determine the exact dates of his birth and death. On the basis of a letter from the Variae, which documents Cassiodore's first official duty during the reign of King Theodorich, A. Franz estimates Cassiodore to have been born around the year 470.[141] Most scholars, however, lean toward a later date of birth roughly around 485.[142] In any event, Cassiodore was 93 years old when he wrote De Orthographia.[143] Since this was his last known work, he probably died within several years after its publication. Unable to be more precise we must be content to accept the customary dating of Cassiodore's life from 485 to 580. As a statesman Cassiodore dedicated himself to the mutual reconciliation of Roman and Germanic cultures. In conjunction with this goal he was active as an author writing chiefly historical works: a chronicle, a history of the Ostrogothic royal family, and a genealogy of his own family. His letters and speeches were also written during this period as well as the philosophical tractate De anima.

Shortly after 540 Cassiodore retired from diplomatic service to take up residence in the monastery at Vivarium, which he himself had established on the grounds of the family estate. He clearly identified this departure from public life as a conversio, although he most probably never became a monk.[144] During this period he ardently pursued learning and scholarship. Since his attempt to establish a theological school in Rome after the model of Nisibis and Alexandria had failed, Cassiodore created a substitute by writing his Institutiones, which consisted of a curriculum of study embracing both the sacred and secular sciences. Because of the central role occupied by the Bible in his educational program Cassiodore wrote several biblical commentaries and reading guides. His lengthy Expositio Psalmorum enjoyed the greatest popularity. He also wrote a commentary on Romans, the now lost Liber titulorum, which was constructed out of excerpts from scripture, and the Complexiones. Finally, he composed textbooks of grammatical rules and orthography and edited the Historia ecclesiastica tripartita.

2. Complexiones in epistolis apostolorum et actibus apostolorum et apocalypsi [145]

a. Date of Composition

As witnessed in his De Orthographia [146] Cassiodore wrote the Complexiones toward the end of his lifetime. The inaccuracy concerning the date of Cassiodore's death makes itself evident in regard to determining the date of composition of this work. Nevertheless, we can set its date in the last third of the sixth century or, presuming the validity of the customary dating procedure, around 575.[147]

b. History of the text

The Complexiones stand alone among the writings of Cassiodore in their complete lack of circulation and influence during the Middle Ages. Any knowledge of their existence seems to have been always through a reference to the work in the preface of De Orthographia. There is only one known manuscript: Verona, Bibl. Capitulare XXXIX-37 (VII) f. 96-110,[148] which was edited and published by S. Maffei in 1721. The editio princeps was republished by Migne in 1865. T. Stangl has indicated that this edition is plagued by inexactness, lacunae, and unnecessary emendations of the manuscript.[149] A. Reifferscheid had already listed approximately fifty readings where the printed edition differs from the original text.[150] Stangl carried this work further in his preparations for a critical edition,[151] which was to have been published in the Vienna corpus but unfortunately never appeared. Since he systematically catalogued his corrections, we have the next best thing to a critical text by simply using the Migne edition and consulting Stangl's research for possible revision.

c. Literary form

Cassiodore wrote several types of biblical commentaries and textbooks. He himself identified his work on the psalms as an *expositio,* which is a commentary of greater length going into some detail about various aspects of a biblical book.[152] His lost commentary on the letter to the Romans was identified in the same way.[153]

In the *Complexiones* he explained the nature of the present work by drawing a comparison with *breves:* *Breves sunt subsequentium rerum particulatim divisa commonitio; Complexiones autem similium rerum juncta copulatio.*[154] The subject matter of the two types of commentaries is the same. The key to understanding the passage lies in the contrast between *divisa commonitio* and *iuncta copulatio* .

(1) *Breves* -- *divisa commonitio*

The word *brevis,* used as a substantive, refers to a short catalogue or summary. Here Cassiodore used the word in the plural, which he identified as synonymous with *summaria* and *tituli.* However, he went into greater detail in his explanation and called the *breves* a *divisa commonitio.* The *commonitorium* was a frequently used literary form in Christian antiquity.[155] Sometimes the word _commemoratorium_ refers to the same literary genus.[156] Cassiodore understood the word _commonitio_ to mean a reminder or an admonition. Here it refers to a little handbook in which one could quickly find a specific fact. In other words, the handbook serves its reader as a reminder. The modifying word _divisa_ should not be overlooked because it forms an integral part of the contrast. The _breves_ are literally a "divided reminder" -- an outline.

(2) _Complexiones_ -- _iuncta copulatio_

The word _complexio_ derives from the deponent verb _complector_ meaning to grasp or embrace in both the literal and figurative sense. Thus Cassiodore made the goal of his _Complexiones_ quite clear when he wrote: _summas rerum in parvitate complectens, non cuncta verba discutiens, sed ad intentiones suas summatim dicta perducens._[157] The _Complexiones_ are a summary of the contents of a biblical book, avoiding a detailed word for word exegesis but leading toward a brief statement of the author's intention. Cassiodore called his work a _copulatio_, which means a joining or uniting; as a grammatical term it also means a contraction. If this is what Cassiodore had in mind when he wrote the sentence, the modifying word _iuncta_ is not a redundancy merely added to the passage for the sake of balance and contrast with _divisa._ On the contrary, the expression _iuncta copulatio_ is very precise and, therefore, the _complexiones_ are a "unified contraction" or, to use an expression from modern scientific literature, an abstract.

d. Structure

Cassiodore laid great value on the symbolic meaning of numbers and divided his work accordingly:

(1,a) The Pauline epistles (14 chapters)

(1,b) The catholic epistles (7 chapters)

(2,a) The Acts of the Apostles (72 chapters)

(2,b) The Apocalypse (33 chapters)

The thirty-three chapters of the section of the Apocalypse refer to the number of years which the Lord lived, where thirty signifies the glorious heights of heaven and three the perfection of the Trinity.[158]

3. References to Tyconius

There are four specific references to the Apocalypse Commentary of Tyconius in the works of Cassiodore, of which three are to be found in the Complexiones and one in the Institutiones:

a. Institutiones, 1,9,3 (ed. Mynors 33,14-20)

Ticonius etiam Donatista in eodem volumine quaedam non respuenda subiunxit, quaedam vero venenosi dogmatis sui fecilenta permiscuit; cui tantum in bonis dictis chresimon, in malis achriston quantum transiens valui reperire, ut arbitror, competenter affixi. quod et vobis similiter in suspectis expositoribus facere suademus, ne lectoris animus fortasse turbetur nefandi dogmatis permixtione confusus.

The first reference reveals two important facts. First, the library at Vivarium had a copy of Tyconius' commentary on the Apocalypse, which Cassiodore had certainly read and with which he was thoroughly familiar. Second, Cassiodore took a rather positive attitude toward Tyconius though not without some reservation. The commentary of the Donatist theologian is not to be spurned. However, one must be careful to sift out poisonous doctrine. Therefore, for the benefit of his students, Cassiodore has made marginal notes in his copy of the work indicating those sections which are "useful" and those which are "useless." Cassiodore handled the works of Origen similarly.[159]

b. Complexiones actuum apostolorum et apocalypsis Joannis, prologus (PL 70, 1382,7-18)

Difficile opus obscure dicta brevius velle perstringere; cum sint latius dicenda, quae volumus explanare: sed quoniam hunc librum Tychonius Donatista subtiliter et diligenter exposuit, providente Deo, qui saluti nostrae antidotum conficit ex venenis; propter brevitatis propositae necessitatem nobis[160] aliqui novi perversi dogmatis sensus praetereundi noscuntur, ut lectorem nostrum non tam satiare quam introducere videamur; quando sine damno intelligentiae suae in illo reperit quod orthodoxus et diligens lector inquirit.

Stangl considers the relationship between the words Tychonius and nobis central to the passage, whereby the contrast of persons highlights the contrasted things, namely their respective commentaries.[161] Therefore, we may deduce three facts from the passage. First, the comparison which Cassiodore makes between the two commentaries is not one of quality but quantity. While presuming that his reader is familiar with Tyconius' commentary, he bemoans the necessary brevity of his own work. Second, Cassiodore does not explicitly name Tyconius as a source. He simply refers his reader to Tyconius, who "subtly and diligently" exposed the book of the Apocalypse. Then he explains that he will not be able to go into as much detail in his own commentary, which is designed as an introduction. Third, Cassiodore takes once again an ambivalent attitude toward Tyconius, calling his work a "remedy for our salvation [made] from poison."

c. Complexiones apocalypsis sancti Joannis, 14
(PL 70, 1410,40-44)

Describitur etiam in mysticam nocendi potentiam positio lucustarum, quod Tychonius minutius et abundanter exposuit: quibus angelum terribilem dicit praeesse, cujus nomen Exterminator est.

The expression positio lucustarum seems to have come from Tyconius' commentary where he wrote confecto praelio locustarum. [162] Nevertheless, nowhere in the passage is there a direct quotation from Tyconius. Vogels questions if the word Exterminator represents the African translation of the Apocalypse used by Tyconius.[163] This can hardly be the case since the commentary of Caesarius and that of Beatus have perdens at Rev. 9:11.[164] The translation of Primasius, which was obviously influenced by the Vulgate at this point, reads Exterminans. [165] However, the word exterminator does appear in one manuscript of the Itala,[166] which is the translation most often used by Cassiodore.[167] Surprisingly, in a passage where Tyconius is explicitly mentioned, neither a direct quotation from his commentary nor traces of his biblical text can be found!

d. Complexiones apocalypsis sancti Joannis, 16
(PL 70, 1411,25-30)

dicens, Deum ascendisse ad caelos, matrem vero ipsius aliquanto tempore in secretioribus locis esse servandum, ut eam illic pascat annis tribus, et semis; quod in magnum sacramentum, sicut Tyconius refert, constat edictum.

Not only the name but also the influence of Tyconius is apparent. Two observations are pertinent. First, although Cassiodore's chapter 16 begins with Rev. 11:15, this passage refers back to Rev. 11:9, where Tyconius understood the three and a half days to mean three and a half years.[168] Under the influence of Tyconius Cassiodore interprets the time reference similarly. Second, Cassiodore explicitly mentions Tyconius, who according to him stated that "the explanation consists in a great sacrament." Unfortunately, no such quotation may be found in the known Tyconian literature. However, one must also concede that Cassiodore does not necessarily identify the passage as a quotation. Actually the situation becomes quite clear when one determines the biblical reference, which is Rev. 17:7. The Vulgate reads <u>sacramentum mulieris et bestiae,</u> while the Tyconian translation substitutes <u>mysterium</u> for <u>sacramentum</u> .[169] Cassiodore's unsystematic approach to the biblical text is disturbing; however, his arbitrary use of various biblical passages in the same paragraph is not inconsistent with his stated goal. In any event, his translation is not that of Tyconius,[170] who remains faithful to the Greek root <u>mysterium.</u> As in the previous instances a Tyconian influence is apparent but no direct quotation may be proven.

4. Use of Cassiodore's <u>Complexiones</u>

Evidently, Cassiodore's work will be of only limited use in reconstructing the commentary of Tyconius. First, Cassiodore knew well the commentary of Tyconius, in which he had made marginal notes for the benefit of his students. However, he had no intention of reproducing or even commenting upon Tyconius' work. Cassiodore wished rather to take an entirely different approach in his Complexiones, which was an abstract of the book of the Apocalypse serving as a brief introduction for students. The literary form of the work itself precludes the extensive verbatim copying from sources. Second, quite concretely in those two passages of the commentary on the Apocalypse text itself where Tyconius is mentioned, there is evidence of a Tyconian influence but no direct quotation. Therefore, in consulting the Complexiones of Cassiodore in the detailed comparison of the Tyconian literature, we could perhaps find some positive indications of Tyconian influence here and there, which would serve as confirmatory evidence in specific cases. However, no extensive passages will be uncovered.

E. Pseudo-Jerome's <u>Commemoratorium</u>

1. Editions and manuscripts[171]

Two editions of pseudo-Jerome's <u>Commemoratorium</u> are available; both are unsatisfactory. The first was published by K. Hartung in 1904 on the basis of just two manuscripts.[172] The second was published by G. Lo Menzo Rapisarda in 1967 using thirteen manuscripts.[173] Since B. Lambert lists twenty-three known manuscripts of the work,[174] neither edition may be judged adequate.

One might be easily led into the trap of considering the more recent edition the more accurate. One might also think that the greater number of manuscripts consulted automatically signifies the greater quality of the resulting edition. These temptations must at all costs be avoided and each edition must be evaluated objectively.

Rapisarda divided the manuscripts into two families which she called x and y. Hartung's edition, relying on Bamberg, Staatliche Bibliothek Patr. 102 (B.V. 18), ff. 101r-110r, represents the y tradition. However, Rapisarda considered x to be the more faithful tradition as witnessed by Erlangen, Universitäts Bibliothek 176, ff. 143v-148v and Heiligenkreuz, Stiftsbibliothek 126, ff. 48r-54r. None of her arguments for this choice is especially convincing.[175] Furthermore, there is contrary evidence based upon external criticism which indicates the superiority of family y. Three examples will demonstrate this.

First, Rapisarda stated that she preferred the reading fluxum to fluxus in the explanation of the word Iezabel. According to her the verb fluo in the sentence fluens fluxum sanguinis is used transitively.[176] In reality the grammatical usage need not be explained because the author copied word for word from Jerome's De nominibus hebraicis.[177] There as well as in family y we find fluxus.

Second, the comments of pseudo-Jerome on Rev. 4:8 correspond to a sermon of Smaragdus. Clearly, both copied from an unknown source.[178] Let us look at the passages more closely:

Hartung 9,18-23 (Family y)

senas alas habent quia per sex aetates mundi predicant evangelium, aut sex leges mundi veteris et novi testamenti adnuntiant, id est: legem naturae, legem littere et legem prophetarum et legem evangeliorum, legem apostolorum, legem ecclesiasticam.

Rapisarda 76,157-161 (Family x)

senas alas habent quia per sex aetates mundi praedicant evangelia aut sex veteris testamenti leges annuntiant id est legem vel naturae ante legem litterae et legem prophetarum, legem evangelii, legem apostolorum et legem ecclesiasticam.

Smaragdus, Collectiones (PL 102, 333,30-37)

Quae animalia senas alas habebant, qui per sex mundi aetates legem Veteris ac Novi Testamenti annuntiare non cessant, quae cum sit Novi ac Veteris Testamenti, lex una in sex videtur esse divisa, id est, in legem naturae, legem litterae, legem prophetarum, legem evangeliorum, legem apostolorum, et legem ecclesiasticam.

Smaragdus, who is usually faithful to his sources, presents the best text. In family x the expression <u>et novi</u> is absent, which changes the entire meaning of the passage. Obviously, x is corrupt and y offers the better reading.

Finally, there exist in family y traces of a pre-Vulgate biblical translation, which have been either revised or eliminated in family x, as in the following two examples:

Rev.	Vulgate	Pre-Vulgate[179]	Hartung (y)	Rapisarda (x)
1:10	tanquam tubae dicentis	tamquam tubam dicentem mihi	Tamquam tubam dicentem mihi	tamquam tubae dicentis mihi
22:19	de libro vitae	de ligno vitae	de ligno vitae	(missing!)

Family y shows archaic elements while family x evidences revision on the basis of the Vulgate. In conclusion, the y tradition and the edition of Hartung, which will be used in this work, are superior.

2. Literary form

Two items help to identify the nature of pseudo-Jerome's work exactly: its title and its contents. Although the text has been edited twice, neither editor has adequately investigated the title of the work. Since Hartung had only two manuscripts at his disposal, he was in no position to handle the problem; he simply calls the work a tractate.[180] Rapisarda unfortunately does not address herself to the problem and opts quite uncritically for the title *commentarius.* [181] It seems strange that something so obviously important as the title of a work should have been consistently overlooked in the research, but indeed it has been.[182]

We may deal with the problem, first, through the process of elimination. The designations *tractatus* and *expositio,* especially in those cases where they belong to a scribe's *Incipit,* may be immediately dismissed as accretions to the original text. This leaves several possibilities which appear in the manuscript tradition: *commentum, commentum compendiosum, commentarius, commentarium,* and *commemoratorium.* Initial indications point to *commemoratorium* as the proper title of the work not only because that word occurs most frequently in the manuscript tradition but also because it does indeed constitute the most difficult reading.[183] Interestingly enough, the same transformation has taken place in the textual tradition of Ambrosius' *De officiis ministrorum,* where *commemoratorium* was simplified to *commentarium* in some manuscripts.[184]

This reading of the text is further confirmed by the structure and contents of the work at hand. For example, let us look more closely at the comments on Rev. 17:

17,1 ista *meretrix* totus mundus intellegitur. *qui sedet super aquas* super populum. 17,3 *bestia* antichristus. *mulier* fornicatio totius mundi. *coccinea* propter sanguinem martyrum. 17,4 *populum in manu* voluptas carnis. 17,7 iste *angelus* Christus.[185]

Hartung's use of italics brings out the true character of the passage by allowing one to differentiate easily between the biblical quotations and the commentary. Notice that pseudo-Jerome's comments are short and pithy. Sentences are for the most part incomplete and nouns are set in the absolute form. One gets the overall impression of a reference work which was designed as a memory aid to the reader, who could check the meaning of a word or expression simply by looking it up. In other words, the _Commemoratorium in Apocalypsin_ is a primitive reading guide to the book of the Apocalypse.

A parallel use of the word in regard to hagiography supports this argument. The _Commemoratorium vitae sancti Severini,_ [186] which was written by the monk Eugippius, is a memory aid listing events in the life of the saint. Thus a _commemoratorium vitae,_ which is a list of biographical facts, differs substantially from a _vita,_ which is a completely developed biography. Similarly, a _commemoratorium in Apocalypsin,_ which is a list of definitions in lexicon form, also differs substantially from a _commentarius in Apocalypsin,_ a completely developed commentary. The word _commemoratorium_ is not used indiscriminately nor may it be considered synonymous with other similar expressions. Its meaning is quite precise referring exclusively to a work which is at the same time both a memory aid and a list.[187] Pseudo-Jerome's work is beyond all doubt a _commemoratorium._

3. The prologue

Perhaps one of the most problematic passages of the entire _Commemoratorium_ is its prologue.[188] On the one hand, the presence of the prologue in the Bamberg Codex only and its absence from the other twenty-two manuscripts might seem to indicate its inauthenticity. On the other hand, the prologue does manifest remarkable factual accuracy.[189]

First and foremost, the prologue correctly identifies four sources of the Commemoratorium: an anonymous author, rightly judged by Hartung to be Hippolytus,[190] Origen, Primasius, and Tyconius.

Second, the prologue is a composite of an Apocalypse prologue[191] and an insert providing information about the Commemoratorium.[192] In addition to the evidence presented previously,[193] further indications support this hypothesis. The insert has a definite beginning and end. The author clearly indicates that he is dealing with another matter. The expression multi quidem inveniuntur is apparently set in contrast to the beginning of the prologue multa quidem obscuritas. Finally, the author closes the insert with the words: Sufficiat quod diximus.

As interesting and informative as the study of the prologue has been, sufficient evidence neither to affirm nor to deny its authenticity exists. The perplexing question remains open.

4. Date and place of composition

Although efforts to determine the authenticity of the prologue have been constantly frustrated by insufficient evidence, inquiry into the date of composition has been much more fruitful.[194] On the basis of concrete literary evidence the parameters of the problem may be clearly delineated and a reasonable conclusion arrived at. Since the author of the Commemoratorium used the commentary of Primasius in writing his work, the date of Primasius' commentary, roughly 540, must be considered the earliest possible date of composition. The first datable evidence of the existence of the Commemoratorium is found in the Apocalypse commentary of Ambrosius Autpertus, where there is a direct quotation: Tres sunt uisiones, una corporalis, altera spiritalis, tertia intellectualis. Ista autem intellectualis est, et ideo sublimior aliis.[195] Although Autpertus attributed the passage to Jerome, it obviously originated from pseudo-Jerome's Commemoratorium.[196] Autpertus wrote his commentary between 758 and 767. Therefore, the Commemoratorium had to be written between the dates of composition of Primasius' and Autpertus' commentaries, namely between 540 and 767.

Since literary productivity during this period was relatively limited, there is sufficient information to build a hypothesis in regard to the place of composition. Two factors are of prime importance. First, the author used the commentaries of Primasius, Tyconius, and Hippolytus, the sermons of Origen, and De nominibus hebraicis of Jerome. In other words, he had access to a rather extensive library. Second, the Commemoratorium is clearly a reading guide or teaching aid or textbook. This would presuppose an academic milieu. Cassiodore indicates three of the five books consulted were available in the library of the monastery at Vivarium, namely the commentaries of Primasius and Tyconius as well as De nominibus hebraicis of Jerome.[197] In addition, a tremendous emphasis was placed on biblical scholarship at Vivarium; many such textbooks grew out of this environment. Therefore, it would be reasonable to propose the hypothesis that the Commemoratorium in Apocalypsin, attributed to Jerome, was actually written by an anonymous monk at Vivarium in southern Italy around the year 600. However, one must concede that Castellum Lucullanum, the monastery of Eugippius near Naples, could also have been the place of composition.

5. Tyconian passages

The foremost difficulty in determining the influence of Tyconius on the Commemoratorium lies in the fact that the author had access not only to the commentary of Tyconius but also to that of Primasius. Thus it is sometimes impossible to determine whether the Commemoratorium was influenced directly by Tyconius or by Tyconius through Primasius. Previously, I stated that the threefold reference to recapitulatio,[198] which is indeed a favorite theme of Tyconius, could have come either from him or from Primasius. Further analysis demonstrates that this statement is not entirely accurate. In one instance only is there a parallel reference in Primasius.[199] The other two references, which are each confirmed by at least one other parallel in the remaining Tyconian literature,[200] are missing in Primasius. Therefore, they had to come directly from Tyconius.

A study of the biblical references also produces some valuable information. Both Primasius and Tyconius used African Apocalypse translations which often differ from their European counterparts. Therefore, those passages where the Commemoratorium agrees with Primasius and Tyconius but differs from the Vulgate indicate a dependence upon one of the two authors:

Rev.	Vulgate	Primasius or Tyconius	*Commemoratorium*
3:4	ambulabunt	ambulaverunt	ambulaverunt
5:13	sub terra	subtus terram	subtus terra
6:4	super illum	super eum	super eum
6:5	super illum	super eum	super eum
10:2	libellum	librum	librum
22:1	fluvium	flumen	flumen

Furthermore, one must remember that there was no single authoritative African translation but rather several translations in circulation. There are four places where the *Commemoratorium* differs from the Vulgate as well as Primasius but agrees with Tyconius. These four passages present definitive evidence that the author of the *Commemoratorium* knew and used the commentary of Tyconius:

Rev.	Vulgate	Primasius	Tyconius	*Commemoratorium*
1:10	tanquam tubae dicentis	sicut tubam dicentem mihi	tamquam tubam dicentem mihi	Tamquam tubam dicentem mihi
1:14	tanquam flamma	ut flamma	velut flamma	Velut flamma
1:16	et de ore eius gladius utraque parte acutus exibat	et ex ore ejus gladius utrimque acutus exiebat	et ex ore eius gladius ex utraque parte acutus procedens	et de ore eius gladius procedebat ex utraque parte acutus
22:19	de libro vitae	de libro vitae	de ligno vitae	de ligno vitae

6. Results

The evidence may be summarized as follows. First, there are

three references to _recapitulatio,_ two of which had to come from Tyconius. The remaining reference could be from either Tyconius or Primasius. Second, the four biblical passages common to the _Commemoratorium_ and Tyconius but at variance with Primasius indicate a direct and immediate use of the commentary of Tyconius itself.

Although positive and irrefutable evidence does indeed show that pseudo-Jerome possessed the lost commentary of Tyconius, the use of his work in Tyconian comparisons will be quite limited. Since pseudo-Jerome adapted his material to the _commemoratorium_ format, sentences are incomplete and the text is extremely abbreviated.

F. Capitulary of the Codex Oratorii B6

1. The literary form <u>capitulare</u>
2. The manuscript
3. Tyconian content
4. Bede's use of the capitulary
5. Date and place of composition
6. Significance

1. The literary form <u>capitulare</u>

When Haußleiter investigated the Apocalypse commentary of Primasius, he did not neglect the <u>capitula</u> contained at the beginning of each of the five books of that work.[201] For purposes of comparison Haußleiter considered other examples of the same literary form. In an appendix he published an anonymous 48 chapter capitulary of the Apocalypse according to the three available manuscripts.[202] His investigation led him to emphasize the importance of the exact number of chapters. Since Rev. 4:4 mentions 24 elders, the number 24 or multiples thereof were frequent. Haußleiter concluded that a capitulary of the Apocalypse or of an Apocalypse commentary which varied from multiples of 24 had often suffered either omissions or additions. In this way he explained the 98 chapters of Primasius and the 39 of the Codex Augiensis.

Since the <u>capitula</u> are normally brief and thus easily overlooked, there has yet to be a systematic investigation of this literary form. A <u>capitulare</u> or capitulary is a series of chapter headings or titles which summarize the contents of any given book.

The *capitula* or individual chapter headings may appear as separate titles before each respective section[203] or may be grouped together at the beginning or end of a book much like a modern table of contents.[204] The *capitulare* was often not written by the same author who composed the book itself but rather by some subsequent teacher or compiler. This is obvious in the case of a biblical book; in other instances, however, the question of authorship may be problematic.[205] As monasteries flourished and monastic schools became centers of learning, many such pedagogical works were written.[206] Although the *capitulare* sometimes came to be circulated independently of the work from which it sprung, it was generally considered part of the original work. Therefore, capitularies have usually not been individually catalogued.

2. The manuscript

In the course of his investigations Haußleiter came across a capitulary which is of major concern here because "of all the summaries of the contents of the Apocalypse, which I know, none breaths so totally the spirit of the exegesis of Tyconius as this one."[207] Haußleiter expressed great interest in finding other manuscripts of this capitulary. However, since he never again mentioned the matter, it appears that he found nothing. The unique witness is the Codex Vallicellanus B 6, which has been described by G. Bianchini[208], who curiously enough did not mention the *capitula* at all. The Carolingian manuscript, which is now located in the library of the Oratorians near the Chiesa nuova in Rome, is more famous for having preserved perhaps the best existing specimen of the Alcuinian

Bible. Bianchini considered the manuscript to be an autograph of Alcuin which had originated from the monastery of Saint Martin at Tours. That would necessarily place the date of the manuscript before the death of Alcuin in 804.

The capitulary is available in the compilation of G. M. Tommasi,[209] who under the title "Cod. Oratorii B. 6." published three items from the Vallicellanus in regard to the Apocalypse: first, the customary Apocalypse prologue, Joannes Apostolus et Evangelista; second, the 38 numbered capitula or chapter headings, which are in every case composed as complete sentences varying in length from two to nine lines; and, finally, 38 quotations from the Apocalypse of roughly three lines each, which do not always correspond to the beginning of each capitulum.

3. Tyconian content

Although the capitula are associated with the book of the Apocalypse, they are obviously much too sophisticated to have come directly from the text of the Apocalypse. They quite clearly reflect a broader elaboration on the biblical book. There can be no question that they are based on the Apocalypse commentary of Tyconius. For example, capitulum 7 describes the threefold war against the gentiles, the false brothers, and the heretics. A comparison with Beatus reveals the same or similar opposing groups in the comments on Rev. 6:8ff.[210]

4. Bede's use of the capitulary

The chapter headings themselves, however, are to be found nowhere in the Tyconian tradition with one exception -- Bede knew them. First, in his Epistola ad Eusebium Bede explains among other things that the Apocalypse should be divided into seven parts. In his description of the first part, Rev. 1-3, Bede paraphrases capitula 1-4.[211] Second, in his Explanatio Apocalypsis Bede quotes capitula 29 and 32 directly.[212] Third, three sections of the text of Bede's commentary manifest strong similarities to capitula 7, 11, and 15.[213]

Perhaps most intriguing is the position of the quotations from capitula 15, 29, and 32 in the text of Bede's commentary. If we look to the corresponding biblical quotations recorded by Tommasi, capitulum 15 refers to Rev. 10:1ff., capitulum 29 to Rev. 16:18ff., and capitulum 32 to Rev. 18:1ff. In all three cases, however, the capitulum forms in Bede's commentary the last sentence of the section preceding the corresponding biblical quotation. In other words the capitulum does not appear as part of the commentary on the biblical text to which it refers, but is so positioned as to introduce the biblical text and subsequent comments. Since these three capitula may well be performing their originally intended function in the commentary, it seems clear that Bede knew the capitulary in its present form.

5. Date and place of composition

This leaves the problem of attempting to determine the date

and place of composition of the capitulary. Some facts are certain. First, the capitulary is based on the Apocalypse commentary of Tyconius. Second, its absence from the Tyconian tradition with the single exception of Bede rules out the possibility that Tyconius himself could have written it. Third, the capitulary had to have been written before Bede composed his Explanatio Apocalypsis, namely before the year 735 when Bede died.

Although these are valuable pieces of information, of equal significance is the appearance of the capitulary in a manuscript which contains an Alcuinian autograph. Alcuin, like Bede, was a Northumbrian monk. Since the capitulary was evidently at the disposal of both Bede and Alcuin, while at the same time appearing nowhere else, the only alternative is to opt for the English, and specifically Northumbrian, origin of the work. This also helps in determining the date of composition. The monastery of Saint Peter was founded at Wearmouth in 673 and the monastery of Saint Paul at Jarrow in 682. The capitulary would have to have been written after the first monastic founding in Northumbria but before the death of Bede, namely between the years 673 and 735.

Therefore, on the basis of the evidence at hand I propose the following hypothesis: The capitulary contained in the Codex Vallicellanus B 6 was written by an unknown monk at a Northumbrian monastery, either Wearmouth or Jarrow, around the year 700.

6. Significance

The Tyconian capitulary is significant on two accounts. First, presenting a summary of Tyconius' commentary, it does stand soundly within the Tyconian tradition. Although the author of the capitulary had the commentary of Tyconius before him, there appear to be no verbatim quotations in the work.

Second, the division of the capitulary into 39 chapters opens the question whether this arrangement reflects the original structure of Tyconius' commentary. Now that the three book hypothesis has been soundly defeated,[214] this possibility must be seriously considered. The number 39 cannot be explained as one of the traditional symbolic numbers frequently derived from the Apocalypse. One solution would be to add or subtract chapters in order to arrive at one of the more customary numbers. However, this procedure seems hardly justifiable, since the capitulary appears to be a rather well composed unity, with neither extraneous chapters nor lacunae. Could the division into 39 chapters have originated from Tyconius himself?

Although 28 out of 39 times the beginning of a storia in Beatus corresponds to the beginning of a capitula, evidence from Beatus, as we will see,[215] indicates a division into broader chapters or books. A compromise solution would be to propose a structure of the commentary according to divisions and subdivisions similar to Primasius' work where there are 5 libri and 98 capitula.[216] Bede mentions one structure of seven parts yet follows threefold division in his own work.[217] At present this problem cannot be solved due to insufficient evidence.[218] However, one is inclined to consider the 39 capitula a non-Tyconian division because it is not supported by other witnesses from the Tyconian tradition.

G. Bede the Venerable

1. The life and writings of Bede

2. <u>Epistola ad Eusebium</u>

a. Occasion and contents

b. Information pertaining to Tyconius

c. New possibilities

3. <u>Explanatio Apocalypsis</u>

a. Structure, method, and procedure

b. Sources

(1) Outside the Tyconian tradition

(2) Within the Tyconian tradition

c. Bede's use of his sources

(1) Verbatim quotations

(2) Modification according to style or context

(3) Simplification

(4) Inserted explanation

(5) Summary

d. Biblical texts

4. Results

a. Structure

b. Text

1. The life and writings of Bede

Although the Venerable Bede was of major significance during the early Middle Ages, biographical information is rather sketchy. One must rely on two sources: a brief autobiographical note in his ecclesiastical history[219] and a letter of his friend and student Cuthbert.[220] Bede was born on the lands of the monastery at Wearmouth in the year 673 or perhaps 674. At the age of seven he was given into the care of the monk Ceolfried at Jarrow, where he spent most of his life dedicated to learning, teaching, and writing. He was ordained a deacon at age 19 and a priest at age 30. He died on May 26, 735.

Of all the writings of Bede the most famous is, of course, his Ecclesiastical History of the English People, which has been a wealth of historical information for subsequent generations as well as a landmark in the history of literature. Bede wrote other historical works, poetry, letters, and pedagogical treatises. However, the major portion of his writings is theological and specifically exegetical in nature. Since in the above mentioned autobiographical note Bede lists his exegetical works first, one might suspect that he considered these most important. In any event, his contemporaries refer to him above all as the theologian and scripture scholar.[221]

2. Epistola ad Eusebium

As in the Migne edition so also in most manuscripts, the Explanatio Apocalypsis does not stand alone.[222] Customarily the commentary is prefaced by a letter to the monk Eusebius and a poem Exsul ab humano.[223] Although the poem is insignificant to the present study,[224] the letter is of major importance and must be considered in some detail.

a. Occasion and contents

The letter is designed to introduce the commentary to the monk Hwaetbert, who is also called Eusebius. Being devoid of personal comments except for the customary greeting and the closing salutation, the letter treats of three matters: first, Bede's division of the Apocalypse into seven parts; second, the use and value of the seven rules of Tyconius; and third, the composition of Bede's commentary which follows in three books. The letter was written before Hwaetbert's succession as abbot of Jarrow in the year 716.[225]

b. Information pertaining to Tyconius

The letter to Eusebius was central in the formerly accepted theory concerning the structure of Tyconius' Apocalypse commentary.[226] The theory is actually quite simple. One must first of all accept three premises. First, Gennadius asserts that Tyconius' commentary encompassed the entire book of the Apocalypse.[227] Second, the Venerable Bede indicates that the commentary contained three books.[228] Third, Beatus of Liebana unwittingly disclosed the contents of Tyconius' second book by mechanically copying Tyconius' title after having written his own title to the same book.[229]

The structure of the lost commentary flows quite spontaneously from the three premises. Tyconius' title of Book II, recorded by Beatus, indicates that his second book encompassed Rev. 4:1-8:1. Since the commentary was complete in three books and the contents of the second book are known, it follows that Book I covered Rev. 1:1-3:22 and Book III Rev. 8:2-22:21.

Although the theory is quite logical, the second premise is simply false. Bede does not assert that the Tyconian commentary contained three books.[230] The final section of the letter to Eusebius is critical. Expressing some reservation in regard to Tyconius' Donatist leanings, Bede confesses that he followed Tyconius' commentary in writing his own work: Cujus quidem auctoris et nos in hoc opere sensum secuti, nonnulla quae extrinsecus posuit, breviandi causa omisimus: plura vero...superadjicere curavimus.[231] The tense of the verbs used by Bede is significant. In the Epistola he is writing about the Explanatio, which he had already completed. After considering his chief source and his method of dealing with that source, Bede presents the structure of his own commentary: Cumque opus memoratum in tres libellos relevandae mentis gratia findi placuisset,...[232] With this sentence the stage was set for the erroneous interpretation. It was generally assumed that the opus memoratum, which may be translated "the previously mentioned work," referred to Bede's source, namely Tyconius' Apocalypse Commentary. The verb placuisset in the pluperfect seemed to confirm the assertion. Most deceptive, however, was the use of the letter as an introduction to the commentary. When the prefatory letter discussed "the previously mentioned work," one would hardly have concluded that "the previously mentioned work" was identical with the commentary which followed. Nevertheless, Bede is clearly referring to his own Apocalypse commentary,[233] which he obviously had completed before he wrote the letter to Eusebius, which he had already explicitly mentioned with the expression in hoc opere and which, by the way, does contain three books. Bede even justifies having divided his Explanatio into three books by citing Augustine, who says, "for some reason the attention of a reader is refreshed by the end of a book in the same way as the traveller's labour is by an inn."[234] In the very same sentence Bede further describes the structure of the work indicating that he followed the unbroken series of chapters of the Apocalypse in order to make finding a passage easier for his readers. Finally, he states that he has written brief and simple sentences because of the inertia of the English, who have only recently received the faith in the days of Pope Gregory.

Thus, an analysis of the Epistola ad Eusebium reveals that both the specific reference, opus memoratum, and the entire context of the passage points to Bede's own previously written Explanatio Apocalypsis, which he is subsequently introducing to Eusebius by letter. Bede wishes to show sufficient grounds for the twofold structure of his work. The division into three books serves the reader's intentio, which occasionally must be refreshed, while following the unbroken series of biblical chapters serves the inventio of anyone who might be seeking a particular reference. To put it in contemporary terms, Bede is stating that he has written both a commentary and a reference work. This being the case, the passage does not, indeed, cannot refer to Tyconius.

c. New possibilities

With the traditional theory concerning the structure of

Tyconius' commentary exploded, one is tempted to search for some new possibilities. In his <u>Epistola ad Eusebium</u> Bede suggests a sevenfold division of the Apocalypse:

1. 1:1-3:22
2. 4:1-8:1
3. 8:2-11:18
4. 11:19-14:20
5. 15:1-17:18
6. 18:1-20:15
7. 21:1-22:21

Significantly, his second section corresponds exactly to Book II of Tyconius as reported by Beatus. The question arises: Does the sevenfold division of Bede find its origin in Tyconius?

Some indications point toward an affirmative answer. Bede does seem excessively preoccupied with Tyconius in the letter to Eusebius. He describes the <u>Liber regularum</u> of Tyconius. He explains the use of Tyconius' commentary in writing his own work. The section of the letter which describes the sevenfold division is filled with Tyconian phrases and thought. In the very first line Bede writes about the <u>bella intestina.</u>[235] We do know that <u>De bello intestino</u> is the title of a lost work of Tyconius.[236] Furthermore, the <u>Liber regularum</u> refers to the same theme in commenting on the struggle of the brothers Esau and Jacob within the womb.[237] Bede mentions <u>recapitulationes,</u> which are central to Tyconius' thought. He also deals with mystical numbers. Finally, the <u>novissima pressura</u> is an Africanism which seems out of place in eighth century England.

Nevertheless, in spite of all these factors one is reluctant to attribute the division to Tyconius. The sevenfold division appears nowhere in the Tyconian tradition outside of Bede. In addition, Bede has much of his description from the Tyconian capitulary[238] especially at the beginning of the work specifically where the _bella intestina_ and the _recapitulationes_ are mentioned. Furthermore, all the references to the _Liber regularum_ are by way of Augustine's _De doctrina christiana._ [239] The Africanism could easily have crept into the work through an archaic biblical translation.[240] Finally and most importantly, one suspects that Bede would have mentioned his source. He has no fear of mentioning the seven rules of Tyconius. He explicitly acknowledges his use of Tyconius' commentary. However, at this point Bede writes _septem mihi videtur esse divisa periochis._ [241] Bede is claiming the division as his own. Because Bede's intellectual honesty and reliability are unquestionable, it seems clear that the sevenfold division, though possibly influenced by Tyconius, is primarily and substantially the work of none other than Bede himself.

3. _Explanatio Apocalypsis_

a. Structure, method, and procedure

The commentary is divided into three books as described in the _Epistola._ Book I deals with Rev. 1:1-8:1, Book II with Rev. 8:2-14:29 and Book III with Rev. 15:1-22:21. Actually, this is not inconsistent with Bede's sevenfold division because he treats two sections in the first book, two in the second and the remaining three in the third:

Book I	1.	1:1-3:22
	2.	4:1-8:1
Book II	3.	8:2-11:18
	4.	11:19-14:20
Book III	5.	15:1-17:18
	6.	18:1-20:15
	7.	21:1-22:21

The commentary follows the biblical text closely although there is no attempt to be complete. Bede usually cites a section of scripture, often not in its entirety but merely several words ending with the indication 'etc.' He then comments on the quoted passage.

b. Sources

In his introductory letter Bede mentions Tyconius, whose work he used extensively in writing his commentary. In addition, Bede used sources other than Tyconius. Some are mentioned explicitly; others are merely cited while their origin is not stated.

(1) Outside the Tyconian tradition

G. Bonner has identified many of the sources used by Tyconius.[242] To his list may be added Jerome's De nominibus hebraicis.[243] Some passages still remain unidentified for example the quotation from Fortunatus at 138,7 and Simon Magnus at 169,43. Finally, some passages appear to have been taken from elsewhere, for example 139,49-50 and 155,47-48. Since these references are either out of context or deviate from the train of thought in the Apocalypse, some literary source is highly probable.

(2) Within the Tyconian tradition

Much more important for this investigation are the sources used by Bede which belong to the Tyconian tradition. These include Jerome-Victorinus, Primasius, Codex Oratorii B 6, and, of course, the lost Apocalypse Commentary itself. Unfortunately, in this regard Bonner's work requires extensive revision. First, he did not have the Codex Oratorii B 6, which is occasionally helpful. Second, he attributed several passages to Tyconius which are taken directly from Primasius. Since Bede had the commentary of Primasius at his disposal, a quotation from Primasius alone is not sufficient to demonstrate Tyconian origin of the passage. Third, Bonner has overlooked many passages which come to light through a diligent comparison of Bede to Beatus, Caesarius, and the Turin Fragment. Therefore, a complete list of the passages quoted directly from Tyconius or at least strongly influenced by him, with the exclusion of indirectly cited Tyconian passages by way of Primasius and Jerome-Victorinus, appears in the complete Tyconian synopsis at the end of this work.[244]

c. Bede's use of his sources

Significant to this study is the way in which Bede handles quotations from other works. In his research of Bede's exegesis A. Willmes[245] treated this question using four different works of Bede. Although he did not consider Bede's Apocalypse commentary, his findings on the basis of randomly chosen passages give us at least a good indication of Bede's use of quotations.

First, Willmes presented the quantitative relationship of Bede's writings to the biblical and patristic quotations contained therein:

Biblical texts	17.47%
Quotations from the fathers and others	32.41%
Personal contribution	50.12%

Although these are mere averages, the results do suggest that Bede was quite fond of his patristic sources. However, we must not approach the statistics too rigidly since in Willmes' sampling quotations from the fathers and others in any given text of Bede varied from 5 to 75%.

Second, Willmes attempted to describe the way in which Bede cited other authors. He arrived at the following conclusion:

Verbatim quotations	58.9%
Modified quotations	41.1%

This indicates that more often than not Bede tends to be faithful to the wording of the quoted text.

At this point the difference between intellectual dependency and literal dependency should be clarified. Bede clearly quotes more extensively from Primasius than from Tyconius. However, this does not mean that he is more intellectually dependent on Primasius than Tyconius. Indeed, quite the contrary seems to be true.[246] Although he quotes abundantly from Primasius, Bede's exegesis was tremendously influenced by Tyconius. He discusses Tyconius at length in his introductory letter. He also mentions Tyconius explicitly nine times in the commentary itself[247] while Primasius is mentioned only once.[248] Bede is very much the student of Tyconius. Primasius' crude analogy of collecting precious gems from a dungheap is changed to a more refined expression by Bede -- "a rose among thorns."[249]

There appear to be five ways in which Bede uses his sources specifically in the Apocalypse commentary. First, he often quotes word for word. Second, he frequently modifies his sources either according to context or for the purpose of stylistic integrity. Third, he simplifies passages for his less intellectual readers. Fourth, he sometimes inserts parenthetical explanations. Fifth, he summarizes his sources. Although this last procedure is strictly speaking not a quotation, it does indicate a significant method which must be considered here. One example of each procedure used by Bede follows.

(1) Verbatim quotations

Since, as Willmes discovered, Bede frequently quotes his sources verbatim, his commentary is most helpful in recovering the text of the lost commentary of Tyconius. The following passage is a good example of a case in which the words of Tyconius would have been irretrievable without the quotation at Bede 177,15-18: Exiit ultio usque ad rectores populorum. Usque enim ad diabolum et ejus angelos novissimo certamine exiit ultio sanguinis sanctorum effusi. The corresponding passage in Caesarius 249,23-25 manifests only minor variations: exiet ultio usque ad rectores populorum; usque enim diabolum et angelos eius novissimo certamine exiet ultio sanguinis effusi. Since Beatus 7,2,35-36 and Jerome-Victorinus 135,10-12 reflect the same Tyconian source with broader revisions, without Bede recovery of the text of Tyconius would in this instance be impossible. Bede's only significant change in the passage is the insertion of the word sanctorum for the sake of clarity, which he copied from Primasius 890,23. On the basis of the essential verbal correspondence between Caesarius and Bede, the exact words of Tyconius are as follows: Exiet ultio ad rectores populorum usque enim ad diabolum et angelos eius novissimo certamine exiet ultio sanguinis effusi.

(2) Modification according to style or context

A comparison of the three passages below indicates that Bede occasionally changed the wording of Tyconius:

Bede 177,44-45

et utriusque Testamenti veritate canora

Caesarius 250,14-15

Haec enim sunt in utroque testamento quod cantant supradicti

Beatus 7,3,16

haec enim sunt in utroque testamento, quod cantant supradicti

The correspondence between Beatus and Caesarius indicates the wording of Tyconius, which was modified by Bede because the reference to the supradicti would have made no sense in his immediate context.

(3) Simplification

The passage below is rather easy to analyze because it was copied directly from Primasius by Bede.

Bede 182,5-8

Sed utrum a parte bonorum, an a parte malorum, an ex utraque parte sibi altrinsecus coeant, non hic satis elucet. Sicut Moysi et magis factum est Pharaonis.

Primasius 897,44-49

sed utrum a parte bonorum falsitate contradicentium, an a parte malorum illa signa quae memorat, perseverent ad exercendum bonos et obdrandum malos, an ex utraque parte signa sibi altrinsecus vocant, non hic satis elucet sicut a Moyse et magis factum est Pharaonis

Clearly Bede has simplified the passage. Less important material has been removed to highlight the basic contrasts which Primasius intended.

(4) Inserted explanation

Bede 149,35-41

Suo quodammodo potentatu omnia praefocantes, nullum pro libitu sui juris respirare sinebant. In terris diversitas provenciarum, in mari insularum, in arboribus diversa hominum qualitas et conditio designatur. Aliter. Qui sunt angeli quatuor, iidem quatuor intelligendi sunt venti, juxta Danielis prophetiam dicentis...

Once again we are dealing with a non-Tyconian passage copied directly from Primasius by Bede. In the corresponding section at Primasius 841,22-29 is the same passage with the middle sentence beginning _in terris_ missing. Since Bede copied from Primasius, he obviously inserted the explanatory sentence.

(5) Summary

Occasionally, Bede summarizes his sources. In two instances he mentions Tyconius and summarizes the lost Apocalypse Commentary by gathering together a series of short quotations.[250] His method is apparent for two reasons. First, the quotations are out of logical order when compared to the book of the Apocalypse. Furthermore, the Tyconian literature indicates a uniform order which is absent from Bede. Second, the collections of quotations are not properly integrated in Bede's commentary. Bede uses one collection to close Book II while the other stands rather awkwardly in the midst of his comments on Rev. 16.

In his comments at the beginning of Rev. 6, Bede presents a short summary of the seven seals at 146,38-50. The contents of the passage are thoroughly Tyconian. Bede presumes that his reader is familiar with the triple war against the church, which may be found described in the Codex Oratorii B 6, 476,7 and Beatus 4,1,24-41. Further similarities are also present in Beatus 4,1,24-41 and Caesarius 226,18-227,2. Bede's explanation of the seven seals is radically different from that of the Spanish tradition.[251] Beatus actually has both the division of Tyconius and Bede scattered throughout Book IV and the division of Apringius at the end of Book III.[252] The Spanish tradition, which seemed to become more popular,[253] is Christological while the division of Bede and Tyconius is historical:

	Apringius	Bede	
1.	corporatio	decus Ecclesiae primitivae	
2.	nativitas		(1) gentilium
3.	passio	triforme contra eam bellum	(2) falsorum fratrum
4.	mors		(3) haereticorum
5.	resurrectio	gloriam sub hoc bello triumphatorum	
6.	gloria	illa quae ventura sunt tempore antichristi	
7.	regnum	initium quietis aeternae	

Once again Bede proves invaluable. Without his summary Tyconius' understanding of the seven seals would have remained unknown.

d. Biblical texts

Generally speaking, Bede would have worked with a pre-Alcuinian Vulgate. For example, in his commentary on Tobit Bede used a biblical text which corresponds to the Codex Amiatinus and which he himself revised on the basis of texts deriving from Italy through Saint Gall.[254] Nevertheless, in his Apocalypse commentary Bede was aware of a text which deviated from his familiar Italian and Northumbrian Vulgate -- namely the text of Tyconius. Bede refers to an alia translatio or alia editio fifteen times.[255] Although the reference to another translation is reminiscent of Primasius, Bede makes his own judgments on the other translation which lies before him. One example demonstrates that the alia translatio is that of Tyconius. In his commentary at 136,31 Bede refers to an alternate translation of Rev. 1:15, which mentions the orichalco Libani. The addition of the word Libani is most unusual, but it corresponds exactly to Beatus 1,T1,15.

D. Results

a. Structure

With the former theory concerning the structure of Tyconius' disproved, Bede's <u>Epistola ad Eusebium</u> will play a less significant role in determining the structure of the lost commentary. However, one problem remains to be solved. To what extent was the sevenfold division, of which the second part corresponds to Beatus' rendition of Tyconius' Book II, influenced by Tyconius? This question may be answered only in conjunction with the other texts of the Tyconian tradition.

b. Text

The commentary of Bede will be of tremendous assistance in recovering the text of the lost commentary. Three factors are of major importance. First, Bede quoted the lost commentary extensively and often verbatim. Second, he also occasionally modified his sources as he deemed necessary. Third, Bede frequently summarized his sources, presenting their contents faithfully albeit in his own words.

H. Ambrosius Autpertus

1. The life and writings of Ambrosius Autpertus
2. *Expositio in Apocalypsin*
   a. Date and place of composition
   b. Form and contents
   c. Preface
3. Explicit mention of Tyconius
4. Unacknowledged use of Tyconius
   a. Literal dependence
   b. Dependence of ideas
5. Results

1. The life and writings of Ambrosius Autpertus

Little biographical information concerning Ambrosius Autpertus is available. Most significant is an autobiographical note at the end of his Apocalypse commentary.[256] Additional information may be gleaned from letters and monastic chronicles.[257]

Ambrosius Autpertus was born in Provence toward the beginning of the seventh century. He migrated to Italy and entered the monastery of S. Vincenzo al Volturno. There he studied the scriptures, church fathers, and the classics. He became abbot on October 4, 777 but was forced to resign on December 28, 778 following a conflict between monks of Lombardian and Frankish origin. Ambrosius died on January 30, 784.

Although he wrote a variety of commentaries, sermons, and pious exhortations, his commentary on the Apocalypse is his longest and most significant work.[258] He is often called the first Maryologist in the history of the western church due to his study of the role of Mary in the history of salvation.[259]

2. Expositio in Apocalypsin

a. Date and place of composition

In the previously mentioned autobiographical note Ambrosius states that he wrote the Apocalypse commentary while at the monastery of Saint Vincent. Furthermore, he states that Paul was the supreme pontiff, Desiderius King of the Lombards, and Arochisus Duke of the same province. This means that the commentary was composed between the years 758 and 787. Both date and place of composition are uncontested.[260]

b. Form and contents

Ambrosius wrote the commentary in two parts as he himself notes at the beginning of Book VI.[261] All known manuscripts also contain the letter of Ambrosius to Pope Stephen III defending his commentary, which is the only piece of correspondence handed down from Ambrosius.[262] There is also a somewhat extensive preface in two parts containing the history of Apocalypse commentaries in the west and a general introduction to the exegesis of the book of the Apocalypse.[263] Except for two longer prologues at the beginning of Book V and IX, there remains a lengthy verse by verse commentary on the book of the Apocalypse according to the following outline:

Book	Verses
Book I	1:1 - 1:19
II	1:20 - 3:13
III	3:14 - 5:14
IV	6:1 - 9:21
V	10:1 - 12:12
VI	12:12 - 14:13
VII	14:13 - 16:21
VIII	17:1 - 19:10
IX	19:11 - 21:8
X	21:9 - 22:21

c. Preface

Since our ultimate goal is to determine the relationship of Ambrosius to his sources and specifically to Tyconius, the preface deserves particular attention because it provides a wealth of information.

First, while giving a brief history of commentaries on the Apocalypse written in Latin, Ambrosius states his reasons for undertaking the task of writing a commentary himself. He is extremely critical of his predecessors indicating that Victorinus' commentary is too literal, Jerome's too short, and Primasius' too obscure while Tyconius was a self-confessed heretic. Since neither Augustine nor Gregory wrote a complete Apocalypse commentary, their comments are fragmentary. Should these arguments be insufficient, Ambrosius finally justifies his work as the impulse of divine grace.[264] Clearly, Ambrosius is doing what continues to be commonplace in scientific research even to the present day. In the face of so many existing Apocalypse commentaries he is attempting to demonstrate a need and thus justify the writing of yet another commentary -- his own.

Second, although Ambrosius does assert his respect for and dependence upon the patristic tradition,[265] he is much more preoccupied with presenting the exegetical method which he intends to follow in writing his own commentary. He explicitly mentions the threefold physical, spiritual, and intellectual sense of the scriptures, which he erroneously believes to have inherited from Jerome and intends to apply in the present work.[266] Once again Ambrosius is doing what one would expect in any kind of serious research. He is presenting his method so that the reader may understand his approach to the biblical text.

Both of these aspects indicate at the very beginning of the commentary that we should not expect Ambrosius to be a mere compiler of earlier authors. His mention of previous commentaries should in no way be considered a simple list of sources -- although these works, of course, did influence Ambrosius -- but rather a history of the research which Ambrosius considers inadequate, thus necessitating his own commentary. In addition, by explaining the method he intends to follow, Ambrosius is indicating that he will be using his own creative talents in writing a rather original commentary.[267]

3. Explicit mention of Tyconius

S. Bovo's investigation of the sources of Ambrosius Autpertus' Apocalypse commentary provides a convenient point of departure for the present study.[268] Here we will deal with the explicit mention of Tyconius and in the next section the use of Tyconius' commentary in those instances when he is not acknowledged.

In addition to the reference to Tyconius in the preface, Ambrosius mentions him twice in the text of the commentary. First, Ambrosius indicates that an alia translatio, that is another translation of the Apocalypse used by Tyconius, has preserved the Greek words in recounting the number of cavalry troops mentioned in Rev. 9:16.[269] Ambrosius then points out a tertia editio of Primasius, which is at variance with the translation used by Tyconius and the Vulgate which he cites. However, Primasius also mentions the alia translatio of Tyconius, referring to the same words at Rev. 9:16.[270] Therefore, it is indeed possible, if not probable, that Ambrosius did not consult Tyconius at this point but based his analysis entirely upon Primasius. Second, in his comments on Rev. 15:6 Ambrosius condemns any interpretation of the passage which would condone schism within the Church and attributes such an approach to the "pernicious mouth" of Tyconius.[271] That Tyconius held for a bipartite church is evident in his Liber regularum.[272] Beatus, also commenting on Rev. 15:6, states that the church has members who are good and members who are bad.[273] Since Ambrosius did not have access to Beatus' commentary, which does represent the Tyconian tradition, and since Primasius contains no such reference at this point, we may safely conclude that Ambrosius directly consulted Tyconius' commentary here.

Significantly, Ambrosius never mentions Tyconius without using the appellative Donatist almost as if it were part of his name. Ambrosius' keen awareness of Tyconius' unorthodoxy and his rather unflattering choice of words when referring to Tyconius' point of view would tend to indicate little positive influence of Tyconius upon Ambrosius.

4. Unacknowledged use of Tyconius

Bovo deals with the sources used by Ambrosius, namely Jerome-Victorinus, Tyconius, Augustine, Gregory, Primasius, and Benedict. In each case Bovo indicates, first, those passages demonstrating a literal dependence upon Tyconius and, second, those demonstrating a dependence of ideas. There is a marked deficiency in Bovo's work in that he has used for comparison only the Turin Fragment, which he presumes to reflect the exact text of Tyconius' lost commentary.

a. Literal dependence

Of the three passages where Bovo indicates a literal dependence upon Tyconius, two may be demonstrated to have been directly copied from Primasius. The first passage manifests word for word similarities between Ambrosius and Primasius which are absent from the Turin Fragment entirely:

Ambrosius Autpertus 146,10-12

Numquid namque priusquam Dominus idolatras atque adulteros in publicum prodat et trudidet, nescit hunc Ecclesia occultorum esse cognitorem?

Primasius 35,283-285

Numquid priusquam prodat adulteros et occidat, nesciunt ecclesiae deum scrutatorum esse renum et cordis...?

Turin Fragment 20

Quis enim(?) Antequam Deus prodat adulteros aut occidat nesciunt ecclesiae Dominum scrutatorum esse renis et cordis(?)

The second passage is similar, for example, in that the word _enarrandum_ is present in Ambrosius Autpertus 203,15 and Primasius 46,5 but absent from the corresponding passage in the Turin Fragment 116.

In one instance, however, Ambrosius clearly relied upon Tyconius. The phrase _tempus ut paenitentiam ageretis,_ present at Ambrosius Autpertus 142,32, may also be found in the Turin Fragment 5 with _agatis_ substituting for _ageretis._ However, the entire sentence is absent from Primasius 33,251-254.

b. Dependence of ideas

Bovo also indicates nineteen passages which reflect the thought of Tyconius -- seventeen by comparison to the Turin Fragment and two by comparison to the _Liber regularum._ This approach of its very nature must be rather tenuous since Primasius also frequently reflects the thought of Tyconius. In this light, only one passage may be demonstrated to have been influenced by Tyconius' Apocalypse Commentary. Ambrosius Autpertus 331,5-6 substantially reflects the

Turin Fragment 150 while being absent from Primasius. The sixteen other references mentioned by Bovo could just as easily have been influenced by Primasius as Tyconius.

5. Results

One might legitimately inquire how it is possible to dismiss such great portions of the work of Bovo. The case is rather simple. Ambrosius acknowledges having had the commentaries of both Tyconius and Primasius. However, we know that Tyconius previously had had a great influence upon Primasius. Therefore, if a passage is present in the Turin Fragment, one may not presume the influence of Tyconius until one has first eliminated the possibility of the influence of Primasius.

However, in spite of our criticism of Bovo, he has made a positive contribution to the research. First, his investigation does demonstrate Ambrosius' general approach to his sources. For example, in the section concerning Jerome-Victorinus, Bovo lists certain passages which were corrected or completed by Ambrosius. Furthermore, the instances of a dependency of ideas in all cases are far greater than the proven literal dependencies, indicating that Ambrosius took great liberty with his sources.

Second, Bovo draws some very enlightening conclusions, with which we may concur. He does acknowledge that most of the supposed references from Tyconius are not literal and bear a greater similarity to the commentary Primasius. Ambrosius has distanced himself from both the interpretation and style of Tyconius, preferring instead the interpretation of Primasius and the style of Gregory which he imitates.

In conclusion, Ambrosius Autpertus is not a mere compiler or copyist. Furthermore, he manifests a definite antipathy toward Tyconius because of his Donatism. We cannot, therefore, expect to find the exact wording of Tyconius frequently in his commentary. The enormous length of Ambrosius' commentary will present much raw material to be evaluated. However, both his goal as stated in the preface and his approach as carried out in the commentary indicate that Ambrosius neither accurately nor extensively reflects the lost commentary of Tyconius. Nevertheless, as an immediate contact with the Tyconian commentary, his commentary may not be ignored and will be of limited use in recovering Tyconius.

I. Beatus of Liébana

1. The life and writings of Beatus

a. Some biographical notes

b. The adoptionist controversy

c. The anti-adoptionist _Adversus Elipandum_

2. The Apocalypse commentary of Beatus

a. Structure

b. Content

c. Sources

(1) Generally

(2) Specifically -- Apringius of Béja

d. Manuscripts and editions

(1) The three groups of manuscripts

(a) Neuss I; Sanders _Third Class_

(b) Neuss IIb; Sanders _Second Class_

(c) Neuss IIa; Sanders _First Class_

(2) Revisions or traditions?

(a) The Delisle-Sanders theory

(b) The Neuss theory

(c) The present state of the problem

e. The effect of this situation on Tyconius research

3. _Summa dicendorum_

a. Composition and style

b. Comments on Rev. 16:13-14

c. References to a previous interpretation

d. Evidence for a Tyconian connection

(1) The Apocalypse text of the _Summa_

1. The life and writings of Beatus

a. Some biographical notes

Unfortunately, little is known about the life of Beatus of Liébana.[274] There is no doubt that he was a priest. His adversary in the adoptionist controversy, Elipando, makes direct mention of this fact in his letter to Charlemagne.[275] That Beatus was a monk and not a secular priest is best demonstrated from his own writings. A reference in his letter to Elipando alludes to his state in life: Vnum fratrem dimisimus in saeculo; ecce quantos invenimus in monasterio.[276] In the dedication of his Apocalypse commentary to Etherius, Beatus uses the words with which Isidore dedicated Contra Judaeos to his sister.[277] The changes, which Beatus makes in the text, betray his monastic state:

Isidore, Contra Judaeos epistola dedicatoria (PL 83, 449-450,12-13)

Haec ergo sancta soror, te petente, ob aedificatunem studii tui tibi dicavi, ut qua consorte perfruor sanquinis, cohaeredem faciam et mei laboris.

praefatio,1,9

haec ergo, sancte pater Etheri, te petente ob aedificationem studii fratrum tibi dicavi, ut quem consortem perfruor religionis coheredem faciam et mei laboris.

A bill of sale from the time of Fruela I has a clear reference to a certain Beatus presbyter,[278] which connects him with the monastery San Martin, later known under the name Santo Torribio. Since Fruela I ruled between the years 756 and 768, Beatus must have lived at San Martin in the second half of the eighth century. In this monastery the holy rule was strictly observed and the sacred scriptures were studied arduously. Beatus' confrere, Etherius, later became his most illustrious student.

The two extant works of Beatus, both of which will be treated in detail below, allow some insight into his character. Beatus published his lengthy commentary on the Apocalypse in 776, probably revising it twice before his death. The work is not the product of a subtle or deep thinker, but rather that of a tireless compiler and polemicist. Adversus Elipandum, of which he was co-author with his former student Etherius, presents another Beatus -- the strong and determined opponent of the adoptionist heresy, which arose in Spain at that time. In spite of Elipando's scathing remarks against him, Beatus was confident and intelligent enough not to become entrenched in a personal quarrel but always addressed himself to the issues at hand. Beatus and Etherius were well aware of the central meaning of

Christ to the essence of practiced Christianity.[279] Because there are strong indications that Beatus was present at the Council of Frankfurt in 794, his death probably occurred between 796 and 800.[280] The Vita sancti Beati [281] is considered historically unreliable.[282]

b. The adoptionist controversy

Adoptionism was that teaching concerning the relationship between the divine and human nature of the one person Jesus Christ, whereby the sonship of the human Jesus is explained as acceptance, that is adoption, by God the Father. The adoptionist controversy[283] was instigated in Spain in the eighth century by a certain itinerant preacher named Migetius, who held the rather unusual belief that the three persons of the blessed Trinity, the Father, Son, and Holy Spirit, are to be identified with David, Jesus, and Paul. The Archbishop of Toledo, Elipando, wrote a pastoral letter condemning the false teaching of Migetius. Although a local synod at Seville agreed with this condemnation, the seeds had been planted for a long and bitter dispute concerning the person of Jesus Christ. In his condemnation of Migetius, Elipando had used the word adoptio to describe the sonship of Christ. Elipando was, of course, a Visigoth and adoptio had quite a different meaning on the Iberian peninsula than in Frankish territory. For him adoptio meant simply assumptio. In Jesus Christ the second person of the Trinity, the Son, had assumed or adopted human nature. Furthermore, he was not the originator of the expression, which is found in the writings of such illustrious fathers of the church as Ambrose, Augustine, Isidore, and

Jerome.[284] There are also numerous examples of adoptio referring to the human Jesus in the Mozarabic liturgy.[285] Nevertheless, many were scandalized by his choice of words and a sharp dispute broke out as Etherius, Bishop of Osma, and the Abbot Beatus took it upon themselves to correct the errors of Elipando. Since Elipando was Archbishop of Toledo and thus Primate of Spain, he was enraged and insulted: Nam nunquam est auditum, ut Libanenses Toletanos docuissent. ...quia ignominia erit mihi, si intra ditione [sic] Toletana hoc malum fuerit auditum....[286] Elipando's response also contained a severe personal attack against the abbot, whom he labeled heretic, founder of a new heresy, and precursor of the antichrist.[287] Such a scathing attack could not go unanswered; Beatus and Etherius countered with Adversus Elipandum.[288] In place of the less eloquent and more volatile Elipando, Felix, Bishop of Urgel, eventually became spokesman for the adoptionist cause. Pope Hadrian I clearly sided with the anti-adoptionist forces. In 792 Felix was condemned at the Council of Regensburg and was forced to confess the true faith before the pope in Rome. He later recanted and fled into the Islamic ruled territory of southern Spain. Alcuin came to the fore as the vociferous defender of th faith. Both sides appealed to Charlemagne, who called the Council of Frankfurt in 794, where the adoptionists once again were condemned. Alcuin and Felix continued their disputes. The Council of Aachen in 799 once again condemned adoptionism and commanded Felix to appear. With great reluctance Felix confessed the true faith and was sent into banishment in Lyon. Since Toledo was in Mozarabic Spain and under Arab domination, the decisions of the councils could not be politically enforced there. Elipando was able to continue his struggle on behalf of the adoptionist cause until his death in 809.

There are several interpretations as to the causes of the adoptionist controversy. First, one may trace the movement back to a simple semantic misunderstanding, whereby the word adoptio was erroneously equated with assumptio and used to refer not to the human nature of Christ but to the human person Jesus. Second, the movement could be considered the self-assertion of the local Spanish church against the foreign domination of Rome. Elipando was always very conscious of his position as Primate of Spain. Third, it is no mere coincidence that the movement was strongest in Mozarabic Spain, that part of Spain under Arab domination. The Arabs brought the Nestorian writings and above all those in Syriac translation into Spain. However, more important were the theological tenets of the Moslem religion in regard to God and Jesus Christ. The Koran presents a rigid monotheism, whereby Jesus is relegated to the role of a prophet. In this context adoptionism could be considered an attempt to reconcile traditional Trinitarian theology with the strict monotheism of the Muhammadans and the Jews. All of these factors certainly played a role in the dispute. However, above all adoptionism seems to have grown out the mutual confrontation of Moslem, Jewish, and Christian religion, whereby the ecclesiastical leaders in Mozarabic Spain were especially anxious to reconcile Christian and Moslem thought in order to insure the survival of the church under a benevolent but nevertheless uncertain Muhammadan domination.

c. The antiadoptionist Adversus Elipandum

The involvement of Beatus in the controversy was strictly on a theological level.[289] He was concerned that the true teaching of the Catholic church was being compromised at the expense of conformity to Muhammadan religious belief. Of the anti-adoptionist writings of Beatus only Adversus Elipandum is extant in two books. The second book, whose size is impossible to determine, seems to break off midstream omitting the ending. M. del Alamo claimed that Etherius wrote Book I while Beatus wrote Book II.[290] Unfortunately, he offered absolutely no evidence to support this claim.

J. F. Rivera pointed out several characteristics of Adversus Elipandum which are important for this study.[291] First, Beatus and Etherius wrote against a concrete, existing heresy. Therefore, words like nunc and nunc etiam or polemic expressions like diximus, dicimus, cognoscimus, and dico are an extremely evident stylistic characteristic of the work. Second, the heresy that they are combating asserts that Christ is the nominal and adoptive son of God, but not the real and true son. The refutation of adoptionism by means of a clear Christology is the goal of the letter. Third, the debate is not academic. They are writing against Elipando, Archbishop of Toledo, even though they avoid mentioning his name. The words hereticus, pseudopropheta, and antichristus are direct references to Elipando.

As we will soon see, these stylistic characteristics are to be found in the Apocalypse commentary of Beatus, his only other extant work. Beatus' preoccupation with adoptionism is also evident in the commentary. Comparing the commentary to the Adversus Elipandum reveals veiled anti-adoptionist references.[292]

2. The Apocalypse commentary of Beatus

a. Structure

The commentary is prefaced by an introduction[293] composed of four parts. First, there is the dedicatory letter to Etherius (1,2-9), who was Bishop of Osma and collaborator with Beatus in writing the anti-adoptionist _Adversus Elipandum._ [294] H. L. Ramsay has researched this dedication in detail and has demonstrated that it is a mosaic of quotations, extracted from various works of Isidore of Seville.[295] Second, there follows the prologue _Iohannes apostolus et evangelista_ (2,1-5), which normally precedes the Apocalypse in the Vulgate manuscripts.[296] Though often attributed to Jerome, this section originates from Priscillian.[297] Third, as second prologue, the letter of Saint Jerome to Anatolius (3,1-7), which was written as an introduction to the Apocalypse commentary of Victorinus of Pettau, follows. Fourth, the bulk of the introduction is a summary of the larger commentary which follows. Though described in the text as _Item interpretatio libri huius,_ H. Florez gave this section (4,1-5,108) the title _Summa dicendorum._ [298] This section is actually a commentary on Rev. 4:1-21:4 with omissions as well as interpolations. In my calculation the _Summa dicendorum_ begins with 4,4, while 4,1-3 builds a transition.[299]

The commentary itself[300] is divided into twelve books and follows for the most part a rather uniform plan. In each book the text of the Apocalypse is explained piecemeal in the same order as it appears in the Bible. At the beginning of each section Beatus writes the _Storia,_ a direct quotation from the Apocalypse. The _Explanatio (suprascriptae storiae),_ the commentary on the preceding text, follows immediately. The stories as well as the explanations are of various lengths.

There are three major exceptions to this pattern. First, at the beginning of Book II is the _Prologus de ecclesia et sinagoga._[301] The first part of the prologue (1,2-8,32) has the characteristics of a lexicon, containing a diversified conglomerate of definitions arranged under the twin heading _ecclesia_ and _sinagoga._ Under the heading church are found Christ, angels as individuals and choirs, patriarchs, prophets, apostles, martyrs, clergy in hierarchical order, monks, and the faithful also in hierarchical order ending with the catechumen. The section is completed with a short description of religion and faith. The antichrist, heresy, sects, schism, superstition, hypocrisy, a catalogue of the various types of sinners, the dragon, the evil horses,[302] the beast, the well, and the woman on the beast are found under the heading synagogue. The second part of the prologue (9,1-10,43) is a description of the relationship between the church and the synagogue. Of special interest here are some lightly veiled anti-adoptionist references[303] as well as a creed with its liturgical introduction.[304]

The second diversion from the normal pattern of commentating is a short digression at the end of Book II, carrying the title:

Expositio septem ecclesiarum, qualiter ex septem nominantur, specialiter per arcam Noae declaratur.[305]

Finally, in Book VI three sections which refer directly to the antichrist appear one after the other. The first, beginning at 6,5,1, is entitled *Magister laterculi huius et ratio litterarum* and is composed of two tables and their explanation. *Qualiter cognoscatur antichristus in toto mundo, dum regnare coeperit* follows immediately at 6,6,1. This section has a longer recension in some manuscripts. The third part of this digression, beginning at 6,7,1, is called *De antichristo,* which is a direct quotation from Augustine's *De civitate Dei.*[306]

b. Content

Within the following schema, Beatus comments upon the entire Apocalypse:

Book	Rev.
I	1
II, septem ecclesiarum	2-3
III	4-5
IV, de septem sigillis	6-7:12
V	8:2-11:18
VI, decem capitularum	11:19-14:5
VII	14:6-15
VIII	16
IX	17
X	18-19:10

XI	19:11-20:10
XII	20:11-22

One should also note that the Apocalypse text of Beatus is an African text of that book representing an old Latin translation predating the Vulgate. This text comes without a doubt from Tyconius.[307]

c. Sources

(1) Generally

As a point of departure in investigating Beatus' sources, I will begin with those he explicitly acknowledges: _quae tamen non a me, sed a sanctis patribus, quae explanata reperii, in hoc libello indita sunt et firmata his auctoribus, id est, Iheronimo, Agustino, Ambrosio, Fulgentio, Gregorio, Ticonio, Irenaeo, Apringio, et Isidoro._[308] From this list the names Tyconius and Irenaeus are omitted from certain manuscripts. Indeed it is difficult to determine whether the two names belong to the commentary as Beatus wrote it and later were omitted in copying, or whether they were missing in the original and later added by Beatus himself or by a scribe who noticed the omission. In any case there is no doubt that both Tyconius and Irenaeus are to be counted among Beatus' sources. The absence of the name Victorinus in all manuscripts except one poses no problem. His name was obviously added in the Codex legionensis (Madrid, Biblioteca Nacional B 31) by an observant scribe who was familiar with Victorinus' work. The name of Victorinus was originally omitted because Beatus attributed his work to Jerome, whose name he dutifully lists. In addition, citing several passages from the _Tractatus_

Origenis as an example, Ramsay points out that Beatus was not constrained to limit himself to authors who appear on his list.[309] However, he does concede that Beatus could have come upon these passages indirectly. Nevertheless, the fact that Beatus' list does not exclude the possibility of other sources is extremely important for investigating Tyconius' text. One may not attribute a passage to Tyconius simply because Beatus is not its author and it is not to be found among the listed sources. The passage could conceivably come from another, unacknowledged source. Hahn, Ramsay, and Alvarez Campos have constructed catalogues of passages from the sources acknowledged by Beatus.[310] These lists are extremely valuable in eliminating passages which have not been taken from Tyconius. However, once again a word of caution -- it is indeed possible that some of these authors also had access to Tyconius' commentary. In this case, the presence of a passage among Beatus' acknowledged sources does not give valid grounds to conclude that the passage is not Tyconian, since both authors may have had Tyconius as common source. Of course, this situation is obvious in the case of Jerome who also copied extensively from Tyconius.[311]

The Apocalypse commentary of Beatus has been described as a catena, a chain of quotations from ancient authors.[312] We have only to look at the works of Isidore, who lived a century before Beatus, to see that such a method was in no way unusual during the seventh and eighth century in Spain. Beatus selected his quotations carefully from each author and wove them into a meaningful whole so that it is often impossible to determine where one quotation begins and the other ends. He sometimes adds a phrase or sentence as a transition, but often one quotation flows immediately into the next. Although he does occasionally express his own thought in his own words, Beatus often modifies his sources molding them into a vehicle for his own ideas. An obvious example is the introductory dedication to Etherius, where only a few key words have been changed in order to adapt the passage of Isidore to his own situation.[313] As Ramsay states, "A dedication so composed does not permit one to expect a great deal of originality in the work which follows."[314]

Indeed, it is this very lack of originality that makes the commentary of Beatus of such great interest. Since the commentary is a chain of quotations from other authors, it reflects above all its sources, among whom Tyconius plays a prominent role. Beatus used three Apocalypse commentaries extensively, namely the commentaries of Jerome-Victorinus, Apringius, and Tyconius. Therefore, these three authors will be singled out in this study of Beatus' sources. Since Jerome-Victorinus has already been treated and Tyconius is the subject of my research, I will consider here only the work of Apringius.

(2) Specifically -- Apringius of Béja

Although Apringius did not have access to the commentary of Tyconius, he remains, nevertheless, important as a major source of Beatus, who copied from him at length. The testimony of Isidore[315] shows that Apringius was Bishop of Béja in Portugal, that he wrote a learned commentary on the Apocalypse of Saint John, and that he flourished during the reign of Theudis, who ruled the Visigoths in Spain from 531 to 548. Further evidence as to the existence of his Apocalypse commentary comes from the correspondence of Saint Braulio, Bishop of Zaragossa, who attempted to procure a copy from the Abbot Emiliano of Toledo.[316]

The most significant manuscript of Apringius' commentary was written in Barcelona in the twelfth century and is to be found today in the library of the University of Copenhagen: Arnamagnaeaske Legat 1927 AM. 795 4to.[317] The commentary has been edited and published twice.[318] The chief problem in regard to the manuscript is the presence of excerpts from the commentary of Jerome-Victorinus. The manuscript itself identifies those sections which originate from Apringius and those which originate from Jerome:

	Chapter designation	Rev.
I	Incipit tractus in ApoKalipsin eruditissimi viri Apringii episcopi Pacensis ecclesie	1:1-5:7
II	Deinde explanatio Iheronimi	5:8-17:3
III	Item in explanatione Apringii episcopi de eadem urbe	18:6-19:21
IV	In explanatione beati Iheronimi presbiteri	20:1-10
V	Item in explanatione Apringii episcopi de eorundem mille annorum obligatione diaboli	20:1-22:20

The scribe has written _Explicit liber primus_ after the remarks on Rev. 3:21, and _Incipit liber secundus_ before the beginning of the commentary of Rev. 4:1. These headings, however, are not entirely accurate. There are isolated verses within the sections attributed to Apringius which actually come from Jerome-Victorinus, for example the last sentence of the comments on Rev. 1:13, 14, and 15 respectively.

The basic problem with the manuscript can be simply stated: Who added the passages from Jerome-Victorinus to the commentary -- Apringius himself or a later scribe? Vega argued that the entire manuscript as it now exists originates from Apringius.[319] The more common opinion is to attribute the combining of Apringius with Jerome-Victorinus to a later redactor, perhaps Renallo, doctor of the cathedral of Barcelona in the early twelfth century.[320] It seems more probable that the combination of Jerome-Victorinus with Apringius is the work a redactor and not of Apringius himself. Vega has no concrete evidence to support his argument that Apringius himself incorporated the sections from Jerome-Victorinus into his commentary. In attempting to demonstrate that sections of Jerome-Victorinus, which allegedly had been modified by Apringius, are contained in Beatus' commentary, Vega made the disastrous error of using the older edition of the Jerome-Victorinus commentary published in Migne[321] rather than the newer and superior edition of the Vienna Corpus published by Haußleiter.[322] As a result of this methodological blunder, his text comparisons are almost useless.[323]

A further problem, which must remain open, is whether the Apringius commentary was originally complete, encompassing the entire Apocalypse. Vega advances the rather convincing explanation that Apringius wrote a partial commentary of a homelitic nature corresponding to the readings between Easter and Pentecost, which were later prescribed in canon 17 of the Fourth Synod of Toledo.[324] A comparison between the Apringius commentary and the Mozarabic lectionary[325] supports his hypothesis since most of the readings do come from the early chapters of the Apocalypse during the short time between Easter and Pentecost:

Liturgia Mozarabica

Day or feast	Rev.
in die resurrectionis Domini	1:1-8
secunda feria pasche	2:1-7
feria tertia post pascha	2:8-11
feria quarta pasche	2:12-17
feria quinta pasche	2:18-29
feria sexta pasche	3:1-6
sabbato pasche	3:14-22
in octava pasche	5:1-13
in tertio dominico post pascha	3:7-13
in quarto dominico pasche	14:1-7
in quinto dominico pasche	19:11-17
in sexto dominico pasche	22:1-6
in ascensione domini	4:1-11
in dominico post ascensionem Domini	7:9-13
in die sancto pentecostes	22:6-18

According to the above schema, the readings of only two days are not included in the part of the commentary written by Apringius. Furthermore, one cannot presume that the commentary was at one time complete since there is no evidence to support this presumption. That would leave the far more difficult problem of explaining how the commentary became abbreviated.

Some conclusions may be drawn regarding the relationship of the Apringius commentary to that of Beatus. First, both the Copenhagen manuscript and Beatus' commentary contain the <u>recensio posterior</u> of the Jerome-Victorinus text.[326] Second, whether Beatus used or did not use the combination Apringius and Jerome-Victorinus contained in the Copenhagen manuscript is unclear. Third, Beatus' copy of Apringius was probably no more complete than the Copenhagen manuscript.[327] Fourth, Beatus, nevertheless, used a text of Apringius which was more correct than that of the Copenhagen manuscript. Alamo cites several examples of corruptions in the form of missing lines and grammatical changes not present in the Apringius text used by Beatus.

Although both F. Fita[328] and I. M. Gómez[329] indicate that Apringius knew and copied from the commentary of Primasius, absolutely no evidence supports this hypothesis. No similarity exists between the commentary of Primasius and that of Apringius.

Thus, except for the question regarding Apringius' relationship to Jerome-Victorinus, which is unresolved, none of the sources of Apringius is known to us. Perhaps his work was completely original and he used no sources. In any case Tyconius was definitely not one of his sources. Therefore, the presence of a passage in Apringius eliminates the possibility of Tyconian origin. His commentary may help in eliminating those passages from Beatus' commentary which could not possibly have originated from Tyconius. In this research, then, Apringius plays an exclusively negative role.

d. Manuscripts and editions

In 1770 Florez published Beatus' commentary for the first time in printed form.[330] His work, based on three, certainly no more than four manuscripts, has no critical apparatus and did not enjoy the benefit of modern scientific methods. However, it served researchers remarkably well until 1930 when H. A. Sanders published a critical edition.[331] Unfortunately, this edition does suffer from some technical flaws.[332] Normally, any research would rely upon the existing critical edition. However, this work would be incomplete, if I were to ignore a serious issue which discloses the way Beatus used his sources. So as not to be distracted by issues which belong to the study of paleography, text linguistics, and art history, I am presenting this very complex problem in an extremely simplified outline. If Beatus himself revised his commentary, then such revision or revisions would mean that he varied his dependence upon his sources by applying them differently as the circumstances of the revision required. This investigation will follow three steps: first, a listing of the three recognized manuscript families and their characteristics; second, the possible interpretations of this fact; third, the effect of this problem upon Tyconius research.

(1) The three groups of manuscripts

One might be surprised to learn that the fundamental classification twenty-seven manuscripts of Beatus' commentary remains undisputed. However, today there are thirty-two known manuscripts,[333] meaning that five have not been considered here. The classification into families is based primarily upon additions and omissions which the various manuscripts have in common. Furthermore, its validity has been proven by an independent text comparison.[334] Therefore, without further explanation, following is a list of the manuscripts in their three groups.[335]

(a) Neuss I; Sanders <u>Third Class</u>

This class of manuscripts has two outstanding characteristics. The three names Etherius, Tyconius, and Irenaeus are omitted from the introductory dedication. Furthermore, the chapter from Augustine is omitted entirely.

1) Madrid, Biblioteca Nacional, Vitr. 14-1 olim Hh 58 (A1)

2) Paris, Bibliotheque Nationale, Lat. 8878 (S)

3) Madrid, Real Academia de la Historia, Cod. 33 (A2)

4) Escurial, Cod. II & 5 (E)

5) Burgo di Osma, Archivo de la Catedral, Cod. 1 (O)

6) Berlin, Staatsbibliothek, Theol. Lat. 561 (B)

7) Paris, Bibliotheque Nationale, Nouv. acq. 1366 (N)

8) Lisbon, Archivo Torre do Tombo (L)

9) Rome, Biblioteca Corsini, Cod. lat. 369 (C)

10) Rome, Biblioteca Vaticana, Cod. Lat. 7621 (Vt)

11) Excurial, Cod. I f 7 (Ex)

12) Santo Domingo de Silos (F)

(b) Neuss IIb; Sanders <u>Second Class</u>

Here the insertion from Augustine is doubled by being added also at the end of the prologue to Book II. In addition, there are changes in the wording of the dedicatory letter.

1) Madrid, Archivo Historico Nacional, S4V6 (T)
2) New York, Pierpont Morgan Library, Ms. 429 (H)
3) Gerona, Archivo de la Catedral (G)
4) Turin, Biblioteca Nazionale, cod. lat. 93 (Tu)
5) Paris, Bibliotheque Nationale, Nouv. acq. lat. 2290 (Ar)
6) Manchester, John Rylands Library, Lat. 8 (R)
7) Madrid, Museo Arqueologico (Pc)
8) Madrid, Biblioteca Privada del Rey, 2B3 (Pp)
9) Santo Domingo de Silos (Fc)

(c) Neuss IIa; Sanders <u>First Class</u>

This class of manuscripts has the chapter <u>De antichristo,</u> which is taken from Augustine's <u>De civitate Dei</u> 20,19 inserted at the end of Book VI plus a shorter addition at 2,2,83-90. Other differences are to be found for example at praefatio,1,9 and 4,5,16.

1) New York, Pierpont Morgan Library, Ms. 644;
olim London, Henry Yates Thompson 97 (M)
2) London, British Museum, Lat. 11695 (D)
3) Valladolid, Biblioteca Sancta Cruz, cod. 1789 (V)
4) Seo d'Urgel, Biblioteca de la Catedral, cod. 4 (U)
5) Madrid, Biblioteca Nacional, B. 31 (J)

6) Madrid, Biblioteca Nacional, B. 31 (Fi)

(2) Revisions of traditions?

(a) The Delisle-Sanders theory

The existence of the three manuscript families may be explained in one of two ways, the first being based upon the hypothesis of L. Delisle, who suggested that Beatus himself could have published two different redactions of the commentary.[336] This theory is based on the premise that the dating of the present era in 4,5,2 corresponds with the time of the writing of the redaction. In A1 and S we find the year 776, but in the other manuscripts the year 786 or thereabouts. Delisle proposed the possibility that Beatus finished his first edition in 776, which is preserved only in A1 and S, and issued a revision ten years later, which served as the prototype for the remaining manuscripts.

This hypothesis was adopted and broadened by Sanders.[337] According to this theory, A1 and S remain the only manuscripts which give the first edition of 776. A2 constitutes a second edition which Beatus finished in 784. All the manuscripts of the first class present the third edition from 786. Finally, the manuscripts of the second class reflect the fourth edition, which is a revision of the third edition after the death of Beatus. All the remaining manuscripts are based on A2, the second edition.

According to Sanders, the first edition contains passages

which Beatus intentionally omitted in writing his second edition, for example the long addition at 6,6,1. However, more important for this study is the summary commentary on Rev. 1:11-3:14 in the preface. Sanders asserts that Beatus wished to retain this passage which had been lost or damaged in his copy of the first edition. Since the sources were no longer available, he had to rewrite the passage for the second edition.

Historical circumstances necessitated a third edition. In 785 Beatus and Bishop Etherius had collaborated in writing the anti-adoptionist Adversus Elipandum. Since passages of the Apocalypse commentary were incorporated into the letter, Etherius became aware of Beatus' monumental work and requested a copy from him. Beatus obliged and inserted the dedication to Etherius. Errors in this edition may be traced to the scribe who made the copy for the bishop.

Sanders explains that Beatus also added the names Tyconius and Irenaeus in this edition. He surmises that Beatus used for his earlier editions a Tyconius text which erroneously carried the name Apringius inserted in its title. By the time he got around to the third edition, he was aware of his previous error. Irenaeus is added because Beatus learned that he was the author of some statements copied from later authors; he was probably not used directly.

(b) The Neuss theory

In his extensive study of the Beatus manuscripts, W. Neuss disagrees radically with the previous hypothesis.[338] On the basis of a carefully researched text and illustration comparison, he builds a genealogy of the manuscripts. After a detailed investigation, which cannot be reproduced here, he concludes that all existing manuscripts originate from a single prototype, written around 785, to which A1 and S stand in very close relationship.

By means of this hypothesis the divergent characteristics of the manuscript families are explainable. Neuss proposed various possibilities to explain the omission of the three names Etherius, Tyconius, and Irenaeus. Since Etherius is mentioned in the dedication, his name must have been in the original text. It could be that Beatus omitted both Tyconius and Irenaeus on theological grounds, the former because he was a schismatic and the latter because he was a chiliast. However, most likely both names were in the original and for some reason were omitted from the prototype of the third class (group I, Neuss). The seemingly arbitrary diversity in the first and second class (group II) may be explained in that a scribe became aware of a manuscript of the first class, where the names were missing.

Neuss explains the existence of two entirely different prologues in the preface as the choice of the scribe of the prototype to A1 and S. Faced with the possibility of including either the letter which was written by Jerome personally or selections of a more general nature taken from the works of his countryman Isidore, the scribe opted for the second possibility as a fitting introduction to a biblical work. Jerome was omitted in favor of Isidore and S reflects this change recording two widely divergent prologues.

(3) The present state of the problem

In his exhaustive study of A1, P. K. Klein has been able to reconcile the two diverging theories to a certain degree. First, he pointed out the major error in the research of Neuss who presumed that the text and illustration tradition must be identical.[339] Klein demonstrated that although the texts of A1 and S are very closely related, the illustrations bear little or no relationship to one another. He agreed with the opinion of Sanders in regard to three redactions, adding the useful information that the first redaction was scantily or not at all illustrated. Second, Neuss' opinion that all the manuscripts may be traced back to a common prototype does not exclude Sanders' theory of a threefold redaction.[340] It is safe to assume that various redactions will also produce variations in the text. In conclusion, Klein supported Sanders' theory concerning a threefold redaction, whereby each redaction manifests certain characteristics in regard to both content and text.

M. C. Díaz y Díaz[341] has rightly stated that the major problems concerning the Beatus manuscripts have not been definitively solved. First, the literary composition of the work remains confused especially in regard to the sources which Beatus used. Second, no genuine consensus has been reached regarding the significance the three manuscript groups. Third, the relationship of the illustrations to the manuscripts still remains unclear. Therefore, he has called for a new collation of manuscripts for the purpose of constructing a new stemma.

e. The effect of this situation on Tyconius research

The possible existence of various Beatus editions or redactions[342] is essential to this research because this factor would of necessity determine their proximity to Beatus' sources. First, if Sanders' theory is acceptable, then A1 and S reflect the very first redaction of Beatus. In the first redaction Beatus exercised less independence and was more faithful to his sources. However, in the later redactions, either out of personal preference or because the sources had become unavailable, Beatus exercised greater freedom in formulation and diverged from his sources as the circumstances required. Therefore, accepting Sanders' theory requires preferring all the A1 and S readings in this research because of their proximity to Beatus' sources, among whom is Tyconius. Second, accepting the theory of Neuss means acknowledging that A1 and S in no way reflect a closer proximity to Beatus' sources but rather variations in the text tradition. If Beatus wrote just one single redaction of his commentary, then a study of the various manuscripts wins no insight into his sources. In this case, working with the best critical edition available, which would present the commentary as Beatus wrote it, would be preferable. Since these problems have yet to be solved, the edition of Sanders is clearly not definitive.

3. <u>Summa dicendorum</u>

a. Composition and style

All researchers have acknowledged the clearly independent

character of the <u>Summa dicendorum,</u> beginning with H. Florez, who appropriately dubbed the introductory summary of Beatus' commentary with this descriptive title.[343] Even a superficial reading of the passage shows an extremely close relationship to the more complete commentary which follows. More than half of the <u>Summa dicendorum</u> is present in the larger commentary within the same literary context. Much of this correspondence is verbatim or reflects only minor changes. Also some sections originate from the writings of Isidore of Seville.

In addition to the rather large verbal correspondence, there is also a close relationship between certain passages where the same meaning is expressed in entirely different words. Two examples follow:

praefatio,4,21

septimum sigillum in hoc signo complet librum septem sigillis signatum.

4,6,79

concludit utramque narrationem septimo sigillo

praefatio,5,84

et vadunt impii in profundum inferni, quem angelus lapidem molarem in profundum maris nominavit, iusti vero in vitam aeternam.

10,3,3

hoc est illud, quod Daniel dicit, quod alii resurgent ad vitam aeternam, alii in opprobrium sempiternum, ut videant semper.

Perhaps most intriguing are those passages which do not correspond in meaning but rather demonstrate a stylistic similarity. The two following passages comment on Rev. 13:1 and 16:19-20 respectively:

praefatio,5,17

in hoc bestia multa demonstrat membra, _aliquando_ diabolum, _aliquando_ sacerdotes malos, _aliquando_ populum malum, _aliquando_ religiosos falsos.

6,3,16

cum et ipsa bestia unum corpus est, sed distincte multa membra habeat. _aliquando_ enim diabolum dicit bestiam, _aliquando_ corpus eius, quod sunt infideles, id est, sine baptismo, _aliquando_ unum ex capitibus ipsius bestiae...

praefatio,5,66

Babilon abominatio est vastationis, quod est Latine generale malum. _sive_ in paganos, _sive_ in Christianos, _sive_ in servos Dei, quicquid malum agitur Babilon dicitur.

8,8,9

Babilon autem generale malum est adversus Ierusalem, _sive_ in gentibus _sive_ in falsis fratribus, sed pro locis accipiendum est, sicut veritate scimus

That little originality is manifested in the _Summa dicendorum_ is abundantly clear. However, several sections do stand out as obvious exceptions. The church is described in 4,43-45 as coming from the circumcision and extending to the four corners of the earth. Elsewhere a primitive style is especially evident, for example in 4,91-93 where _quod autem dicit_ is quite redundantly repeated three times. The two longest passages without parallels elsewhere are 4,115-117, which describes the antichrist, and 5,60-61, which considers the various false prophets. Finally, besides these longer passages, there are dispersed here and there throughout the text a great number of shorter sentences, which are to be found neither in the larger commentary of Beatus nor in Isidore.

The aim here is, of course, to determine by investigating

three types of passages to what degree, if any at all, Tyconius influenced the composition of the Summa dicendorum. First, the commentary on Rev. 16:13-14, contained in 5,48-62, stands out as unique and presents special difficulties. Large sections have been copied directly from Isidore. The circumcelliones, an exclusively African phenomenon, are mentioned. However, a great amount of material is original, being neither in the larger commentary nor in Isidore. Second, there appears twice in the text a reference to a previous literal interpretation of Elijah's testimony which is now being spiritually interpreted. There is no doubt that these two references, 4,72 and 5,23, are related to one another. It is also possible that other shorter references to the same theme share the same source. Finally, there are several short but extremely important passages, namely 4,58; 4,96; 4,99; and 5,67, which clearly show a connection with Tyconius other than through Beatus.

b. Commentary on Rev. 16:13-14 (praefatio,5,48-62)

Here is undoubtedly the most problematic passage of the Summa dicendorum. Haußleiter used it to support the theory that Jerome wrote the entire preface while relying upon Tyconius as a source.[344] Jerome's authorship would account for the apparent repetition of information which is presented by Tyconius in the following commentary. The reference to circelliones in 5,54 led Hahn to jump to the unwarrantable conclusion that this specific passage and thus the entire Summa dicendorum is of African and, therefore, Tyconian origin.[345] Ramsay correctly expressed great skepticism in regard to both theories since he discovered that a major portion of this section is taken directly, often verbatim, from Isidore of Seville.[346] Finally, the situation is further complicated in that a substantial part of the passage is peculiar to the Summa dicendorum, having no parallels in other Apocalypse commentaries.

The first task must be to investigate the Isidorian passages. They are definitely not the same, but fall into three distinct categories. First, two passages appear also in the larger commentary of Beatus within the same context, namely in regard to Rev. 16:13-14. Second, three passages are also found in the prologue of Book II where a similar structure is also apparent. Third, the remainder of the Isidorian passages is not to be found in the larger commentary of Beatus.

The first set of passages appropriately belongs to the comments on Rev. 16:13-14, and they are also present in Isidore's Exodus commentary. The passages appear three times in the writings of Beatus:

praefatio,5,49-50

et nihil aliud prodest animal ipse, nisi quod sonum vocis improbis et importunis clamoribus reddet.... etiam et ipsa aqua scripturarum inflata modulatione, velut ranarum sonis et cantibus huic mundo deceptionis fabulas inferent.

8,7,5 and 7

rana est enim loquacissima vanitas. nihil enim ad aliud animal ipsud utile est, nisi quod sonum vocis improbis et importunis clamoribus reddet.... quasi ranas e caeno, voces emittunt, quo inani quadem et inflata modulatione, vel ranarum sonis et cantibus, modo hic deceptionis fabulus inferunt.

Adversus Elipandum 52 (CChr.SL 59, 38,1429-1438)

Rana est loquacissima vanitas. Nihil enim cibo aptum est animal istud, quoniam inmundum est. Nihil aliud animal ipsut utile est, nisi quod sonum uocis, improuis et importunis clamoribus reddet.... quasi ranas e caeno uoces emittunt, qui inani quadam et inflata modulatione superuiae uelut ranarum sonis et cantibus nouis deceptionis fabulas scribunt.

Isidore In Exodum 14,3 (PL 83, 292,42-48)

qui inani quadam, et inflata modulatione, velut ranarum sonis et cantibus mundo huic deceptionis fabulas intulerunt. Rana est enim loquacissima vanitas; ad nihil enim aliud animal ipsum utile est, nisi quod sonum vocis improbis et importunis clamoribus reddit.

Both in writing the preface and in writing the larger commentary, Beatus copied directly from Isidore. However, the sections, as they appear in the Adversus Elipandum, have been copied from Book VIII of the Apocalypse commentary. This is apparent because the words quasi ranae e coeno, voces emittunt are present in the letter to Elipando and with a slight variation in Book VIII but not at all in Isidore.[347]

One is above all impressed by the fact that the passages seem to fit so well into the commentary and prologue of Beatus at this point, especially because the frogs are mentioned in Rev. 16:13. A comparison with the commentary of Caesarius[348] and that of Primasius[349] demonstrates clearly that Tyconius himself did address some of his comments to these frogs. The question, of course, arises: Since Isidore is often not very original, is it possible that he copied from the commentary of Tyconius? Actually, no evidence supports this hypothesis. Most likely Isidore did not even have a copy of Tyconius' Liber regularum, but was familiar with this work only through Book III of Augustine's De doctrina christiana.[350] However, there appear to be indications that Isidore did know the commentary of Primasius:

Primasius 232,165-233,201

bestiam antichristum cum suis, pseudoprophetam praepositos et doctores dogmatum noxiorum. Ranae enim et loco et uisu molestoque strepitu sic odibiles habentur.... cum de ore illorum immundos spiritus in modum dicit prodire ranarum.... usque ad signum enim ranarum suis magi incantationibus....

Isidore, In Exodum 10,14 (PL 83,292,34-46)

Aquae Aegyptiae erratica, et lubrica philosophorum sunt dogmata.... velut ranarum sonis et cantibus mundo huic deceptionis fabulas intulerunt. Rana est enim loquacissima vanitas; ad nihil enim aliud animal ipsum utile est....

Therefore, it is very possible that some material from Tyconius has made its way through Primasius and Isidore to end up next to its original source in Beatus' commentary. The interdependence of the commentaries may be described schematically as follows:

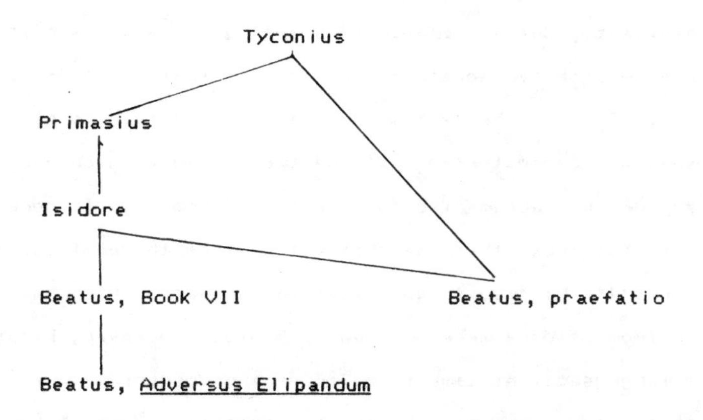

For this very reason many researchers were deceived into believing that Tyconius was the author of the entire Summa dicendorum. The two passages from Isidore fit surprisingly well into the total context because their content is indeed Tyconian.

The next set of Isidorian passages is those which appear both in the Prologus libri II and in the Summa dicendorum, where they describe the four members of the pseudoprophet, namely the heretic, schismatic, superstitious person, and hypocrite.[351] Since, as we will soon see, any judgment in regard to these passages depends to a great extent upon the origin of the prologue, we must investigate its authorship before considering the Isidorian passages contained therein. The prologue carries the heading De ecclesia et sinagoga, which accurately describes its contents. It serves to introduce Book II, which deals with the seven churches, namely Rev. 2-3, although the end of Book I already touches upon this theme.

The question concerning authorship of the prologue is most significant. While prematurely praising it as a new historical source, Haußleiter advanced the argument that Tyconius is its author.[352] This theory has been permanently laid to rest by Ramsay, who demonstrated that the two passages which Haußleiter used to support his argument originate from Jerome and Isidore.[353] Bousset has shown that the greatest part of the prologue comes from Isidore.[354] He also thought that any passages which had not been taken from Isidore were written by Beatus. However, Ramsay indicated that large sections come from Jerome and Gregory as well. Furthermore, a comparison with the commentaries which have been influenced by Tyconius shows no correspondence. Therefore, it is safe to conclude that there is no evidence to support the theory of Tyconian authorship. On the contrary, a far more feasible hypothesis is that Beatus wrote the prologue, drawing upon Isidore, Jerome, and

Gregory as sources. An introduction to Book II does fit appropriately into this scheme. Beatus wished to collect definitions from various sources in regard to church and synagogue before starting the commentary on the seven churches. What was not available from other sources, he wrote himself. Having set the theory of Tyconian authorship of the prologue to rest, we may now turn our attention to the three Isidorian passages which are common to the preface and the prologue.

The third of these Isidorian passages promises to shed some light on the situation. Below is the passage as it appears in the preface and prologue of Beatus:

praefatio,5,51

quod unusquisgue id sibi eligat et faciat arbitrio suo, quod melius _illi_ esse videntur

prologus,7,2

nam heresis Graece, Latine electio _vocatur,_ quod scilicet unusquisque id sibi elegat, quod melius _ille_ esse videtur

The corresponding passage in the Etymologies of Isidore is strikingly similar. Its source is to be found in the Titus commentary of Jerome:

Etymologiae 8,3,1 (BAC 433, 688)

Haeresis Graece ab electione _vocatur,_ quod scilicet, unusquisque id sibi eligat quod melius _illi_ esse videntur

Ad Titum 3 (PL 26, 597,26-28)

Haeresis Graece ab electione _dicitur,_ quod scilicet unusquisque id sibi eligat quod _ei_ melius esse videatur

The second two passages are almost identical. However, Isidore introduced two major changes into the text. First, he substituted *vocatur* for *dicitur.* Second, he changed *ei* to *illi.* Unfortunately,the word *ille,* as it appears in the prologue, makes no sense whatsoever. However, the preface is correct with *illi* as a personal dative following *videtur.* We may safely presume that *illi* is the correct reading in the prologue. Quite clearly Beatus wishes to refer not to an abstract heretic, but to none other than his specific opponent in the adoptionist controversy, Elipando. It is apparent that Isidore copied from Jerome, and Beatus in turn copied from Isidore. It is also most likely that the preface was written on the basis of the prologue.

The next step is to consider the structure of all three passages. The schema below makes the situation most clear:

praefatio	prologus	*Etymologiae*
hereticus	de heresibus	haeresis
	de secta	secta
schismaticus	de scisma	schisma
supprestitiosus	de supprestitione	superstitio
hypocrita	de hypocrita	

The prologue builds a bridge between the Etymologies and the preface. Beatus, who wrote the prologue, took the four items from Isidore and added hypocrisy, whose description he copied from Gregory the Great. Indeed these five items are just the beginning of a very long series of definitions. The interpolator of the preface, probably Beatus himself, took four of the five items from the prologue. In the preface the items are no longer abstractions but concrete persons. He is describing the false prophet, namely Elipando. The personalization of the word secta into sectator would not only have been unusual and confusing but also downright misleading. In Tit. 2:14, for example, the word sectator has a fully positive meaning. Therefore, Beatus dropped the grouping and omitted the word. If one would assert that the preface was written before the prologue, then one would have the difficult task of explaining how the word secta reappears exactly where it belongs as in the Etymologies. Therefore, these Isidorian passages must have found their way into the preface by way of the prologue. Tyconius is not their author, but rather Beatus depending upon Isidore.

The final set of Isidorian passages is those which appear in the Summa dicendorum but nowhere in the longer commentary of Beatus.[355] Before Ramsay rightly expressed his own reservations in regard to Tyconian authorship,[356] most researchers assumed the African and, therefore, Tyconian origin of this passage simply because the circelliones are mentioned. Haußleiter fell headlong into this trap which led him to the conclusion that the author of the Summa dicendorum was someone familiar with the work of Tyconius.[357] Working with the same erroneous principle, Hahn concluded that Tyconius himself wrote this specific passage and the entire Summa dicendorum.[358] The overwhelming evidence is on the side of Ramsay because the passage does originate from Isidore.[359] Actually, the key to understanding the passage is the work cotopitas. Whoever interpolated the passage into the preface, probably Beatus, states that the word is Greek, which of course it is not. On the other hand, Isidore does not make this mistake. He could have invented the word; however, this is most unlikely. Isidore sometimes does invent an etymology in order to make a point. Here the problem is not the etymology but the word itself. In fact, he gives no etymology and in no way attempts to justify his use of the word. The other possibility is that Isidore took the word from an African source. In this case, the word could very well be of Punic origin especially if the circumcelliones came from that section of the population. Haußleiter rightly points out that the Latin translation of the word is agrestes, namely farmer. R. Lorenz brought some light to the situation when he investigated the semitic words that sound like cotopitas. In Hebrew the word qatap and in Syriac the word q'tap come from the same root and mean to "gather" or "harvest." This meaning is indeed not far from agrestes in Latin.[360]

How then did the circumcelliones become identified as a type of monk? Although the circumcelliones of Africa were not monks but migrant field workers,[361] they came to be treated as a type of monk in the later Christian literature due to a false understanding of Augustine's Enarrationes in Psalmos.[362] Isidore lists the circumcelliones as a specific type of monk.[363] In the Regula magistri and the Rule of Benedict the gyrovagi are a group of monks with similar traits.[364] Although the passage in the Summa dicendorum obviously comes from Isidore, there is a very close similarity to Cassiodore's commentary on Psalm 132.[365] All of these authors describe the circumcelliones similarly in regard to three aspects: first, their activity as wanderers; second, their attempt to live together as brothers, especially as described in Acts

4:32; and finally, their failure as monks. Therefore, there appear to be no grounds to assert that the passage in Beatus is of African or Tyconian origin. However, it does have very much in common with the monastic tradition of the West.

The next step is to consider those passages which are unique to the *Summa dicendorum.*[366] The monastic flavor indicated above is especially evident in these passages. Toward the end of the section on the hypocrites, the quotation from Isidore is interrupted and the following sentence is inserted: *ita hoc genus monachorum intus sunt mali sed foris boni ostendunt.*[367] That is indeed an accurate description of hypocrisy. However, the author wrote "this kind of monks," which is most unusual since the passage is supposedly a description of the pseudoprophet. Suddenly out of nowhere the author addresses himself no longer to the hypocritical false prophets but to the hypocritical false monks. The word *monachus* is to be found neither in the *Liber regularum* nor in the other Tyconian literature. Furthermore, there is a grammatical characteristic present which indicates that the passage is of late origin. The verb *sunt* is plural under the influence of the word *monachorum.* However, the subject of the sentence is *genus* in the singular. A collective noun with a plural verb is definitely characteristic of medieval style. The passage could not have been written in the fourth century, and thus does not come from Tyconius.

A closer reading of the passages indicates other monastic references. For example, the word *fratres* appears three times.[368] With this word Tyconius is not referring to his brother Donatists, as

Hahn asserts,[369] but rather Beatus is referring to his brother monks. Reference to communal living appears also three times,[370] in each case as a negative expression to show that this certain type of false prophet or monk is unable to live in peace and concord. The author uses the word consilium three times in its usual monastic meaning.[371] Finally, there is a reference to the traditional activities of monks: vigilare, laborare, and ieiunare.[372]

One could safely conclude that the entire commentary on Rev. 16:13-14 was written or at least revised by a monk or someone addressing himself to monks. Most likely Beatus himself, who was an abbot as well as a priest, added the quotations from Isidore in addition to his own comments. The passage also fits in well with the anti-adoptionist polemic of Beatus. Elipando, who as Archbishop of Toledo and Primate of Spain, was also a monk.[373] Quite clearly Beatus was continuing his criticism of this leader of the adoptionist cause.

c. References to a previous interpretation

Next to be investigated are two specific passages in the Summa dicendorum, which refer explicitly to a previous interpretation. I believe that these two passages do not stand in isolation, but that they rather represent two of the many interpretations which come from the hand of Beatus. The two passages are contained in the comments on Rev. 11:4 and Rev. 14:6;8 respectively:

praefatio,4,72

Hi sunt duae olivae et duo candelabra. haec secundum litteram de Elia diximus. sed nunc spiritualiter de duo testamenta, quod est lex et evangelium, dicamus.

praefatio,5,23

et alium angelum sequentem illum, id est, Eliam et qui cum eo venturus est, qui anticipat praedicatione sua regnum antichristi. haec secundum litteram diximus. mystice autem angelum in caelo volantem et alium sequentem legem et evangelium dicit....

According to Haußleiter, the author of these two passages "confesses that he presented in an earlier interpretation an opinion different from the one which he now holds."[374] A comparison with the commentary of Jerome-Victorinus reveals the earlier interpretation of the author.[375] The repetition of the words Heliam, qui anticipat praedicatione sua regnum Antichristi leaves no doubt that the corresponding passage of Jerome-Victorinus was modified in its transfer to the Summa dicendorum. This change is explainable only if the same author wrote both commentaries making his revision in the second as he explicitly concedes. Thus, according to Haußleiter Jerome must be the author of the Summa dicendorum, since he is the one responsible for the later recension of the Victorinus commentary.

Hahn countered with a series of references from other parts of the Summa dicendorum in order to disprove the hypothesis of Haußleiter and support his own argument that Tyconius is its author.[376] Although I agree with Hahn in rejecting Haußleiter's hypothesis, unfortunately his argument suffers from two serious defects. First, some of the evidence which he presents, for example the reference to the circumcelliones and to the brother Donatists, may hardly be used, since this material represents later additions to the text. Second, he does not handle the legitimate problem which Haußleiter raises, namely how to understand two explicit references to a previous interpretation which is now intentionally being altered.

Examining these two passages more closely may help solve this problem. The author makes two basic affirmations. First, he is changing his exegetical method, which allows him to arrive at a different conclusion. The striking contrast between <u>diximus</u> in the perfect tense and later <u>dicamus</u> in the present makes the situation absolutely clear. What was previously literally interpreted is now being spiritually interpreted. Haußleiter seems to assert that the author is forced to withdraw an earlier opinion because his present opinion contradicts what he held earlier. This is not at all the case. The later spiritual interpretation in no way invalidates the earlier literal interpretation. The two opinions, that is the two interpretations, can exist side by side without causing the least difficulty. In other words, the assertions are not mutually exclusive. Therefore, the author does not have to feel himself obliged to withdraw his earlier opinion. He merely explains the basis for his new interpretation in order to avoid confusion.

Second, the more basic affirmation of the author goes beyond the problem of the change and on to the content of this new interpretation. This is indeed his foremost intention. The comments about the change are merely a justification of the new interpretation which he is now eager to present. Unfortunately, Haußleiter stops with the fact of the change and ignores the content of this new interpretation entirely, although it is absolutely necessary for a proper understanding of the passage. According to the literal understanding of Rev. 11:4 in the light of Matt. 17:3-4 and parallels, the two witnesses are Moses and Elijah. According to the spiritual sense of the passage, the two witnesses are _lex et evangelium._ Since the words are absent from the corresponding passages of Jerome-Victorinus, they obviously constitute a new spiritual interpretation of the text. The expression _lex et evangelium_ appears twelve times in the _Summa dicendorum,_ [377] while being considerably less frequent in the larger commentary. Especially evident is the total absence of the expression _lex et evangelium_ from the Tyconian literature; it can be found neither in the Turin Fragment, nor in the commentaries of Jerome-Victorinus, Caesarius, and Primasius, nor in the _Liber regularum._ However, the letter of Beatus to Elipando contains a similar preoccupation with _lex et evangelium,_ where the expression appears eleven times.[378] In his letter to Elipando Beatus asserts that the articles of faith are contained in the _lex et evangelium,_ where the adoptionist theories of Elipando are not to be found. On the basis of the foregoing evidence, the possibility that Tyconius or Jerome wrote the passages is eliminated. A far more feasible hypothesis is that Beatus wrote the two passages in support of his anti-adoptionist polemic against Elipando.

In connection with this problem Haußleiter introduces another passage to support his argument in favor of Jerome's authorship.[379] He correctly affirms that praefatio,4,64 contains a phrase from a symbol of faith: _templum metire est patrem confiteri omnipotentam et Iesum Christum filium eius, qui natus est de spiritu et Maria virgine._ He asserts that the phrase could have come neither from Tyconius, since it is not African, nor from Beatus, since Beatus cites an entirely different symbol in his letter against Elipando.[380] Therefore, he concludes that the phrase comes from an old Roman symbol which was introduced into the text by Jerome. However, Haußleiter fails to mention that the phrase natus (est) de Spiritu sancto et Maria uirgine appears six times in the letter to Elipando.[381] This corresponds exactly to the intention of Beatus, who wishes to affirm the physical birth of Jesus from Mary as well as Jesus' conception by the Holy Spirit.[382] Once again all indications point to the anti-adoptionist polemic of Beatus against Elipando. Quite clearly Beatus also inserted the credal formula into the commentary.

d. Evidence for a Tyconian connection

The above investigation of both the much disputed passage on Rev. 16:13-14 and the reference to a previous interpretation demonstrates two facts. First, at least certain sections of the Summa dicendorum originate from the literary activity of Beatus, who either composed his own comments or copied passages from the works of other authors, adapting them to his own specific intention. Second, the hypothesis that Jerome could have written the Summa dicendorum has no basis in reality. With this information in mind we are now in a position to delve further into the question of authorship and in the light of the available facts to propose a solution to this problem. Solving this problem depends entirely upon understanding of the literary history of the text. There can be only three possible solutions to the problem. First, one could assert that Beatus wrote the Summa dicendorum in its entirety as a summary and introduction to his larger commentary. If this were the case, the introduction would have had to been based exclusively upon the larger commentary which follows. In other words, the entire content of the summary would have to be attributed either to the larger commentary or to the imagination of Beatus. The second possible alternative is that Tyconius himself wrote the Summa dicendorum as an introduction to his commentary. In other words, the original structure of Tyconius' lost commentary encompassed this lengthy introduction which preceded the actual commentary itself. The third and final possibility is that the Summa dicendorum is a summary of the original Tyconian commentary, which was written neither by Beatus nor by Tyconius but by a third party. The third alternative, which will be explained in detail and substantiated by means of three arguments below, is most defensible.

My hypothesis follows: Tyconius wrote his original commentary possibly either with no introduction at all or with a short forward similar to the one which precedes his Liber regularum. Several copies were made of the commentary which was passed down in manuscript form. One of these manuscripts came into the possession of someone who made a short summary or epitome of the original work. At least two Tyconian manuscripts came into the hands of Beatus, the normal longer Tyconian commentary and the epitome. The larger Tyconian commentary was integrated into the larger commentary of Beatus, who used the epitome as an introduction. To the epitome he prefixed his own introduction encompassing the dedication to Etherius, the Apocalypse prologue, and the letter of Jerome to Anatolius. He then interpolated several quotations from Isidore into the entire introduction. Finally, he added here and there his own comments, for example naming his sources and polemicizing against the adoptionist Elipando.

Actually, a parallel situation may found in the _Expositio_ of Caesarius, where it is evident that two manuscript traditions have been incorporated into the commentary.[383] In this way, one can account for the fact that several passages are commented upon twice. In Beatus' commentary, the situation is somewhat different: first, the two manuscript traditions are substantially different from one another, one manuscript presenting a complete Tyconian commentary and the other an epitome; second, the two manuscripts have not been integrated into a single whole but rather are presented separately and sequentially, that is one after the other with the shorter manuscript serving as the prototype of the introduction. The proposed hypothesis will be substantiated by the Apocalypse text of the _Summa dicendorum_, the content of its Apocalypse commentary, and its abbreviated character.

(1) The Apocalypse text of the _Summa dicendorum_

Vogels has demonstrated that Beatus' commentary contains a text of the Apocalypse that originated from Tyconius. Especially helpful in proving this point are the _storiae_, where Beatus brought together the corresponding scripture passages of the commentary and presented a single flowing Apocalypse text. A comparison with the _Summa dicendorum_ indicates that we are dealing here with an abridged Tyconian text.[384] As Vogels concluded, the Apocalypse text of the _Summa dicendorum_ is an abridged Tyconian Apocalypse text, of which the longer version is presented in the subsequent _storiae_ and _explanationes._ In other words, from the point of view of the Apocalypse text alone, the _Summa dicendorum_ is an abbreviated version of what appears in the larger commentary of Beatus.

(2) The Apocalypse commentary of the _Summa dicendorum_

The evidence to be presented now serves a twofold goal. First, it will demonstrate that the _Summa dicendorum_ presents a Tyconian text, which occasionally differs from the one in the larger commentary. Second, this being the case, the presence of material which comes from another Tyconian tradition within the _Summa dicendorum_ eliminates the possibility that the larger commentary of Beatus could have served as a model for the shorter introduction.

A three way comparison between the _Summa dicendorum,_ the larger commentary of Beatus and the Turin Fragment will achieve this end. The Turin Fragment is especially suitable for this comparison because of its totally separate transmission independent of the Spanish tradition of Beatus. Indeed further comparisons could be made, for example with the commentaries of Primasius or Caesarius. However, such comparisons would be much more complicated, since it would be necessary to refer to Jerome-Victorinus in order to eliminate the material Beatus could have obtained from that source, which is common to Beatus, Primasius, and Caesarius. Limiting the comparisons to the Turin Fragment simplifies the problem, while nevertheless being sufficient to achieve the goal. Demonstrating that there are passages which the _Summa dicendorum_ and the Turin Fragment have in common and which at the same time diverge from the corresponding readings in the larger commentary will fulfill the twofold goal stated above. This would mean that the Summa dicendorum and the Turin Fragment share a common source which differs from the source of the larger commentary of Beatus. In this way, a direct contact between the original text of Tyconius and the Summa dicendorum will be demonstrated, and the possibility that the Summa dicendorum is a summary of the larger commentary of Beatus will be eliminated. In other words, the Summa dicendorum, the larger commentary of Beatus and the Turin Fragment represent three independent manuscript traditions of the one Tyconian commentary.

The first passage to be compared comes from the comments on Rev. 10:9:

5,10,34

hic liber amaritudinem ventri tuo faciet, cum praedicare et operare coeperis, quod intellexeris.

praefatio,4,58

hic liber lex est et evangelium. sed cum eum coeperis legere, dulcis est in ore, sed amaritudinem senties, quum praedicare et operare coeperis, quod intellexeris.

Turin Fragment 319

Id est, dum perceperis delectaberis eloquii diuini dulcedine, et amaritudinem senties cum operari et praedicare coeperis quod intellexeris.

The last part of the passage is common to all three with the exception that the words operari and praedicare are inverted in the Turin Fragment. Previous research shows that the words hic liber lex est et evangelium were added to the preface by Beatus. The passage which is critical to the issue has been italicized. It is especially obvious that only the word _amaritudinem_ in the larger commentary of Beatus agrees with the corresponding passage in the preface. However, in the Turin Fragment this word is within its original context. Apparently _dulcedine_ has been corrupted into _dulcis est in ore_ or visa versa. In any event, the agreement between the preface and the Turin Fragment indicates Tyconius as a common source. Above all, the text of the preface is not based upon the text of the larger commentary in Book V.

Agreement between the preface and the Turin Fragment with divergence from the larger commentary is evident in several other passages:

5,13,6

quo modo _poterant_ habitantes terram de duorum _morte_ gaudere, si una civitate _morerentur?_

praefatio,4,96

quomodo _poterunt_ habitantes terram de duorum _nece_ gaudere, si in una civitate _morientur?_

Turin Fragment 400

Nam quomodo _poterunt_ habitantes terram de duorum hominum _nece_ gaudere, si in una ciuitate _morientur?_

The preface and the Turin Fragment agree exactly with the only exception being the omission of the word _hominum_ from the preface. On the other hand, a comparison of Book V to the preface shows that the two verbs suffered inflectional changes in the larger commentary and the noun _nece_ has been replaced with _morte._ A final example follows:

5,13,13

hora est enim omne tempus

praefatio,4,99

in illa hora, quod dicit, omne tempus significat

Turin Fragment 409

In hora quod ait, omne tempus significat

Once again the similarity between the preface and the Turin Fragment is apparent, while the larger commentary presents another reading. On the basis on these comparisons I conclude that the larger commentary of Beatus could not have served as a model for the shorter introduction in the preface. The shorter introduction or Summa dicendorum, as it is called, is rather an epitome of the original commentary of Tyconius.

(3) The abbreviated character of the Summa dicendorum

The fact that the Summa dicendorum is missing both a beginning and an end is significant. The abbreviated commentary actually begins with Rev. 4:1. After a short introduction taken from Isidore, the first four chapters of the Apocalypse are summarized in several lines. An alternate and somewhat longer summary is present in the S manuscript. Actually, the absence of the original beginning presents no great problem. It is not at all unusual that the outer leaves of a manuscript be damaged or lost. Faced with this situation and not wanting to begin his commentary midstream, Beatus added some introductory material. Two sentences were necessary to fill the gap with a summary so that the work would flow smoothly.

However, more important than the lack of a beginning is the obvious lack of an end. If indeed the Summa dicendorum had served as the introduction to the original Tyconius commentary, then its end would have to have been in the middle of the manuscript. How then did the ending become lost? If the Summa dicendorum was not an introduction but a separate manuscript, then its ending would indeed have been the last leaves of a book. Just as the beginning of a manuscript tends to suffer damage or loss, so also the end. The missing end of the Summa dicendorum is easily explainable if the work was transmitted separately and later appended to the beginning of the commentary.

Several observations in regard to the end of the Summa dicendorum support this hypothesis. The work seems to have two endings, neither of which continues to the last chapter of the Apocalypse. The first ending is found after the comments on Rev. 19 and is indicated by the words: hic facit finem et recapitulat ab origine. [385] Since these words do not appear in the other commentaries of the Tyconian tradition at this point, they were most likely added at a later date. After three more pages of commentary, the Summa dicendorum ends with the direct quotation of Rev. 21:3-4.

The solution to this problem corresponds well to the proposed hypothesis. Since the Summa dicendorum was at one time a separate manuscript, the first as well as the last portion was lost or damaged. This unfortunately left the work with the rather unusual characteristic of ending with a question, to which the above mentioned editorial remark was appended. Since the words of Rev. 21:4 do offer a very appropriate ending to an Apocalypse introduction, the comments on Rev. 20:1-21:4 were added to bring the work to a more satisfactory close. It appears that the comments in praefatio,5,92-107 were added by Beatus himself, who used in this case his own longer commentary and a Vulgate Apocalypse text. Indeed the Apocalypse text of this section shows far greater similarities to the Vulgate than to the Tyconian text of Beatus' commentary. Rev. 20:9-10 and 21:4 are examples:

Apocalypse text from praefatio,5,101; 108

Et descendit ignis de caelo et devoravit eos, et diabolus, quo seducebat eos, missus est in stagnum ignis et sulforis, ubi est bestia et pseudo-propheta; et cruciabuntur die ac nocte in saecula saeculorum....
et absterget Deus omnem lacrimam ab oculis eorum, et mors ultra non erit, neque luctus neque dolor. quae prima fuerant abierunt.

Apocalypse text from 11,T.20,9-10; 12,T.21,4

Et descendit ignis a Deo de caelo et comedit inimicos suos. et diabolus seducens eos missus est in stagnum ignis et sulfuris, ubi et bestia et pseudopropheta, et punietur die ac nocte in saecula saeculorum....
et absterget omnem lacrimam ab oculis eorum; et mors non erit amplius, et luctus non erit. iam prima transierunt.

Vulgate text of Rev. 20:9-10; 21:4

Et descendit ignis a Deo de caelo, et devoravit eos: et diabolus, qui seducebat eos, missus est in stagnum ignis, et sulphuris, ubi et bestia, et pseudopropheta cruciabuntur die ac nocte in saecula saeculorum....
et absterget Deus omnem lacrymam ab oculis eorum: et mors ultra non erit, neque luctus, neque clamor, neque dolor erit ultra, quia prima abierunt.

The two examples are abundantly clear. At this point the Apocalypse text of the Summa dicendorum is no longer the African text of Tyconius but rather the Vulgate. This evidence supports the assertion that Beatus added praefatio,5,92-107 to the epitome of Tyconius' commentary in order to bring the introduction to his commentary to a fitting end.

In any event, even with the additional ending of Beatus, the Summa dicendorum is incomplete. Both the beginning and end are lacking. This fact, especially the missing ending, lends great support to the hypothesis that the Summa dicendorum was a separately transmitted epitome of the original Tyconius commentary.

4. Assistance in determining the structure of Tyconius' lost commentary

a. Beatus and the previous hypothesis

The commentary of Beatus of Liébana had provided a significant piece of information in regard to the formerly accepted theory concerning the structure of the lost commentary of Tyconius.[386] That theory was based on three premises. First, Gennadius asserted that Tyconius commented upon the entire book of the Apocalypse. Second, Bede the Venerable indicated in his letter to Eusebius that Tyconius' commentary contained three books. Third, Beatus of Liébana unwittingly disclosed the contents of Book II by mechanically copying Tyconius' title after having written his own title to the same book. The second premise has already been proven false.[387] Careful investigation will reveal that the others are also false.

First, Gennadius does not assert that Tyconius commented on the entire book of the Apocalypse. Gennadius states: Exposuit et apocalypsin Iohannis ex integro. [388] The phrase ex integro has been erroneously interpreted to mean that Tyconius commented on the entire book of the Apocalypse.[389] This is false. The phrase ex integro should rather be translated "in a new way."

Second, the one line error in the commentary of Beatus reads as follows: <u>Hic liber continet quattuor animalia et quattuor equos, animas interfectorum, quattuor ventos et duodena milia.</u> [390] This is totally inconsistent with the title of the section written above this line by Beatus: <u>Liber secundus septem ecclesiarum.</u> [391] However, the erroneous line, describing the contents of Rev. 4:1-8:1, more likely originates from Apringius rather than Tyconius. Beatus used Apringius of Béja as a source in writing his commentary. The Copenhagen manuscript published by Ferotin is probably not as accurate as the manuscript used by Beatus. The question whether the work of Apringius was ever complete has never been adequately answered. In any event, the Copenhagen manuscript contains a scribe's incipit before the comments beginning at Rev. 4:1 which states: <u>Incipit liber secundus.</u> [392] The possibility arises that the sentence incorrectly identifying the contents of Beatus' Book II could actually have had its origin in the commentary of Apringius. This does not mean that this sentence is a direct quotation from Apringius. However, it could be a description of Apringius' Book II, which found its way into the commentary of Beatus in the wrong place, at the beginning of Beatus' Book II rather than at the beginning of the comments on Rev. 4:1ff. The hypothesis is quite reasonable. Among the known sources of Beatus is a text where the beginning of the second book of the commentary and the beginning of the comments on the fourth chapter of the Apocalypse coincide. This known possible source, Apringius, should reasonably be preferred to the unknown hypothetical source, Tyconius. A similarity may be found at the beginning of Book VI where Beatus copies a section of Tyconius' commentary as a heading.[393] That passage, confirmed by the Turin

Fragment as Tyconian, is also obviously out of place.

Thus, neither the reference by Gennadius nor the one line error in Beatus provides any evidence in regard to the structure of the lost commentary.

b. A new hypothesis

Asserting that Beatus imitated Tyconius in structuring his commentary, S. Alvarez Campos has advanced a new hypothesis that the lost commentary of Tyconius contained twelve books.[394] Alvarez Campos limits himself to only one passage to prove his point:

plenas dixit fialas, quas supra in nono libro septem exposuimus effusas, ut si, hic legens non intellexeris, ibi plenissme intellegas. unde manifestum hunc librum duodecimum, sicut supra diximus, recapitulatum a Christi passione.[395]

Alvarez Campos insists that Tyconius "without a doubt" wrote the passage because Beatus unconsciously copied sections from Tyconius without concerning himself with previous or subsequent allusions. In addition, Alvarez Campos states that the ending of a book of Beatus, at least Books I, II, and XI, according to external criticism always comes from Tyconius. However, neither does he cite specific passages nor does he attempt to prove this assertion.

Alvarez Campos' position is vulnerable on several grounds. First, the passage which he cites proves nothing. Beatus in writing his twelfth book refers to his ninth book. There is no inconsistency and no error. The passage is not out of place; there is no problem which needs to be explained. Second, the passage which he cites is found nowhere else in the Tyconian tradition. In other words, there is no external control to prove that the passage has its origin in Tyconius. Third, the passage addresses the reader in the second person. Nowhere is this a characteristic of Tyconius' style. In the Liber regularum Tyconius customarily refers to his reader in the third person.[396] Fourth, Alvarez Campos' hypothesis, like that of Hahn before him, is based on the presupposition that Beatus is a mere copyist who was incapable of exercising any creativity in writing his commentary. Beatus has been constantly underestimated in much previous research. However, Beatus is capable of expressing his own thought in his own words and frequently does so. Fifth, the prologue of book two, which was not at all influenced by Tyconius, is preoccupied with the number twelve as symbolic of the true church, as in the following example: iste praefiguravit ecclesiam, ex quo sunt nati duodecim patriarchae, quae est ecclesia in duodenario constituta, unde et duodecim tribus Israel ducuntur.[397] The number twelve is also associated with the preservation of the faith. After citing a liturgically formulated creed, Beatus writes: haec est fides apostolica, quem in toto mundo tenet ecclesia a sole Christo et a duodecim horarum apostolorum numero inluminata.[398] This certainly may be interpreted as an expression of his anti-adoptionist polemic.

Finally, by way of rebuttal one might look at Beatus 9,2,40-44:

denique et in sexto libro de hos septem montes et septem reges iam diximus, sed de hac muliere tacuimus, cum et in istoria tractando eam minime invenimus. in eo libro tres bestias diximus ascendentes, unam de abysso, alteram de mari, tertiam de terra. in hoc libro diximus... in illo sexto libro diximus... in quo libro nomen et notam antichristi expressimus. in hoc libro mulierem corruptelam dicimus, quam in illo libro civitatem Romanam nominavimus. illuc specialiter septem montes, hic vero septem vitia; illuc specialiter septem reges, hic vero speciales reges cum ipsis vitiis disseremus, ut spiritualiter et carnaliter miscendo tempus praeteritum, praesens, et futurum aperte declaremus...

Here is a detailed explanation by Beatus of certain inconsistencies of interpretation between his sixth and ninth books. He specifically refers to the mixing of a spiritual and carnal interpretation of time. Nothing can be more distant from the approach of Tyconius who interprets biblical references to time in terms of the relationship between the part and whole.[399] Furthermore, according to Gennadius Tyconius finds nothing carnal in the Apocalypse but understands everything in a spiritual way.[400] Certainly one may not legitimately presume that any internal reference in Beatus to a previous or subsequent passage is necessarily of Tyconian origin.

In conclusion, therefore, the lengthy commentary of Beatus provides no information which may assist in determining the structure of the lost Apocalypse Commentary of Tyconius.

5. Results

1. In no case may a passage which has been influenced by Tyconius be presumed to be a word for word repetition of that commentary. Such a conclusion can only be based upon an exact comparison with the other commentaries of the Tyconian tradition.
2. There is no reason to believe that the entire Tyconian text is present in Beatus' commentary. In the course of this research both large and small omissions have become apparent.

3. The Summa dicendorum and the larger commentary of Beatus should be collated as two separate sources because, as has been demonstrated, they represent two separate manuscript traditions.

4. Although the Summa dicendorum was not written by Tyconius but rather is a summary of his commentary, substantial sections of Tyconius' commentary are contained therein.

5. Although Beatus copied from various works and added his own comments as he saw fit, his commentary still remains the most extensive source of Tyconius' commentary.

6. Apringius of Béja, whose Apocalypse commentary was known and used by Beatus, did not use Tyconius' commentary in writing his work. Therefore, Apringius' commentary serves only the secondary function of eliminating those sections which could not possibly come from Tyconius.

7. Beatus' commentary provides no information which may help in determining the structure of the lost Apocalypse Commentary of Tyconius.

Chapter III

Investigation of manuscripts attributed to Tyconius

A. The Turin Fragment

1. Description

a. Physical characteristics of the manuscript

b. Paleography

2. Contents

a. The Turin Fragment and other texts of the Tyconian tradition

(1) Primasius

(2) Bede

(3) Beatus

b. Interpolations in the Turin Fragment

3. Results

1. Description

Codex Taurinensis F. IV. 1. 18 (olim Bobiensis 62) has been described in detail by A. Peyron and F. Lo Bue.[1] The manuscript, first published by the Benedictines at Montecassino in 1897,[2] is now available in the critical edition of Lo Bue, who has followed sound methodology presenting an accurate text with an extensive introduction, complete critical apparatus, and an appropriate index. Only two factors need to be considered here because of their significance in our research, namely the physical characteristics of the manuscript and its paleography.

a. Physical characteristics of the manuscript

The codex consists of two fascicles, the first commenting on Rev. 2:18-4:1 and the second on Rev. 7:16-12:6. Due to the absence of a title page the manuscript is anonymous. Lo Bue advances the hypothesis that the outer pages of the first fascicle were lost, thus creating the internal lacuna between Rev.4:1 and 7:16 as well as the absence of the initial portion of the commentary from Rev. 1:1 to 2:17. The hypothesis seems to be quite reasonable since it does explain the evidence at hand.

b. Paleography

Lo Bue strangely identifies the paleography of the manuscript as "book gothic" which is impossible. Bonner recognized this and received an opinion from B. Bischoff who examined the four plates published with Lo Bue's edition.[3] Bischoff concluded that the manuscript was written in a northern Italian hand in the first half of the tenth century. Clearly, this opinion is correct, representing, as it does, a balanced analysis of the data. In addition to the evidence advanced by Bischoff I would add that the ligatures re and ae, the e caduta, and the abbreviations are equally representative of the Carolingian miniscule.[4] Bischoff specifically opts for the first half of the tenth century on the basis of the narrow spacing of the lines indicating not a scarcity of vellum, as Lo Bue asserts, but rather greater stylization and thus lateness. That the manuscript has been dated and its origin geographically located with reasonable accuracy is significant for two reasons. First, a ninth century inventory of the library at Saint Gall still recorded the presence of a copy of Tyconius' Apocalypse commentary.[5] The historical connections between Bobbio and Saint Gall place the commentary in a geographical area where Tyconius enjoyed some popularity as evidenced by other works of the Tyconian tradition. Second and more important, knowing the date and location of the manuscript, we will be able to deal with the crucial question of emendations and interpolations in an historical context.

2. Contents

Two problems must be addressed concerning the contents of the manuscript. First, there are noticeable differences and similarities between the Turin Fragment and other works of the Tyconian tradition. Second, there are possible interpolations. Although Hahn[6] entirely rejected the Turin Fragment as useless in a Tyconian reconstruction, Pincherle[7] thought that it should be collated in the first place. Such a wide diversity of opinions is possible only because the above mentioned problems have not been solved. However, there is sufficient data to deal with both of these problems and arrive at reasonable hypotheses if not solutions.

a. The Turin Fragment and other texts of the Tyconian tradition

Lo Bue treats of the Turin Fragment's relationship to the commentaries of Jerome-Victorinus, Primasius, Bede, and Beatus. For the present we will not consider Jerome-Victorinus because it offers no assistance in solving the problem at hand. In regard to the other commentaries, however, we will consider some of the same texts presented by Lo Bue and review his conclusions.

(1) Primasius

Lo Bue's treatment of Primasius is extremely important because he has uncovered an intricate relationship among the various works of the Tyconian tradition. For example, in the comments on Rev. 8:5a Lo Bue has found greater similarities between the Turin Fragment and Primasius than between the Turin Fragment and other works of the Tyconian tradition. The passages below are significant:

Turin Fragment 161

Partem uero quam dixit habentem animam mori, homines dicit spiritaliter mortuos, et a regno Dei separatos.

Primasius 140,114-115

Alia editio dicendo "habentium animas" ostendit euidenter spiritali eos morte necatos.

Caesarius 230,12-13

Habentium animas dixit, ut ostenderet in carne vivos, sed spiritaliter mortuos.

Bede 156,31-32

Quae habent animas dixit, ut ostenderet vivos spiritualiter mortuos.

Beatus 5,3,4

habentia animas dixit, ut ostenderet vivos et mortuos dixisse.

In the light of this comparison Lo Bue comes to the tentative conclusion that the discrepancy might be attributed to the author of the pseudo-Augustinian homilies, on which both Bede and Beatus may depend.[8] The conclusion may be summarized schematically as follows:

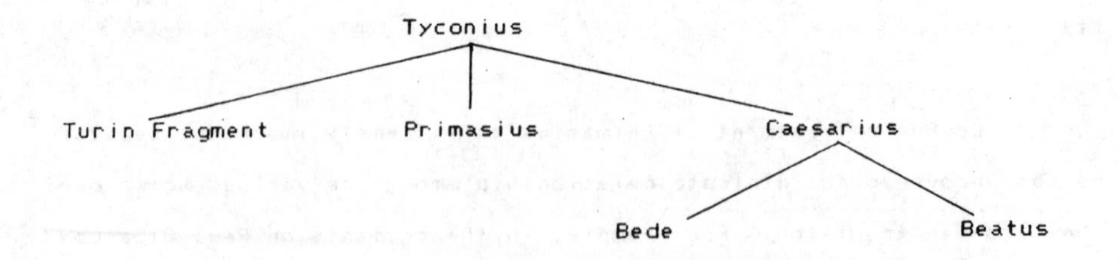

At this point it is imperative to introduce a necessary distinction which Lo Bue seems to have overlooked. There is a difference between the interrelationship among the various commentaries in the Tyconian tradition and the relationship of each of these commentaries to the Tyconian archetype. In other words, we may with accuracy determine that various authors knew and used the lost commentary to greater or lesser degrees in writing their own commentaries. In so doing some modified the text of Tyconius to suit their own goals while others quoted or simply copied the Tyconian text. However, there is also a manuscript tradition to the lost commentary. These authors had various exemplars of the Tyconian text. For example, Beatus appears to have used an epitome for the Summa dicendorum while Caesarius had two manuscripts. Beatus in writing his commentary, Primasius, and Bede probably had complete manuscripts. The relationship of these various authors to the Tyconian archetype is an entirely different problem than their relationship to one another.

Lo Bue has perhaps unwittingly gone beyond the initial questions of the interrelationship of the various Tyconian texts to one another to the second and deeper question concerning the relationship of the various texts to the Tyconian archetype. Since there is no evidence to demonstrate that either Bede or Beatus had access to the pseudo-Augustinian homilies, Lo Bue's conclusion would best be stated in terms of the Tyconian manuscript tradition as follows:

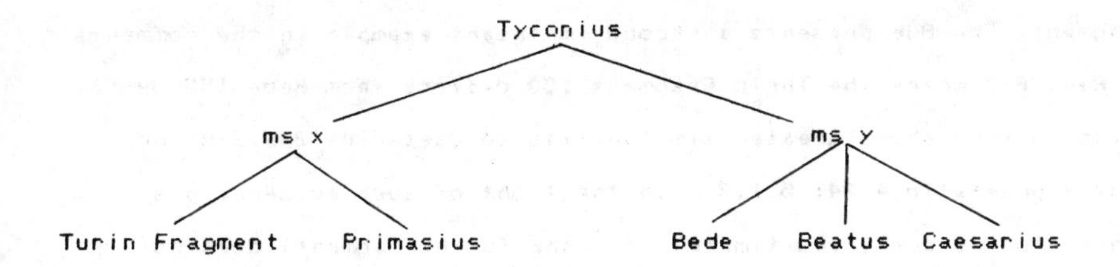

However, even with this distinction introduced, the conclusion would be somewhat premature on the basis of one passage alone. Furthermore, there are other works of the Tyconian tradition to be taken into consideration as well as the obvious double manuscript tradition in the cases of Beatus and Caesarius.

(2) Bede

In the comments on Rev. 8:7 Lo Bue discovers that the Turin Fragment differs from Bede and other works of the Tyconian tradition:

Turin Fragment 152

In arboribus et in terra homines, id est hostes ecclesiae internos dicit, quos futuro iuditio per[h]enni supplicio condem[p]nabit. In foeno autem carnem delictorum uitiis saginatam expressit, cuius uirtus et gloria solis ardore[m] arescit. Partem uero terciam quam dixit combustioni contraditam hereticos designauit. Quia qui foris a uera ecclesia inuenitur, cum diabolo qui hui<u>s partis est auctor, poenis perpetuis condem[p]nabitur.

Bede 156,8-16

Omnis caro fenum, quae nunc luxus mollitie saginata, sole judicii fervente, florem decoris amittit.... Tychonius de tertia parte sic in hoc loco inquit. Tertiam hostes intestinos dicit. Caeterum quidquid praeter Ecclesiam est, tertia pars dicta est, et Ecclesia tertia, quae contra geminum malum pugnet.

Parallel passages at Caesarius 230,6-8, Beatus 5,2,1, and Primasius 138,82-139,90 show greater similarities to Bede than to the Turin Fragment. Lo Bue presents a second important example in the comments on Rev. 8:7 where the Turin Fragment 150 differs from Bede 155,54-56, which in turn shows greater similarities to Caesarius 230,3-4 and Beatus praefatio,4,24; 5,1,7. In the light of such evidence his conclusion is quite legitimate: "T [the Turin Fragment] does not preserve the Tyconian text which other commentators had before them, but a text which at a certain period of its history underwent some degree of modification."[9] Lo Bue's observations may summarized graphically as follows:

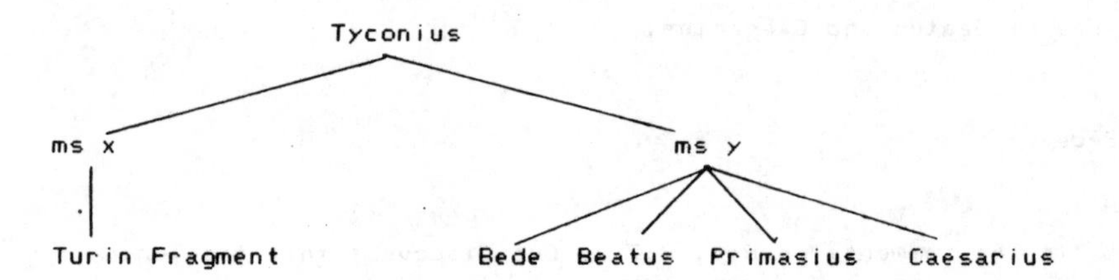

Since in this case the Turin Fragment's independence from the other Tyconian works including Primasius appears to conflict with the evidence presented in the previous section, the manuscript tradition is obviously extremely complex.

(3) Beatus

There are two sets of passages to deal with in the commentary of Beatus. First, there are the so-called "African passages" containing specific historical references to Africa. Second, there is a single enigmatic reference to a compendium of ten chapters in both Beatus and the Turin Fragment.

First, several passages in the commentary of Beatus explicitly mention Africa. In two instances the Turin Fragment presents parallel passages:

Beatus 2,6,80-81

sicut tunc non Filadelfia sola servata est, licet soli promiserit, ita et nunc; nam si sola Filadelfia aut nunc Africa verbum patientiae Dei servavit, quod postea in totum orbem promittit temptationem venturam? aperte dicimus, quia non est in toto orbe, qui temptetur praeter ecclesiam. et hoc quod Filadelfiae dicit, omni ecclesiae dicit, et qui sua ecclesia est, tutelam protectionis cotidie promittit, dicens: servabo te ab hora temptationis quae ventura est in universum mundum. sicut enim in Africa factum est, ita fieri oportet in toto mundo revelari antichristum, sicut et nobis ex parte revelatum est, et hoc esse novissimae persecutionis genus eo tempore quando venerit antichristus; nihilque aliud fieri nisi pressura, qualis non fuit ab initio, ex quo gentes esse coeperunt...

Turin Fragment 72-73

Non Philadelphia sola seruata est cum soli promiserit. Nunc dicendum est <quia> per totum orbem futuram temptationem promisit. Non enim est in toto orbe praeter ecclesiam qui temptetur. Vniuersae ecclesiae dicit: Seruabo te ab hora temptationis quae in uniuerso orbe uentura est. Et hoc esse nouissimae persecutionis genus in mundo, dum aliquanti se a uera ecclesia quae in toto mundo est separant, et alli in ea[m] immobili fide permaneant

Beatus 5,10,37-38

sed quia tempus describit, quod post Africanas persecutiones futurum est, ut ostenderet eius modi esse novissimam praedicationem et reparationem certaminis, proinde dixit iterum. et quia postea non in Africa tantum eodem genere sed in omne mundo praedicabit ecclesia, propterea adiecit: in populis et linguis et gentibus et regibus multis. una est ecclesia in toto orbe, quae praedicat in Africa; ipsa ubique similiter praedicabit, propterea velut Africanae dixit: oportet te iterum praedicare.

Turin Fragment 322-323

Sed in toto mundo quae antea praedicauerat iterum praedicare in populis iubetur et tribu<bu>s et linguis et regi[oni]bus multis. Una est enim ecclesia in toto mundo diffusa quem sua praedicatione impleuit.

Clearly, the text of Beatus is more faithful to the Tyconian archetype while the text of the Turin Fragment has been altered. In each case the Turin Fragment has omitted any concrete reference to Africa appearing in Beatus and the Tyconian archetype. If this were not the case, then we would have to assert that Beatus writing in Spain during the ninth century invented and inserted concrete references to Africa of the fourth century, which is of course absurd. In addition, Tyconius did not hesitate to make at least one reference to his contemporary situation in the *Liber regularum* explicitly mentioning Africa.[10] Therefore, we can only agree with the conclusion of Lo Bue that the so-called "African passages" in Beatus' commentary are of Tyconian origin and were systematically eliminated from the Turin Fragment.

Second, both Beatus and the Turin Fragment contain a reference to a compendium of ten chapters which is remarkably absent from all other works of the Tyconian tradition:

Beatus, inscriptio, p. 456

Scire autem opus est, omnem hanc periocham decem capitulis esse distinctam. quae capitula non a se actus ecclesiatici, quae per tempora sequuntur, ordinata sunt, sed unum quoque capitulum totius est temporis. sunt capitula haec.

Turin Fragment 467

Scire autem opus est omnem hanc periocham decem capitulis esse distinctam, quae capitula non ut se actus ecclesiastici per tempora sequuntur ordinata sunt, sed unumquodque capitulum totius temporis significat praecedentia et futura. Quae capitula hoc modo uidentur esse signata.

Concerning this passage we may affirm three facts. First, in spite of the passage's absence from all other works of the Tyconian tradition it is definitely Tyconian in origin. There is no way the single passage can appear in both Beatus and the Turin Fragment unless it was also present in the archetype. Second, both documents have the passage introducing the comments at Rev. 11:19, which must, therefore, be the original location of the passage. Third, both works appear to have the passage introducing an enumeration or description of the ten chapters.

Although the passage refers to a compendium of ten chapters, one is hard pressed to find any rational explanation for the number ten in the text of the Apocalypse. There is a reference to the dragon with ten horns at Rev. 12:3 as well as a reference to a tenth of the city falling into ruins at Rev 11:13. However, both of these references are obviously too remote. In his Liber regularum Tyconius calls ten, like three, a complete number indicating that they are interchangeable in the gospels.[11] In Rev. 13:4 the dragon sweeps a third of the stars from the sky and hurls them down to earth. Once again the reference hardly provides an explanation.

Actually, one should not be surprised by the problem because it obviously caused difficulties in antiquity as well. Beatus places the passage at the beginning of his book six to which he gives the title decem capitularum. Although the passage ends sunt capitula haec, no enumeration or description follows. In other words, the passage is out of place in Beatus' commentary. However, the passage is equally out of place in the Turin Fragment where ten chapters are briefly described in paragraphs 468-474. Obviously, someone composed the summary, which is entirely without parallels in the Tyconian tradition, and inserted it into the Turin Fragment so that the passage would make sense.

In conclusion, this leaves one in the rather uncomfortable situation of having a problem with no reasonable solution. The passage definitely stands in the Tyconian archetype at Rev. 11:19. However, its significance remains elusive.

b. Interpolations in the Turin Fragment

Lo Bue identifies nine passages as "probably interpolated."[12] Although Bonner summarily dismisses Lo Bue's conclusion as a "pure hypothesis,"[13] it would appear rather that Lo Bue is being overly cautious in this judgment while Bonner is denying reality. Let us begin by listing the passages identified by Lo Bue:[13]

1) On Rev. 2:24 -- "Necesse est eos diuersis erroribus uinci, qui radicem uertatis dimiserint et se diabolo subiugarint" (Turin Fragment 32).

2) On Rev. 3:9 -- "Hinc ergo quamuis omni ecclesiae promiserit, incassum laborant qui angustam nituntur facere ecclesiam Dei, in qua tamen altior latet ratio futuri scilicet sacramenti" (Turin Fragment 66).

3) On Rev. 3:10 -- "(Et hoc esse nouissimae persecutionis genus in mundo) dum aliquanti se a uera ecclesia quae in toto mundo se separant, et alii in ea[m] immobili fide permaneant" (Turin Fragment 73).

4) On Rev. 3:12 -- (scismatici) "se a corpore totius ecclesiae quae in toto mundo est segregarunt, et inaniter gloriantes in se omnem ecclesiam esse confidunt, cum in tota esse ipsi non possunt" (Turin

Fragment 87).

5) On Rev. 8:7 -- "Quia qui foris a uera ecclesia inuenitur, cum diabolo qui hui(u)s partis est auctor, poenis perpetuis condem[p]nabitur" (Turin Fragment 152).

6) On Rev. 9:10 -- "(Potestas igitur locustarum pseudoprophetarum dicit esse personam,) qui falsidicis ac uenenosis doctrinis ueram non desinunt impugnare ecclesiam" (Turin Fragment 228).

7) On Rev. 11:6 -- "quia qui fide unius ecclesiae Dei permanserit, potestate[m] sibi a Deo conlata p[a]enitus non carebit" (Turin Fragment 353).

8) On Rev. 11:8 -- "Odiunt disciplinam qui impietate repleti ueram et in toto mundo positam spernunt et contem[p]nunt ecclesiam, et dum in se totam esse confidunt simulato eius corpore separati sunt" (Turin Fragment 374).

9) On Rev. 11:9 -- "ut quia ipsi nolunt pacifice in eam (*scil.* in ecclesiam) intrare et in unum cum fratribus habitare, alios ne intrent non desinunt impugnare" (Turin Fragment 386).

Even a cursory reading of the passages indicates an obvious similarity in style, vocabulary, and content. All evidence supports the conclusion that the passages are interpolations.

First, none of the passages is present in any of the Tyconian literature. Furthermore, when a parallel is available, it is substantially different from the Turin Fragment as in the case of Beatus 2,6,80-83 and Bede 156,8-16 which correspond to Turin Fragment 72-73 and 152 respectively.[15] In both of these cases, as we have already seen, the Turin Fragment has been altered.[16]

Second, the passages manifest a vocabulary and style which are foreign to Tyconius. In fact, there are even traces of vulgarisms indicating a date of composition later than the fourth century. For example, the expression *foris a vera ecclesia* bears greater similarity to the modern Italian *fuori della chiesa* than to the customary theological expression _extra ecclesiam_ which appears in Cyprian.[17] The adverb _pacifice_ also represents a later usage.

Third, the content of the passages is also non-Tyconian. Lo Bue correctly points out the ecclesiological nature of the passages. Although Tyconius' contribution to ecclesiology is famous, the approach of the interpolated passages is substantially different from that of Tyconius. The passages are concerned with those who have separated themselves from the true church whereby great emphasis is placed on the separation itself and the qualification "true" in regard to the church. However, Tyconius writes of the bipartite church -- _unum corpus_ consisting of _inimici et dilecti._[18] Furthermore, the references to errors, doctrine, and faith in the passages would indicate an antiheretical polemic.

Where then do the passages come from? To no avail Lo Bue has searched other writings attempting to find possible direct transcriptions.[19] Given the date and location of the manuscript as well as the date and place of composition of Tyconius' commentary, the interpolations would have to have been written in North Africa or Italy between the fourth and tenth centuries. Greater precision may not be possible but there are some good indications. During the time and in the geographical area specified, the most pressing theological and, for that matter, political problem facing the church would have been Arianism spread far and wide by migrating Germanic tribes such as the Vandals, Goths, and Lombards.[20] Uniting this information with what has already been stated concerning the content and style of the passages, we may legitimately speculate that the interpolations were an anti-Arian polemic directed against the Lombards in northern Italy perhaps during the seventh century.

3. Results

Having thoroughly investigated the data, we must now judge the value of the manuscript in reconstructing the lost commentary. On the one hand, Hahn's speedy rejection of the Turin Fragment may be considered rash and impetuous. On the other hand, Pincherle's assertion that the manuscript should be collated in the first place is an overstatement. Although the Turin Fragment will be of substantial value in arriving at the lost commentary, it cannot be considered the best representative of the Tyconian archetype.

B. The Budapest Fragment

1. Description of the manuscript

2. Contents of the manuscript

3. Comments on the text

a. The corrected abbreviations

b. The lacunae

4. Partial reconstruction of the text

5. Conclusions and consequences

1. Description of the manuscript

The Budapest Fragment of Tyconius' Apocalypse Commentary,[21] identified as S. Fr. l. m. 1.,[22] was discovered in 1974 during the cataloging of recoverable fragments of manuscripts found in archives and libraries of Hungary. This page of an Apocalypse commentary together with other medieval manuscripts of a liturgical nature had been used in the binding of books which are now located in the Central Catholic Seminary at Budapest.

The fragment, though scanty, is nevertheless a valuable discovery. It consists of one folio written in two columns. On the recto there are 21 legible lines with the left column being complete while only one or two letters at the beginning of each line in the right column survive. On the verso the situation is, of course, reversed. There are 20 legible lines with the last one or two letters of most lines in the left column surviving along with the entire right column. In addition, as we will see below, the bottom two lines of each column appear to have been cut off the folio during the binding process.

Paleographically the manuscript is readily identifiable as Carolingian.[23] The parchment was written either in France or most likely in northern Italy during the ninth century, which interestingly enough places the manuscript in close geographical and chronological proximity to the Turin Fragment of Tyconius' Apocalypse Commentary.[24]

2. Contents of the manuscript

Mezey edited the fragment and published his findings along with a facsimile reproduction, which has proved extremely helpful. The obvious quotation from the sixth chapter of the Apocalypse in verso B 20 was Mezey's point of departure, which led him to investigate Apocalypse commentaries. Having compared the recovered fragment to Primasius and pseudo-Augustine (Caesarius), Mezey found enough evidence to suggest that he had actually discovered a fragment of the lost commentary of Tyconius. Pincherle took the research one step further by publishing the fragment side by side with the corresponding passages of Beatus' commentary. The similarities were so extensive as to definitively confirm the Tyconian nature of the fragment.

Now we are in a position to continue the research in two areas. First, although Mezey paid close attention to the paleography and the punctuation, both he and Pincherle have either misinterpreted or not deciphered several abbreviations. Second, since the fragment is clearly Tyconian, we may legitimately use the parallel passages of the extant Tyconian literature in attempting to fill the lacunae in the manuscript. Of course, one must exercise due caution in this endeavor.

3. Comments on the text

a. The corrected abbreviations

In recto A 2 both Mezey and Pincherle have written *dominus* for *domini,* which has been abbreviated *dni* in the manuscript. For the last word of the same line Mezey suggests *ait* and Pincherle *dici,* where one should read *au,* the normal Carolingian abbreviation for *autem.* In recto A 7 both Mezey and Pincherle leave a lacuna, where one can read *a* and faint traces of *u;* once again we have *au* for *autem.* All of these corrections are corroborated by comparing the fragment to Beatus 4,1,15-16. In recto B 11 there is *p̍* for *pre* and in verso A 16 *é* for *est* rather than *em* as recorded by Mezey.

b. The lacunae

Even more important than the abbreviations are the lacunae in the text which can be filled by using Beatus 4,1,18-19 in conjunction with Primasius 95,91-96,99. Two obvious cases will demonstrate the method. Each complete line has between 14 and 19 letters, symbols, or ligatures. On the basis of Beatus 4,1,15 and Caesarius 226,16 we can complete recto A 1, which begins _unc._ Since the next line begins _nem,_ the missing letters are obviously _-tionem et sanqui-,_ which would make the line 16 letters long. The fit is perfect. Another example is recto A 21, where we read a single _l_ toward the end of the line. We can complete the whole line orienting ourselves on the last two letters of the previous line _mo_ and the hanging _l._ Therefore, line 20 reads _doctrinam ex mo-_ and line 21 _dico omnem populum._ With 16 letters the fit is once again perfect.

As we go to recto B, where there is only the initial letter or two letters of each line, the task becomes more difficult. Recto B 1 begins with the ligature _et._ Reading Beatus we come across _et_ after seven words: _sacri numeri, quod est trinitas implere. sed._ Primasius has a similar but nevertheless distinctly different expression at this point: _mystico indiuiduae trinitatis numero consecrari. Sed._ Since Beatus customarily was more faithful to his source than Primasius, I would suggest that the seven words of Beatus formed the last two lines, 22 and 23, which have been lost from recto A. With each line having 18 letters, the seven words fit quite well leading us into the _et_ of recto B 1. Beginning with _et_ and counting every 14 to 19 letters, we search for the initial letter or two letters of the subsequent line.[25] Eliminating only the words _denario, id est,_ which are also absent from Primasius, we can copy word for word from Beatus up to line 9 of the fragment. The further away one comes from the concrete material of the first column, the more difficult it becomes to fill the lacunae of the manuscript. Nevertheless, we can make a tentative and partial reconstruction of the second column up to line 14. Unfortunately we can come no further.

However, we do have verso B 1-20, which corresponds extensively to Beatus 4,1,23-24. In attempting to work backwards to the bottom of verso A, we hit an immediate and definite dead end. The initial word of verso B 1, fuerunt, can be found neither in Beatus nor in any other Tyconian parallel. Therefore, it is impossible to uncover a single line of verso A. Beatus 4,1,21-23, which is also without parallels in the Tyconian literature, appears to be entirely non-Tyconian, having been written by Beatus himself who substituted this section in place of Tyconius' text at this point.

4. Partial reconstruction of the text

Since my emendations of Mezey's and Pincherle's text are extensive, the four columns of the fragment follow in their entirety. The recovered sections are in brackets.

S. Fr. 1. m. 1. recto A

1 unc[ti]o[nem et sangui]
2 nem domini[. In] tritico autem
3 et h[o]rd[e]um ecclesiam
4 dixi[t] si[v]e in mag[n]is et
5 min[i]mi[s] sive in prae
6 posi[t]is et [pop]ulis et [n]on
7 est a[utem] m[inu]s una bili
8 bris a [tribu]s quia et
9 in un[i]on[e] perfecta est
10 et in [t]rin[it]ate. Sic enim
11 in fa[ri]nae mensuris tri
12 bus f[er]m[ent]um dici[t] ab
13 scon[d]itum. Quod si ra
14 tion[is] non esset, suffi
15 cer[et] in [fari]na abscon
16 ditu[m ...] per alium
17 eva[n]gel[ista]m farinae
18 men[su]r[is] dicere.
19 [Osten]di[t fermentum
20 id est] doctrinam ex mo
21 [dico omnem popu]l[um]
22 [sacri numeri, quod est]
23 [trinitas, implere. Sed]

S. Fr. 1. m. 1. recto B

1 et [pretium docet unum]

2 es[se triticum et]

3 ho[rdeum. Si enim]

4 p[usilli sunt et magni]

5 qu[od merito in sanctita]

6 te [unus praecellat alte]

7 r[um utrique uno per]

8 f[ecto pretio redemp]

9 ti [sunt. ...]

10 d[onationis ...]

11 pre[tium tamen aequat]

12 et [meritum sive ma]

13 g[nos et minimos ...]

14 si[(ve) ...]

15 li

16 d

17 et

18 r

19 q

20 r

21 li (?)

S. Fr. 1. m. 1. verso A

1 [...] a

2 [...] s

3 [...] e

4 [...] r (?)

5 [...] le

6 [...] o

7 [...] e

8 [...] (?)

9 [...] es

10 [...] (?)

11 [...] s

12 [...] c

13 [...] (?)

14 [...] s

15 [...] (?)

16 [...] est

17 [...] ri

18 [...] e

19 [...] (?)

20 [...] un

21 [...]

S. Fr. 1. m. 1. verso B

1 fuerunt, nobis magis
2 proficiet aliena curio
3 sitas [... qu]amque ma
4 teriam unam proba
5 re. Ut sicut in hor
6 deo ostendit duodecim
7 apostolos, ita et in tri
8 tico etiam septiformes
9 populos, ubique enim
10 septinarius numerus
11 plenitudo est eius rei
12 qua agitur. Sicut
13 in figuram ecclesiae
14 sub israhelita persecu
15 tore dictum est: "Re
16 liqui mihi septe[m] milia
17 virorum." Describit
18 et hipocrisin revela
19 tam.
20 "Et cum aperu[isset]
21 [...]

5. Conclusions and consequences

First, the fragment gives us a pristinely preserved section of the lost commentary of Tyconius. Unfortunately, one folio is not very much. Nevertheless, the variance of the fragment from the known Tyconian parallels in conjunction with extensive similarities leads us to conclude that the Budapest Fragment is not a quotation from another author who used Tyconius but a complete section of the lost and illusive commentary itself.

Second, the fragment confirms various previous findings. Beatus added to the commentary and introduced his own ideas into the text. A prime example of this is given in the parallels presented by Pincherle. Primasius also changed the Tyconian text extensively. For this short section the Budapest Fragment must be considered our best witness.

Third, it is clear that the missing section from recto B 15 to verso A 21 will never be recovered. Beatus, Primasius, Caesarius and every other Tyconian parallel omit the passage. Quite clearly, barring the discovery of a complete manuscript of Tyconius' commentary, some passages will be lost forever. We must acknowledge this limitation.

Chapter IV

Investigation of other works attributed to Tyconius

A. The non-Tyconian authorship of the sermon <u>In natali</u>

1. Description of the sermon

2. History of the research

a. Arguments for Catholic authorship

b. Arguments for Donatist authorship

c. The work of Romero Pose

3. Tyconius and the sermon

a. The impossibility of Tyconius' authorship

b. The Tyconian connection

(1) The passage from the sermon

(2) The passages of the Tyconian tradition

(3) Comparison of the passages

c. Analysis of the sermon in respect to the pre-Tyconian hypothesis

(1) Concrete literary evidence

(2) Liturgical practice

(3) Historical context

(4) Other Donatist literature

(5) Date of composition

d. Conclusion and summary

(1) The validity of the pre-Tyconian hypothesis

(2) Uselessness of the sermon in a reconstruction

1. Description of the sermon

Sermo in natali sanctorum innocentium, generally considered to to be the oldest extant Christmas sermon, has been handed down in two manuscripts: Orleans 154 (131), pp. 78-87, which alone attributes the sermon to Optatus of Mileve, and Wolfenbuettel 4096, fols. 8v-12r. The recent attempt of E. Romero Pose[1] to associate the sermon with the Tyconian tradition requires that it be treated here. A. Wilmart[2] in his critical edition divided the text into thirteen paragraphs, whose contents follow in outline form:

1. Introduction -- the mystery of the birth of Christ
2. Summary of the history of the magi -- Matt. 2

Part I -- Herod the persecutor (3-7)

3. Following Christ
4. Glory of the murdered infants
5. Persecution of the just
6. Our being persecuted
7. Herod's persecution of Christ as prototype

Part II -- Example of the magi (8-12)

8. Our gifts
9. Gold
10. Frankincense and myrrh -- the smell of holiness

11. The smell of death

12. Our following the magi's example

13. Conclusion -- future hope

The work is a homelitic masterpiece, in which the author has used his literary ability and pedagogical awareness to convey his specific theological message.

2. History of the research

Although opinion is unanimous concerning the African origin of the sermon, the question of authorship has been the object of intense debate. Basically, there are two schools of thought in this regard with some minor variations within each approach. The critical question is whether one attributes the sermon to an author of the Catholic or of the Donatist tradition.

a. Arguments for Catholic authorship

On the basis of his investigation of the Wolfenbuettel manuscript, Morin[3] proposed the authorship of Quodvultdeus, the Catholic bishop of Carthage. The subsequent discovery of the Orleans manuscript, which had originally come from Fleury, tipped the scales in favor of Optatus of Mileve, whom the manuscript identifies as the author. Delisle[4] was content to accept the testimony of the manuscript. Wilmart[5] extensively developed the case for Optatus' authorship on the basis of stylistic similarities between the sermon and the known works of Optatus; his conclusions remained unchallenged for years.[6] Taking a novel tact, P. Courcelle[7] attempted to place the sermon in the context of the Arian persecution of the Catholics at the hands of the Vandal King Geneserith, whom he identified with Herod in the sermon. Courcelle would affirm the accuracy of the designation of authorship in the Orleans manuscript, attributing the sermon to Optatus II, bishop of Mileve around 420.

b. Arguments for Donatist authorship

Being the first to question the Catholic origin of the sermon, A. Pincherle[8] made a tremendous contribution to the research on three accounts. First, he recognized the weakness of Wilmart's arguments and exposed the inaccuracy of many presumed similarities of style between the sermon and the works of Optatus. Second, he reasonably explained the designation of Optatus as author of the sermon in the Orleans manuscript. A scribe, recognizing the African characteristics of the sermon, attributed it to Optatus after the sermon had already been associated with the feast of Holy Innocents in the Gallican calendar. Third, perceiving the Donatist spirit of the sermon, Pincherle suggested that its author was an unknown Donatist bishop of a diocese somewhere in Numidia. He furthermore asserted that the complete lack of polemic in the sermon will probably hide the identity of its author forever. His research, which to this day remains the most lucid and insightful work on the sermon, marked the beginning of a new approach, whose validity is now generally accepted in most quarters.[9]

Building upon Pincherle's theory of Donatist origin, F. Scorza

Barcellona[10] indicated that certain aspects of the sermon depend upon either Tyconius or his ideas. He surveyed the question of authorship, arriving at no conclusion but leaving open the possibility of attributing the sermon to Optatus of Thamugadi.[11] Finally, Romero Pose claimed to have found many specifically Tyconian characteristics in the sermon.[12]

c. The work of Romero Pose

Since Romero Pose is the only scholar to have uncovered extensive specifically Tyconian characteristics in the sermon, I will limit myself to an evaluation of his research. Of course, in this endeavor we must not lose sight of our goal -- the possible reconstruction of Tyconius' commentary on the Apocalypse. We are interested in the sermon only to the extent that it sheds light on the lost commentary of Tyconius.

Three major deficiencies mar the work of Romero Pose. First, he is not clear in regard to his method. He announces two ways of determining the identity of the unknown author of a specific work. One way is internal criticism or the analysis of the contents of the work; the other is external criticism or the investigation of the literary form. His explanation of the distinction between internal and external criticism is not accurate. Internal criticism may be literary; external criticism may be applied to the contents of a work. Actually, Romero Pose himself analyzes the contents of the sermon and compares its ideas to those of Tyconius. Therefore, his analysis of the sermon is based on external criticism because he compares it to the known works of Tyconius. However, his approach is not literary because he limits himself to the ideas or contents of the writings. Thus, all his evidence must of necessity be limited to non-literary intellectual similarities. Second, he makes no attempt to judge the significance or insignificance of the material which he uncovers. In other words, he is not sufficiently selective. The reader finds himself overwhelmed by a mass of data comparing the works of Tyconius to the sermon. Romero Pose in no way differentiates between more or less important similarities. His research is inflated with superfluous material while at the same time significant findings are not completely analyzed. For example, Romero Pose indicates similar vocabulary where there is nothing especially unusual about the words selected or their context which would offer decided evidence of a relationship between the sermon and Tyconius' writings.[13] Stylistic similarities are once again remote resemblances not peculiar to the works in question.[14] On the other hand, on at least one occasion very striking literary parallels between the sermon and Tyconius' works were not completely investigated.[15] Third, after having presented his evidence, Romero Pose draws no conclusion. The reader is forced to ask himself: <u>cui bono?</u> Why investigate the sermon if one does not wish to draw some kind of conclusion? Romero Pose had several valid options available: he could have drawn either a tentative conclusion or a limited conclusion or a negative conclusion. A tentative conclusion would have offered the various possible solutions to the "enigma" as Romero Pose calls it. A limited conclusion would have more clearly delineated the parameters of the problem. A negative conclusion would have at least narrowed the field of research by eliminating untenable possibilities. Romero Pose simply tells us that the writings of Tyconius and the sermon are similar.

3. Tyconius and the sermon

a The impossibility of Tyconius' authorship

At this point we must allay once and for all any suspicion that Tyconius could have written the sermon. This must be explicitly stated in order to eliminate all confusion in this regard. First, the work in question is a sermon. According to the African tradition a sermon could be preached normally by a bishop or possibly in extraordinary circumstances by a simple priest.[16] Tyconius, however, was a layman. No ancient writer attributes an ecclesiastical office to him. Nowhere is he mentioned in connection with a specific town which could be regarded possibly as his episcopal see. Someone might object that Tyconius could have been a bishop, but no one ever mentioned it.[17] This is hardly possible. Gennadius certainly would have identified Tyconius as a bishop if he were one. His stated aim was to provide a catalogue of authors and their writings. He calls Tyconius simply "Afer" -- the African.[18] Nor does Augustine in his many references to Tyconius ever indicate that he was a priest or a bishop.[19] Once again one would suspect Augustine to have stated this if it were the case. Certainly Augustine, who lavished praise upon Tyconius, would have mentioned anything to highlight the rift within the Donatist community. A recalcitrant bishop among the Donatists would have helped Augustine's cause tremendously. Tyconius was neither a priest nor a bishop. He is generally acknowledged to have been a layman. This being the case, he certainly neither wrote nor preached a sermon.

Second, in spite of Romero Pose's assertions, there are absolutely no _stylistic_ similarities between the sermon and the works of Tyconius. The clumsiness and unimaginative correctness of the _Liber regularum_ is a far cry from the rhetorical balance and artistic finery of the sermon. These two very different works could never have been written by the same person. For these reasons even the remote possibility that Tyconius could have written the sermon must be denied.

b. The Tyconian connection

Nevertheless, there is at one point in the sermon a definite _literary_ similarity to certain passages of the Tyconian tradition. These passages merit further investigation.

(1) The passage from the sermon

The exquisite balance and the frequent use of rhetorical devices expose the passage as a carefully constructed unity typical of the sermon. The passage is presented here in schematic form in order to highlight its literary characteristics:[20]

1 A Hinc et Herodes

B furit insanus;

immo vero diabulus

in Herode deiectus

C dolet ecclesiam

suis faucibus ereptam

et deo coniunctam.

2 A Subdolis tamen subtilitatibus

B adoraturum se dominum simulat,

ut hominem deo mixtum, si fieri possit, occidat:

3 A quem spiritus sancti gubernatione

B subtractum invenire non meruit;

et infantium caedem cruentes indixit.

A cursory glance over the text reveals the repeated use of alliteration[21] and assonance.[22] The antithesis of comparison[23] and contrast[24] permeate the entire passage. All in all we have a very precisely constructed symmetrical literary piece.

(2) The passages of the Tyconian tradition

The corresponding passages from Beatus and the Turin Fragment share in essence the same contents but are composed in an entirely different manner:

Beatus 6,2,11

sic denique Herodes, intestinus hostis, in oriente viso signo, consentiens simulat se Christum adoraturum, quem spiritus sancti gubernatione totis viribus quaerebat occidere. Herodes diabolus est.

signum in Oriente Christus est in ecclesia, qui nos orire facit ad lucem.

Beatus prefatio,5,6

caelum ecclesia est; draco diabolus simulat se Christum adoraturum per suos ministros in ecclesia ut sicut Herodes intestinus hostis, quem adorare simulabat occidere quaerebat; ita diabolus natum mulieris ecclesiae per malos Christianos simulando sanctitatem Christum in pectore nostra conatur occidere.

Turin Fragment 453-454

Id est diabolus. Aliud autem signum quod dixit, contrarietatem ipsius diaboli designauit, qui Herodum liuoris incendio inflammauerat ut Christum occideret, quem Iudaeorum regem natum cognouerat, et sum simula<re>t adorare eum quem totis uiribus qu<a>erebat occidere.

Tyconius's style is quite evident. The passages are dull and unimaginative but nevertheless precise in their message and grammatically correct.

(3) Comparison of the passages

By comparing the sermon to the Apocalypse Commentary of Tyconius, Romero Pose came to the conclusion that both works share a common literary heritage.[25] That we know already. Pincherle had already definitely proven that the sermon originated in the Donatist community; it was written by a Donatist author.[26] Since Tyconius was a Donatist, one should not be surprised to find a common literary heritage. One would expect to find certain similarities in works written in the same place at roughly the same time by men who share the same theological tradition.

However, these specific passages, which are quoted above, indicate more than a mere similarity of ideas. There are very strong literal similarities. Romero Pose has entirely overlooked these common elements. In both passages there are references to Herod as the devil, to the governing of the Holy Spirit, and to Herod's pretense of adoring Christ. In some instances both works use the same words and modes of expression. Therefore, one must in this specific case look beyond the possibility of a common literary heritage because it does not sufficiently explain the very close similarities. The evidence calls for dependence upon a <u>written</u> source.

This leaves us with three possibilities. First, Tyconius copied from the sermon. Second, the author of the sermon copied from Tyconius. Third, they both copied from a common source. Admittedly the evidence is extremely limited. However, there can be only one conclusion: Tyconius knew the sermon and used it as a source!

Let us consider the various possibilities in reverse order. If we choose the third option and assert that the author of the sermon and Tyconius copied from a common source, then we are left with the question as to what source. More problems are created than solved. Who wrote this unknown source? Where did it come from? What was the nature of the work? Why was it subsequently lost? Why does it not manifest itself elsewhere?

If we choose the second option and assert that the author of the sermon copied from Tyconius, then we face a literary problem. We have already seen that the sermon is a tightly knit literary piece. The sermon is as literature much more sophisticated than the Apocalypse Commentary of Tyconius. Words and expressions in both works are very similar indicating some type of interdependence. The problem follows: How could the author of the sermon have used Tyconius' work as a source while at the same time integrating Tyconius' words and expressions into the literary and rhetorical context of the sermon? The answer is, of course, he could not and he did not.

If we choose the first option and assert that Tyconius knew and copied from the sermon, we have the most reasonable explanation of the evidence. We are not forced to posit the existence of an unknown phantom source. We can also account for the literary finery of the sermon, whose mode of expression was subsequently adopted by Tyconius for use in his commentary. The question now to be answered is whether or not other aspects concerning the sermon are compatible with this hypothesis.

C. Analysis of the sermon in respect to the pre-Tyconian hypothesis

On the basis of the literary evidence available to us, we have formed the hypothesis that Tyconius knew and used the sermon as a source in writing his commentary. Since Tyconius flourished at about 380, the sermon would have had to have been written sometime before that date. Actually, the kernel of the problem specifically concerns the date of composition of the sermon. A pre-Tyconian date is necessary for our hypothesis to stand.

(1) Concrete literary evidence

The first step in dating the sermon must be in terms of the concrete literary evidence which the sermon offers. Direct quotations within the sermon and of the sermon appearing elsewhere allow us to establish the parameters of the problem. The sermon's author quoted from Epistola 56 of Cyprian,[27] which was written around 250. This is fully consistent with the nature of the sermon because it would not have been unusual for a Donatist to have quoted Cyprian, who enjoyed tremendous popularity in the Donatist church. The only other known quotations contained in the sermon are biblical. However, we do find several lines of the sermon cited in a homily of Maximinus the Arian.[28] In 383 Maximinus first appears as author of Dissertatio contra Ambrosium.[29] He is also mentioned in the account of a debate with Augustine in 427.[30] Whether or not Augustine's debating partner was the same Maximinus who wrote the tract against Ambrose is questioned in some quarters.[31] In any event, even if Augustine's Maximinus were not the same man, Ambrose's Maximinus could not have lived far beyond 427. On the basis of concrete literary evidence, which in no way can be refuted, we may set the rough outer limits of the time of composition -- neither earlier than 250 nor later than 430.

(2) Liturgical practice

The next step is to consider the sermon in regard to the liturgical practice of the day. Although the title of the sermon relates it to the feast of Holy Innocents, it clearly a Christmas sermon. Christmas was first introduced into the liturgical calendar at Rome in order to compete with the pagan emperor worship.[32]

There is reference to this aspect of the origin of the Christmas feast in the sermon, where christianus invictus [33] reminds one of sol invictus, the emperor's title. Most scholars believe that Christmas was introduced into Africa sometime before the Great Persecution under Diocletian beginning in 303. Since the sermon refers to the magi, we may conclude that whoever wrote the sermon did not celebrate Epiphany. The celebration of Epiphany was a custom in the East, which came to Rome at about 330 and to Africa at about 360. However, Augustine explicitly states that the Donatists did not celebrate Epiphany.[34] In other words, the sermon could have been written after 360 by a Donatist but certainly not by a Catholic after that date. Thus the evidence on the basis of liturgical practice gives us the year 300 as a terminus a quo. In regard to the terminus ad quem no further specification is possible.

(3) Historical context

The third step is to consider the sermon in its historical context. Unfortunately, there are no concrete historical references to contemporary persons or places. However, since the sermon was written by a Donatist, we must date it after the outbreak of the Donatist schism in 312. The contents of the sermon lead us to believe that it was written at a time of persecution. Pincherle has considered this fact in the light of the Donatist nature of the sermon, leading him to suggest two possible times of composition.[35] The Donatist church was persecuted between 317 and 321. On November 10, 316 Constantine issued an edict ordering the Donatists to return all seized property to the Catholic church. The edict of toleration on May 5, 321 rescinded the previous order. Pincherle even suggested the great orator and founder of the schismatic movement, Donatus himself, as a possible author. The Donatist church then remained relatively free until 347 when the edict of unity was proclaimed by order of the emperor Constans as a result of the visit of the imperial legates Paul and Macarius. The Donatists were most certainly in an extremely difficult position from that time until the year 362 when the emperor Julian granted them the right to exercise their religion once again. The period 347 to 362 was looked upon by the Donatists as a period of persecution as dastardly as the Great Persecution itself.

(4) Other Donatist literature

Although this sermon is unique, there are other Donatist documents concerning martyrdom and persecution. The Sermo de passione Donati et Advocati [36] was written before 321. Both the Passio Marculi [37] and the Passio Maximilliani et Isaac [38] were written during the hated Macarian persecution. Other Donatist martyrologies, or more accurately Donatist revisions of existing martyrologies, predate these works. There are no extant Donatist sermons or martyrologies written after the tempora Macaria, which ended with the rescript of Julian in 362. Subsequent Donatist literature is restricted to letters and polemical essays, sentences of councils, and the theological writings of Tyconius. It is apparent that the Donatists were most preoccupied with martyrdom during the Macarian persecution. At that time their own major acts of the martyrs were written. Since this sermon was written by a Donatist bishop during a time of persecution, it would seem most logical to attribute it to that period of time which was regarded by the Donatists as the worst persecution of their church.

(5) Date of composition

Therefore, the sermon was definitely written after 312 and before 430. Any theory of authorship that goes outside of these dates is certainly false. Furthermore I would strongly suggest that the sermon was most likely written between 347 and 362, namely during the persecutio Macaria.

d. Conclusion and summary

(1) The validity of the pre-Tyconian hypothesis

A convergence of evidence supports the hypothesis that the sermon was written before the floruit of Tyconius. First, a comparison between the sermon and the Apocalypse Commentary of Tyconius indicates that Tyconius probably knew the sermon and used it as a source. Second, the sermon was most likely written during the persecutio Macaria. I must emphasize that these conclusions are hypothetical. Since the sermon offers little concrete literary evidence and since there are no historical references to contemporary persons or events, a conclusion must remain hypothetical. Nevertheless, there is no evidence to refute the hypothesis, and further this hypothesis is the most reasonable explanation of the evidence available. In summary, the sermon was written by an unknown Donatist bishop of a diocese somewhere in Numidia probably during the persecutio Macaria, that is, between the years 347 and 362. Any attempt to further specify the author of the sermon or its time of composition must at this time be considered mere speculation.

(2) Uselessness of the sermon in a reconstruction

Since according to my hypothesis the sermon was composed before 362, Tyconius could have in no way influenced the sermon. On the contrary, it appears rather that Tyconius was influenced by the sermon in regard to his ideas on martyrdom and persecution. Therefore, the sermon cannot be used in the reconstruction of Tyconius Apocalypse Commentary.

B. Characteristics of the Liber regularum

1. Style

    a. Sentence structure

    b. Doublets or parallel expressions

    c. Organization

2. Content

    a. Exegetical method -- typology

    b. Theological approach -- ecclesiology

3. Liber regularum and the Apocalypse Commentary

    a. Similarities of style

    b. Similarities in content

    c. Value of the Liber regularum in a reconstruction

B. Characteristics of the Liber regularum

A detailed study of Tyconius' Liber regularum is certainly beyond the scope of this work. The Liber regularum will be considered only to the extent that it will assist in investigating the lost Apocalypse Commentary. Indeed, one may reasonably expect that the text of the Liber regularum will be of no direct help in retrieving the text of the lost Apocalypse Commentary. However, through this only complete extant work of Tyconius, we will be able to identify some typically Tyconian characteristics which are repeated in his Apocalypse Commentary. Therefore, I will limit myself here to some necessary observations on the content and style of the Liber regularum and their consequences on the research at hand.

1. Style

There appear to be three significant traits in Tyconius' writing style. First, his sentence structure is absolutely correct in all respects, but terse and somewhat stilted, reflecting an economy of words. Second, Tyconius is quite fond of doublets for the purpose of either clarifying or reinforcing a point. Third, his organization, though often not apparent, is nevertheless definite.

a. Sentence structure

Tyconius does not waste words. Let us take, for example, the beginning of rule three on promises and the law:

Auctoritas est diuina neminem aliquando ex operibus legis iustificari potuisse. eadem auctoritate firmissium est numquam defuisse qui legem facerent et iustificarentur.[39]

These sentences are typical. It would be difficult, if not impossible, to make the same statement using fewer words. There are no vulgarisms; the idiom is thoroughly classical.

Whenever Tyconius uses a second example to illustrate the same point, the example always indicates some new and different aspect of the topic being discussed. Tyconius, for example, uses the customary <u>id est</u> for the purpose of providing an illustration. However, in such cases he always presents a further development or conclusion and never a mere repetition in different words. Tyconius writes: <u>qui filios Dei uelut per communem utilitatem, id est disciplinam legis.</u> [40] Although the statement would have been clear without the word <u>disciplinam,</u> that word does substantially add to the content of the sentence. Elsewhere he writes: qui negat Christum in carne, id est odit fratem. [41] Once again further information is provided.

Finally, Tyconius does not hesitate to play on words, thus making his style even more frugal: qui nos cogeret studere fidei, qui nos cogeret in Christum. [42] The verb cogere has a double meaning -- to force and to unite. The law forces (cogeret) us to faith, which unites (cogeret) us with Christ.[43] Another example is found in a reference to 2 Thess. 2:3 as Tyconius writes: sed aperte dicantur, inminente discessione quod est reuelatio hominis peccati, discedente Loth a Sodomis. [44] The contrast between inminente and discedente [45] is so apparent in reinforcing his intention that no further explanation is necessary. The chapter ends with this sentence.[46]

b. Doublets or parallel expressions

Tyconius is extremely fond of doublets, which are sometimes used in parallel expressions. The first paragraph of the Liber regularum provides a clear example:

Necessarium duxi ante omnia quae mihi uidentur libellum regularem scribere, et secretorum legis ueluti claues et luminaria fabricare. sunt enim quaedam regulae mysticae quae universae legis resessus obtinent et ueritatis thesauros aliquibus inuisibiles faciunt; quarum si ratio regularum sine inuidia ut communicamus accepta fuerit, clausa quaeque patefient et obscura dilucidabuntur, ut quis prophetiae inmensam siluam perambulans his regulis quodam modo lucis tramitibus deductus ab errore defendatur.[47]

A diagram of the essential elements of the paragraph indicates the parallelism of double predicates, objects, or modifiers:

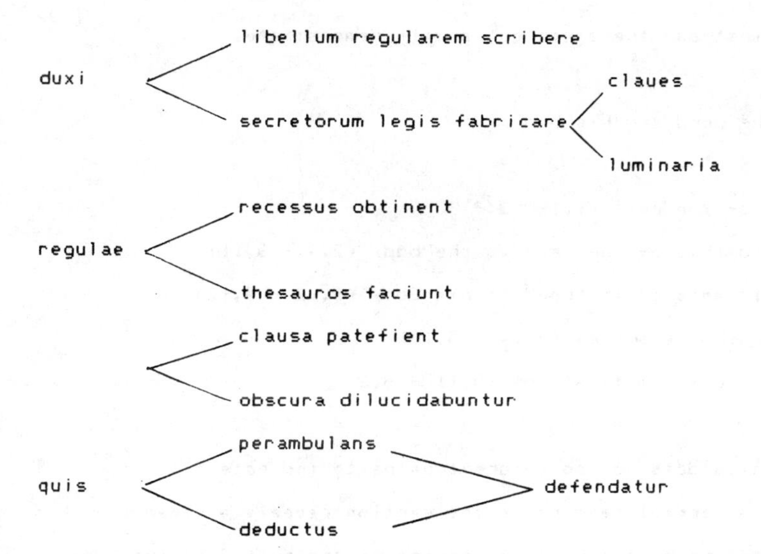

By stating that "doors will be opened and the obscure things will be brought to light"[48] Tyconius is referring to his earlier statement concerning keys and lamps. In fact had Anderson been more attentive to the structure of the passage, he would not have translated luminaria incorrectly as "windows."[49] Clearly keys (claues) open doors (clausa patefient) while lamps or lanterns (luminaria) illuminate the darkness (obscura dilucidabuntur).

c. Organization

Since Tyconius does not specifically enumerate subdivisions within each rule, one might be tempted to jump to the conclusion that organizational principles are lacking. Tyconius certainly does not present a haphazard series of biblical quotations selected at random. On the contrary, in each section he follows a careful plan, as an outline the first and the sixth rules will demonstrate.

Rule One -- The Lord and his body

(1) Statement of the rule (1,19 -2,3)

(2) The relationship of the head to the body (2,4 - 3,11)

(3) The relationship of the Lord to his Body (3,12 - 4,12)

(4) Some less clear examples (4,14 - 5,10)

(5) Ecclesiological ramifications (5,11 - 8,3)

Although Tyconius does not go to great pains to indicate his organization, a careful reading of the section reveals a clear outline. For example, after the statement of the rule Tyconius does not introduce the second part concerning the relationship of the head to the body but immediately quotes Isaiah. However, he does provide a definite conclusion before returning to the original proposition: _non ergo caput, quod ex origine idem est, sed corpus crescit ex capite._ [50] The third part begins: _Ad propositum redeamus._ [51]

Rule Six -- Recapitulation

(1) Statement of the rule (66,11-14)

(2) First kind of recapitulation (66,15 - 67,6)

(3) Future likenesses (67,7-28)

(4) Statements without allegory or mystery (67,29 - 70,9)

Here the organization is apparent because after the statement of the rule each part has its own introduction:

(1) Inter regulas....[52]

(2) Aliquotiens enim sic recapitulat....[53]

(3) Aliquotiens autem non sunt recapitulationes huius modi sed futurae similitudines....[54]

(4) Nec illud praetereundum puto, quod Spiritus sine mysteriis uel allegoria aliud sonare aliud intellegi uoluit....[55]

Clearly, Tyconius is describing three different kinds of recapitulation. The sentences indicated above establish his outline.

2. Content

In its content, the Liber regularum manifests two significant characteristics. First, Tyconius had developed an exegetical method in order to formulate some objective rules universally applicable in interpreting the scriptures. Second, his theological approach grew out of the contemporary Donatist crisis of which he was a part.

a. Exegetical method -- typology

Without totally abandoning the allegorical method which was popular in both the east and west during the fourth century, Tyconius initiated a radically new development based on typology.[56] This resulted in several achievements in exegesis.

First and foremost, the typological method enabled Tyconius to integrate the Old Testament with the New Testament, no small achievement. Obviously, the Jews were God's people and the Old Testament was the record of God's revelation to them. However, the tensions between Jewish Christian and Gentile Christian communities in the early church had left their mark. Paul had written definitively against the possibility of justification through observance of the law. Aside from the tremendous linguistic, cultural, and historical differences between the two testaments, a serious theological problem remained. What does the Old Testament mean to the Christian? The letter of Barnabas attempted to solve the problem allegorically. Circumcision of the flesh refers to the hearing of God's word; the sacrifice of animals refers to the contrite heart. According to the letter of Barnabas the Jews unfortunately did not understand this. Under the influence of Philo, the Alexandrian School and specifically Origen brought the allegorical method to its apex. However, this approach was not totally satisfactory. Marcion, for example, considered the Old and New Testaments antithetic and wished to purge the Bible of the Old Testament and all Jewish elements. The problem obviously persisted in Christian North Africa since Tertullian's longest work was Adversus Marcionem. Tyconius finally overcame the problem not primarily on theological but exegetical grounds. The Old Testament is the type of the New. In other words, the old convenant of God with the Jews prefigured and pointed toward the new covenant in Jesus Christ. Therefore, the two testaments could be interpreted in relationship to one another without recourse to primitive allegory while preserving their essential unity.

Second, the typological method enabled Tyconius to apply the scriptures to his contemporary historical situation. In other words, to use an expression of today, he could be relevant. Montanism, which as evidenced in the writings of Tertullian and in the Passio sanctarum Perpetuae et Felicitatis enjoyed great popularity in Africa, sought relevance through new prophecy, which was actually new revelation. Therefore, when Tyconius mentions the "immense forest of prophecy"[57] in the introduction to the Liber regularum, Anderson is false in interpreting this as "another general reference to the Old Testament."[58] It would seem rather that prophecy refers to the entire Bible in contrast to the new prophecy of the Montanists. His typological method made the Bible relevant and Montanist prophecy both unnecessary and irrelevant. If the Old Testament could prefigure the New, then both the Old and New Testaments could prefigure contemporary historical events. For example, in explaining the sixth rule Tyconius wrote: "But what Daniel said is going on now in Africa."[59] Far from ivory tower speculation, Tyconius' method was real, historical and concrete.[60]

Third, the typological method enabled Tyconius to solve an acute theological problem -- millenarianism. Based on eschatological expectations in the Old Testament and Jewish apocalyptic literature, millenarianism found its way into Christianity especially through the Apocalypse, where Rev. 20:6 was the central locus of millenarian theology: "The second death will have no claim on them; they shall serve God and Christ as priests, and shall reign with him for a thousand years."[61] Montanism was strongly millenarian and perhaps influenced Tertullian when he wrote: "For we do profess that even on earth a kingdom is promised us."[62] However, according to Tyconius one need not posit a thousand year reign in a strict sense because a part may stand for the whole or visa versa. In this way Tyconius put an end to millenarian speculation by interpreting numbers in a spiritual way.[63]

Fourth, the typological method enabled Tyconius to interpret the scripture objectively and universally. This was certainly his intention as stated in the introduction to the Liber regularum: "For there are certain mystical rules which hold the secrets of the whole law...; so that anyone...with these rules...may be guarded from error."[64] The law refers to the entire scriptures and not just the Old Testament.[65] The rules are designed to guide one free from error through the whole Bible. Augustine understands the passage in this way and bristles at Tyconius' universal claim:

If he had said here, "There are certain mystic rules which reveal what is hidden in some of the Law," or, indeed, "in much of the Law," and not "in the whole Law," as he put it, and if he had not said, "Whatever is closed will be opened," but "Much that is closed will be opened," he would have spoken the truth.[66]

Was Tyconius being somewhat arrogant in claiming to have the keys of interpretation to the whole law? Perhaps Augustine thought so. However, Augustine failed to understand Tyconius' intention. In the theological controversies of the day Tyconius had experienced the need for scientific biblical exegesis. He strove to formulate objective rules with a universal application. He wished to avoid the arbitrary judgments of the systematist and the prejudices of the polemicist. His rules were to apply to the entire Bible and protect the reader from error. In Tyconius' approach the typological method was for the fourth century what the historical critical method is for the twentieth -- scientific biblical exegesis.

b. Theological approach -- ecclesiology

The unifying theological principle of the Liber regularum is the Church. Tyconius did not concern himself with theological debates about the nature of Christ or the question of salvation and justification. For him, as for his fellow Donatists, the church was central. Tyconius is sometimes identified as a 'Reform Donatist' because of his ambivalent relationship to the Donatist party.[67] In fact Augustine even compliments him for writing against the Donatists.[68] A conflict with the Donatist Bishop Parmenian led to Tyconius' eventual excommunication from the Donatist community.[69] However, Tyconius never parted with the Donatists to join the Catholics. In spite of differences, conflict, and ultimately excommunication, his personal self-identification with the Donatists was simply too great.

As significant as these facts are, for our purposes we need to limit ourselves to the ecclesiological statement of the Liber regularum. Rule II summarizes Tyconius' entire theological approach. There are two sides to the Church, the body of the Lord. The contrasts are apparent -- fusca et decora, dilecti et inimici, pars dextera et pars sinistra. [70] In other words, the Church is composed of saints and sinners. Once again Augustine takes exception.[71] However, his reservations are not in regard to having a mixed Church composed of both saints and sinners,[72] but in regard to too close an identification between sinners and the Lord.

Rule VII picks up the same theme again in regard to the devil and his body. The devil and Christ are engaged in a continuous struggle with one another until the end of the world. Good and evil are engaged in a life and death fight. Perhaps his fellow Donatists took exception to Tyconius' assertion that this struggle was going on within the one universal or world wide Church. There are two kingdoms, two societies, two cities, but only one Church. The influence on Augustine was of course enormous.[73] This then was the _bella intestina,_ which one of Tyconius' lost works treats.[74] North struggles against South, Rome against Africa. The brothers Cain and Abel are divided while Esau and Jacob fight within the womb.[75]

Tyconius was above all an ecclesiologist and on this very point he departed from the Donatist ideal. Perhaps no other movement in the history of the church with the possible exception of New England Puritanism[76] had such a low toleration of human sinfulness. The Donatists thought themselves a church of saints. They remained loyal during the great persecutions at the hands of the pagans and they continued to be persecuted for their beliefs by the Catholics. The _traditores_ had through their sin lost all ecclesial power and meaning.[77] However, Tyconius opted for a bipartite Church composed of visible and invisible saints and sinners.

3. _Liber regularum_ and the lost Apocalypse Commentary

Information provided by Gennadius[78] shows that Tyconius was born around the year 330. The _Liber regularum_ was written after his polemical works around 382 while the Apocalypse Commentary was completed around 385 about five years before Tyconius' death.[79] Since Tyconius presented exegetical theory in the Book of Rules, he obviously applied this theory in writing his Apocalypse Commentary during the next three years. Why of all the books of the Bible did Tyconius choose to write a commentary on the Apocalypse? He does not answer this question. Perhaps the Apocalypse presented him with a unique twofold possibility. First, he could apply his exegetical method of typology using the many and varied images of the Apocalypse. Second, he could present his favorite theological theme, namely the Church, while dealing with the question of millenarianism. In any case, one may reasonably expect that works written by the same author will manifest definite similarities.

a. Similarities of style

It will be of course very difficult to draw any conclusions concerning the style of a work that is available in a corrupt state and then only in bits and pieces. Nevertheless, in the light of our study of the *Liber regularum* certain similarities may be found in the lost commentary. For example, doublets are also common: *sine ullo timore uel pudore peccandi* [80] or *et fumo et igne armati.* [81]

However, Tyconius' awareness of organization is even more evident. For example, his comments on Rev. 7 end with the following statement: *Concluditur namque septimi sigilli narratio quam ante praetermiserat ennarrando.* [82] Another example may be found at the beginning of the comments on Rev. 8: *hic narrandi finis fuisset.* [83] Such comments indicate a sensitivity to organization within the Apocalypse itself. In addition, they might also indicate the structure of the lost commentary. Primasius ends his Book II with the above quotation *hic narrandi finis fuisset* plus one sentence announcing the next book.[84] Since Hahn's theory concerning the structure of the lost commentary has been disproved,[85] such indications may prove to be helpful in attempting to understand the order and structure of Tyconius' lost commentary.

b. Similarities in content

Although there are no parallels in the Tyconian literature, Hahn correctly identified a passage of Beatus commentary as substantially Tyconian:

draco potestam dedit bestiae, quia intra ecclesiam habet falsos fratres, qui ecclesia videntur esse, et ecclesia non sunt.[86]

Agreement with Hahn's designation is possible because of a similar passage in the Liber regularum:

numquam autem Iacob, id est Ecclesia uenit ad benedictionem non comitante dolo, id est falsis fratribus.[87]

Here is not only a similarity of content but also the same vocabulary.

Lo Bue indicates, for example, similarities between Turin Fragment 165 and Liber regularum 71,23-72,2. Since the Turin Fragment is at this point without clear parallels in the Tyconian literature, the comparison to the Liber regularum is extremely helpful in demonstrating the Tyconian content of the passage.

c. Value of the Liber regularum in a reconstruction

First, the Liber regularum will be most valuable in attempting to ascertain whether or not a passage is Tyconian in those cases where no parallel is available in the Tyconian literature. In this regard the contents or thought of the passage will usually provide a better indication than stylistic similarities which will likely be more difficult to determine.

Second, the Liber regularum has provided certain characteristics of both content and style, which will be of assistance dealing with passages when one or more parallels are available in the existing Tyconian literature. Knowing something of Tyconius' thought and writing habits will aid in eliminating accretions written by later authors.

Third, the Liber regularum has indicated definite but obscure organizational elements. This may be helpful in determining the structure of the lost commentary.

Of course, solid linguistic evidence provided by textual comparison is most reliable. However, indications and tendencies through comparison to the Liber regularum may in some instances be the only evidence available.

Chapter V

Conclusions based on the previous research

A. Dependence, independence and interdependence of the various works influenced by Tyconius

Studying of the thirteen texts available has demonstrated that each is unique, manifesting both advantages and disadvantages in regard to its possible use in recovering the text of the lost Apocalypse Commentary of Tyconius. However, some texts do portray certain similarities and may be grouped for analysis. First, two of the texts are manuscripts of the lost commentary, the Turin Fragment and the Budapest Fragment. Second, one text, In natali, will be of no use at all because of its non-Tyconian origin. Third, the Liber regularum, the only complete extant work of Tyconius, will help in indicating typical characteristics of style and dominant themes of Tyconius. Fourth, due to their brevity the commentaries of both Cassiodore and pseudo-Jerome will be of minimal assistance. Fifth, Jerome-Victorinus is necessary not only because of its Tyconian content but also because it frequently identifies passages which are non-Tyconian. Finally, there is a group of works by authors who used Tyconius' lost commentary to a significant degree in writing their own commentaries -- Beatus, Caesarius, Primasius, Bede with the Codex Oratorii, and Ambrosius Autpertus. This sixth group of commentaries together with the two manuscripts mentioned above will be the primary basis for establishing the text of the lost commentary.

However, even within this sixth group there are considerable differences. Some authors cited Tyconius directly with an acknowledgment. Others copied from him word for word without an acknowledgement. Others modified his commentary to suit their own ends. Yet others did all three of the above. Therefore, any attempt at recovering a passage of the lost commentary will require careful analysis and accurate judgment. In addition, neither manuscript may be considered an archetype. Both are fragmentary and the Turin manuscript has been subjected to interpolation.

This chapter will summarize the results of the present study. Figure 1 illustrates the dependence, independence, and interdependence of the various texts in regard to one another. The oldest commentary is that of Victorinus which predates Tyconius. However, Jerome revised this work integrating some sections of Tyconius' commentary into the original work of Victorinus. Caesarius had access to both the lost commentary of Tyconius and the original unrevised commentary of Victorinus. Primasius also had access to Tyconius and to Victorinus but in its Hieronymian recension. However, it must also be noted that Cassiodore, pseudo-Jerome, Bede, and Ambrosius Autpertus in turn had access to Primasius. Both Cassiodore and pseudo-Jerome knew the commentaries of both Primasius and Tyconius. The capitulary of the Codex Oratorii B6 was influenced by the commentary of Tyconius and was known to Bede, who also knew and used the commentaries of Tyconius, Primasius, and that of Victorinus in its Hieronymian recension. Beatus had access to Tyconius and Jerome-Victorinus. Finally, Ambrosius Autpertus used the commentaries of Tyconius, Primasius, Jerome-Victorinus, and pseudo-Jerome.

Figure 1 -- Interdependence of the various Tyconian Texts

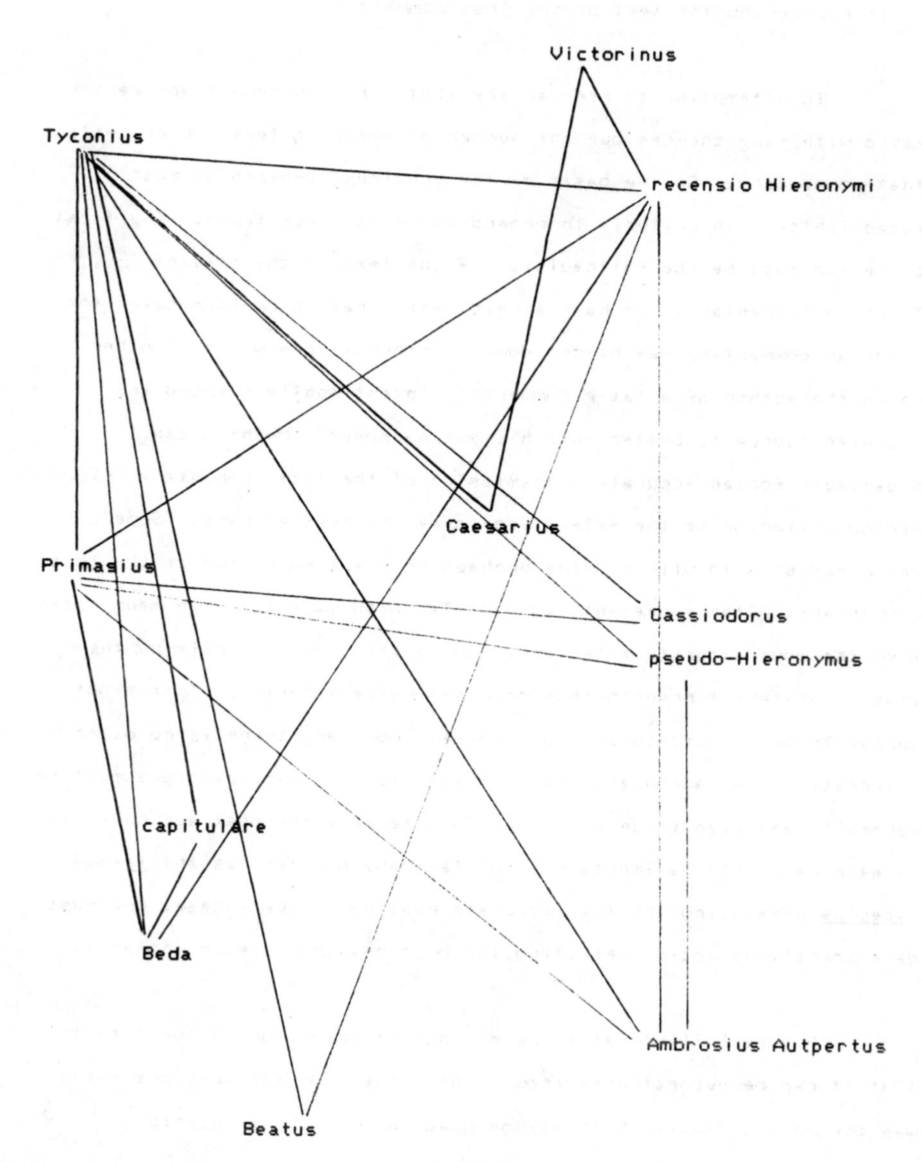

B. Use of the works influenced by Tyconius and the extant manuscripts in recovering the text of the lost commentary

In attempting to recover the lost Tyconian commentary we are faced with many choices due the number of existing texts which reflect that commentary. On the basis of the previous research we must establish certain criteria in regard to using these texts. The first criterion must be the faithfulness of the text to the original Tyconian commentary. We have already seen that in certain cases the Tyconian commentary was handed down in corrupt form while in other cases the author of a later commentary intentionally changed the Tyconian source to better suit his own purposes. Nothing can substitute for an accurate transmission of the lost commentary. The second criterion is the extensiveness of the text at hand. Some of the works studied will provide perhaps only a line or two of the lost commentary. Others present pages of Tyconian material. In many cases when the more accurate material is too brief, one must rely on the less accurate but nevertheless more extensive material. This might appear to be an unfortunate compromise. However, there is no other alternative. As a consequence of this situation many passages must be carefully analyzed in detail so as to determine the most accurate text in each case. It is impossible to claim any one text as the _textus receptus_ presenting the most accurate reading in every case. One must be extremely eclectic, selecting the best reading in each instance.

Figure 2 illustrates the manuscript tradition to the extent that it can be reconstructed now. The subject of the previous section was the various texts which may be used in recovering Tyconius' commentary. The subject of this section is the manuscripts used by the authors of these texts. Thus, all manuscripts except the Turin and the Budapest fragments are hypothetical. In addition, Jerome-Victorinus, Ambrosius Autpertus, Cassiodore, pseudo-Jerome, and the capitulary provide insufficient data to categorize the manuscripts used in those works. Once the interpolated sections of the Turin Fragment are omitted, it manifests remarkable similarities to the *Summa dicendorum* of Beatus, indicating the use of a common archetype. Certain similarities are also evident in the Budapest Fragment and the commentary of Primasius, indicating a second stem. However, the fragment represents the commentary of Tyconius and not Primasius. Caesarius, Bede, and the commentary of Beatus used manuscripts derived from a third stem. Finally, the two manuscripts used by Caesarius obviously share a common origin.

Figure 2 -- Reconstructed Manuscript Tradition

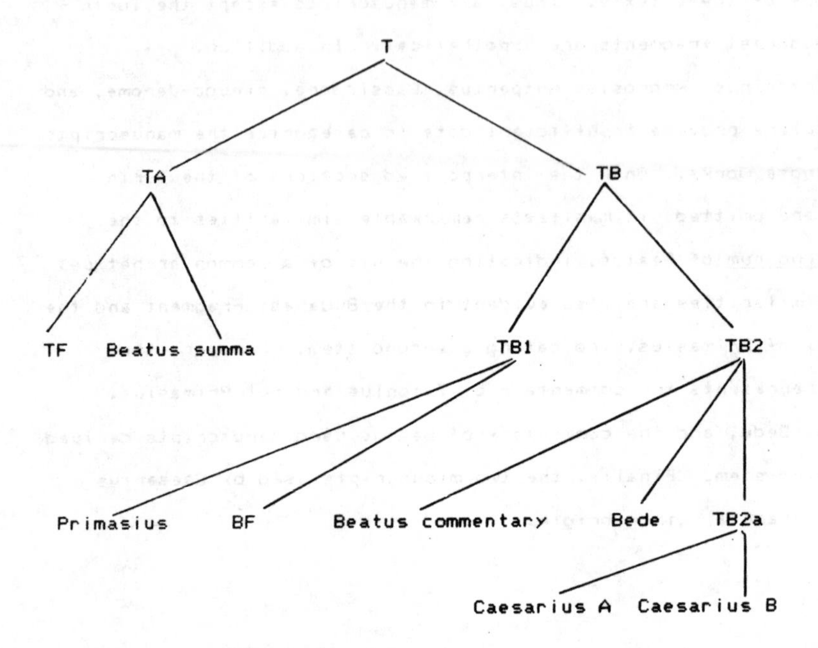

Note 1: All manuscripts except the Turin Fragment (TF) and Budapest Fragment (BF) are hypothetical.

Note 2: Jerome-Victorinus, Ambrosius Autpertus, Cassiodore, pseudo-Jerome and the capitulary provide insufficient data to be placed in the genealogy.

In the light of the previous information concerning the texts influenced by Tyconius and the manuscripts used in these texts, some conclusions may be drawn taking into consideration the threefold criteria. First, the Turin Fragment, with the exception of the clear and intentional interpolations, will generally be most faithful to the original text of Tyconius. However, the manuscript is brief. Second, the commentary of Beatus contains by far the greatest amount of Tyconian material. Although Beatus did exercise some originality in his commentary, much of the Tyconian material is intact. Third, although the commentary of Primasius contains extensive Tyconian material, his originality will often force reliance on other texts as being more accurate in many cases. Fourth, the commentary of Caesarius relied on rather corrupt Tyconian manuscripts and is itself fragmentary and disunited. However, the extensiveness of Tyconian material in the commentary forces us to consider it carefully. Fifth, the direct quotations from Bede will be very helpful as well as the other Tyconian material, which is sufficient to be recognized as important. Sixth, the Budapest Fragment, Cassiodore, pseudo-Jerome, the capitulary, and Ambrosius Autpertus are all admittedly brief in their Tyconian content although the accuracy of the Budapest Fragment makes it somewhat more significant than the others.

There are two matters of methodology to consider. First, Jerome-Victorinus enjoyed a certain degree of popularity in antiquity and was circulated extensively. In comparing the texts of Bede, Beatus, and Ambrosius Autpertus either to others or among themselves, one must always eliminate material which could have originated in Jerome-Victorinus and not in Tyconius. Second, the extent to which

Primasius' commentary was circulated also creates difficulties. It was known by Cassiodore, pseudo-Jerome, Bede, and Ambrosius Autpertus. Once again one must carefully eliminate material in the later commentaries which could have originated in Primasius rather than Tyconius.

C. Structure of the original commentary

This study has disproved two hypotheses concerning the structure of the lost commentary. First, the hypothesis of Hahn and Monceaux asserted that the lost commentary was written in three books.[1] Second, the hypothesis of Alvarez Campos asserted that the lost commentary was written in twelve books.[2] Neither hypothesis may be substantiated by the evidence at hand.

Can a positive hypothesis be offered in regard to the structure of Tyconius' Apocalypse Commentary? Let us enumerate the facts. First, Gennadius makes no mention of the structure of the lost commentary. Since he frequently indicates unusual characteristics of a work, his failure to do so suggests that Tyconius' commentary manifested no unusual physical characteristics. Second, in all the works investigated, which were definitely influenced by Tyconius, there is no mention of a number of books in the lost commentary. In addition, neither Augustine nor contemporary Donatist literature gives any assistance in this regard. Third, in all the works investigated, which were influenced by Tyconius, there are no two works which either mention or follow the same outline.

The lack of development of a tradition in regard to the structure of subsequent commentaries would lead one to believe that there was no single source of influence. This fact, coupled with the total absence of any specific reference to the structure of Tyconius' commentary, indicates a distinct disinterest in the matter. Nevertheless, some subsequent authors were very much preoccupied with the question of structure. However, Tyconius is neither mentioned nor imitated. The only logical conclusion would be to posit the absence of a coherent structure in Tyconius' commentary. However, his Liber regularum indicated good organizational ability. We know that Tyconius wrote a verse by verse commentary of the Apocalypse. Therefore, the lost commentary appears to have been written continuously without internal divisions.

D. The Tyconian Synopsis

After all this research one might legitimately ask himself why we must be content with a mere synopsis. Why not attempt a critical edition? Admittedly, a critical edition should be undertaken at some time in the future. However, I have decided not to begin this undertaking for two specific reasons.

The present work represents a detailed study of the lost commentary of Tyconius from a literary point of view. Because of the complicated historical and textual situation an extensive prolegomenon was necessary prior to any attempt at a detailed reconstruction and possible critical edition. My first goal was to determine if the reconstruction of the lost commentary is at all possible. I have answered this question affirmatively with some reservations. My second goal was to indicate how this might be accomplished. I have stated some clear and definite conclusions in this regard. Therefore, the goals of the present work have been achieved.

However, a much more important reason for not undertaking a critical edition of Tyconius' Apocalypse Commentary exists. My investigation has indicated that the present state of the research does not allow us to proceed any further. Good critical texts are not available in several instances. The lack of a critical edition of Cassiodore is a minor problem. However, serious difficulties manifest themselves in the commentary of Bede, which might be solved by a critical text. An example of this is the relationship of Bede to the capitulary. Above all, however, the textual problems in Beatus of

Liébana bring us to a complete standstill. Beatus contains by far the greatest amount of raw Tyconian material. Without adequate critical texts any attempt at a word for word reconstruction and edition of Tyconius would be premature.

A synopsis offers three clear advantages at the present time:

1. In many cases, we will find Tyconian parallels and will not have enough evidence to reconstruct the exact word for word text although it will be abundantly clear that the passage originates in Tyconius. In such instances a synopsis offers the Tyconian material in an unbiased manner.
2. Progress in researching the thought of Tyconius has been hampered for years by the inaccessibility of his Apocalypse Commentary. While some scholars relied exclusively on one work of the Tyconian tradition, for example Beatus or the Turin Fragment, others avoided the problem all together by limiting their research to Tyconius' _Liber regularum._ Once again the synopsis presents the Tyconian material without commitment to a specific wording.
3. Finally, when adequate critical texts are available, the synopsis indicating all the identifiable Tyconian passages will provide a convenient point of departure for the reconstruction of the lost commentary.

In conclusion, the synopsis summarizes the present research, provides Tyconian passages for those interested in studying his thought, and serves as a prolegomenon to any future critical edition of the lost Apocalypse Commentary.

Rev. 1:9

Bede	135,27
Beatus commentary	1,3,37

Rev. 1:12

Caesarius A	211,7-10
Caesarius B	213,20-21
Primasius	800,24-51
Pseudo-Jerome	6,22-23
Ambrosius Autpertus	68,39-70,1
Beatus commentary	1,4,28-31;34-35;41-42
Liber regularum	11,1-5

Rev. 1:13

Jerome-Victorinus	23,4-6
Caesarius A	211,11-18
Caesarius B	213,22-25
Primasius	801,4-20
Ambrosius Autpertus	72,36-38
Beatus commentary	1,4,42-47;50-52

Rev. 1:14

Caesarius A	211,23-28;212,2-4
Primasius	801,30-31;35-43
Beatus commentary	1,4,63;65;67-70

Rev. 1:15

Caesarius A	212,4-13
Primasius	801,46-802,2
Cod. Oratorii B6	475,1-3
Bede	136,26-36;129,48-51
Ambrosius Autpertus	76,30-37
Beatus commentary	1,4,74-77;81-82

Rev. 1:16

Caesarius B	213,1-3;214,6-10
Primasius	802,9-22;30-41
Cassiodore	1406,9-11
Pseudo-Jerome	7,12
Ambrosius Autpertus	84,1-7
Beatus commentary	1,4,86-89;112-114

Rev. 1:17

Primasius	802,51-56
Beatus commentary	1,5,2

Rev. 1:18

Caesarius A	215,7-11
Primasius	803,10-24
Beatus commentary	1,5,21-23
Liber regularum	77,12-14

Rev. 1:19

Caesarius A	215,25-216,14
Bede	137,11-14
Beatus commentary	1,5,27
Liber regularum	10,13-11,11

Rev. 1:20

Caesarius A	215,11-25
Primasius	803,28-42
Beatus commentary	1,5,30-31;45-46
Liber regularum	59,20-25
Augustine, De doctrina Christiana, 3,30,42	102,18-103,20

Rev. 2:1

Caesarius A	216,2-7;14-19
Primasius	23,1-24,27
Cassiodore	1406,31
Cod. Oratorii B6	475,4
Bede	129,44-45;129,51-130,45
Beatus commentary	1,5,51-55;61;65;68-69;71;72-73
Gennadius, _De viris inlustribus,_ 18	68,4

Rev. 2:3

Primasius	24,31-37
Beatus commentary	2,1,10-11;2,1,24

Rev. 2:4

Primasius	24,45-25,52
Beatus commentary	2,1,30-31

Rev. 2:5

Caesarius B	216,20-27
Primasius	25,52-60
Beatus commentary	2,1,48-51

Rev. 2:6

Primasius	25,60-62
Beatus commentary	2,1,55

Rev. 2:7

Caesarius B	216,28-30
Primasius	25,62-26,71
Cassiodore	1406,40-45
Pseudo-Jerome	7,18-19
Bede	137,50-53
Ambrosius Autpertus	111,39-113,133
Beatus commentary	2,1,63-66;77-82
Liber regularum	81,21-23

Rev. 2:9

Caesarius B	216,30-217,1
Primasius	26,73-87
Beatus commentary	2,2,2-3;6-12;13

Rev. 2:10

Caesarius B	217,2-3
Primasius	26,87-88
Bede	138,17-19
Beatus commentary	2,2,81;93

<u>Liber regularum</u>	60,7-10

Rev. 2:12

Primasius	30,174
Pseudo-Jerome	7,21
Ambrosius Autpertus	125,4-6
Beatus commentary	2,2,101

Rev. 2:13

Caesarius B	217,5-8
Primasius	29,152-170
Bede	138,50-53
Beatus commentary	2,3,1-3;8-9

Rev. 2:17

Caesarius A	217,8-12;13-14
Primasius	30,176-192;31,198-200
Bede	139,9-11
Beatus commentary	1,5,89;2,3,42-44;63;69
<u>Liber regularum</u>	65,1-6

Rev. 2:20-21

Caesarius B	217,18-21
Primasius	32,222-33,261
Bede	139,33-42;140,2-4
Ambrosius Autpertus	138,36-40;142,31-41
Beatus commentary	2,4,8-48
Turin Fragment	1-15
<u>Liber regularum</u>	31,7-32,4

Rev. 2:23

Primasius	35,283-291
Beatus commentary	2,4,60-61
Turin Fragment	20-22;26
<u>Liber regularum</u>	55,4-5

Rev. 2:24

Caesarius A	217,22-26
Primasius	35,292-36,298
Bede	140,9-15
Beatus commentary	2,4,65-69;71-73
Turin Fragment	27-31;33-35

Rev. 2:27

Caesarius A	218,2-5
Primasius	36,306-311
Bede	140,20-23

Turin Fragment	37-39

Rev. 2:28

Primasius	36,311-316
Bede	140,29-31
Beatus commentary	1,5,91;2,4,79
Turin Fragment	40-41
Liber regularum	71,28-29

Rev. 3:1

Caesarius A	218,9-12
Primasius	37,6-10
Beatus commentary	2,5,4-6
Turin Fragment	44-46

Rev. 3:2-3

Beatus commentary	2,5,16-19
Turin Fragment	47-50

Rev. 3:4

Primasius	38,20-21
Beatus commentary	2,5,57
Turin Fragment	51

Rev. 3:5

Primasius	38,22-26
Beatus commentary	2,5,76-80
Turin Fragment	52-55

Rev. 3:7

Caesarius A	218,14-18
Primasius	38,32-37
Beatus commentary	2,6,4
Turin Fragment	58-61

Rev. 3:8

Caesarius A	218,18-22
Primasius	39,42-45
Bede	141,14-16
Beatus commentary	2,6,14-15;32
Turin Fragment	62-64

Rev. 3:9

Primasius	39,52-58
Bede	141,17-21
Beatus commentary	2,6,74-78
Turin Fragment	65;67-71

Rev. 3:10

Primasius	40,68-74
Bede	141,28-30
Beatus commentary	2,6,80-84;91
Turin Fragment	72-75

Rev. 3:11

Primasius	40,77-41,86
Bede	141,37-41
Beatus commentary	2,6,93-97
Turin Fragment	76-82
<u>Liber regularum</u>	24,7-16

Rev. 3:12-13

Caesarius A	218,22-26
Primasius	41,99-102;41,104-42,110;42,112
Bede	141,51-58
Beatus commentary	2,6,98-101;103-108;1,4,65
Turin Fragment	83;85-86;88-97

Rev. 3:14

Caesarius A	218,26-27
Beatus commentary	2,7,6
Turin Fragment	99

Rev. 3:15

Primasius	43,142-144
Beatus commentary	1,5,97-98

Rev. 3:16

Bede	142,16-17
Beatus commentary	2,7,3;7
Turin Fragment	100

Rev. 3:17

Caesarius A	218,27-219,1
Primasius	42,131-43,133
Beatus commentary	2,7,9-10
Turin Fragment	101-102

Rev. 3:18

Caesarius A	219,1-4
Primasius	44,157-163
Bede	142,21-23
Beatus commentary	2,7,14-15;26
Turin Fragment	103-106;218

Rev. 3:19

Primasius	44,170-173
Bede	142,29-30
Beatus commentary	2,7,25
Turin Fragment	107

Rev. 3:20

Primasius	44,173-45,179
Turin Fragment	108

Rev. 3:21

Primasius	45,179-182
Cassiodore	1408,26-28
Bede	142,40-43
Beatus commentary	2,7,28-29
Turin Fragment	110-112

Rev. 3:22

Primasius	45,185-191
Bede	142,52-55
Beatus commentary	2,7,30;3,inscriptio (p. 264)
Turin Fragment	113-114
Liber regularum	4,20-23

Rev. 4:1

Caesarius A	219,4-12
Primasius	46,1-14
Cod. Oratorii B6	475,4
Bede	142,55-57
Beatus preface	4,4
Beatus commentary	3,1,3-5;9
Turin Fragment	115-117
Liber regularum	64,7-10

Rev. 4:3

Caesarius A	219,14-15
Primasius	47,31-35
Beatus preface	4,5
Beatus commentary	3,2,10

Rev. 4:4

Caesarius A	219,18-23
Primasius	48,43-57
Bede	143,26-34
Beatus commentary	3,2,22-30

Rev. 4:5

Caesarius A	219,23-220,2
Primasius	48,61-63;49,65-66
Beatus commentary	3,2,31

Rev. 4:6

Caesarius A	220,7-13
Primasius	50,92-51,112
Cassiodore	1408,41-44
Pseudo-Jerome	9,11-12
Bede	144,21-24
Beatus preface	4,6
Beatus commentary	3,3,1-2

Rev. 4:7

Caesarius A	220,10-19
Primasius	54,188-55,199
Beatus commentary	3,3,22;24-27

Rev. 4:8

Caesarius A	220,19-27
Primasius	55,199-208:94,56-57
Bede	144,21-22
Beatus preface	4,7
Beatus commentary	3,3,28-29;32;4,1,2

Rev. 4:10

Caesarius A	221,12-14
Primasius	58,262-267
Bede	144,58-59

Rev. 4:11

Caesarius A	221,15-20
Primasius	58,267-274
Bede	145,1-2
Beatus commentary	3,3,131-132

Rev. 5:1

Caesarius A	221,22-25
Primasius	61,1-6;62,19-20
Cod. Oratorii B6	475,6
Beatus commentary	3,4,1-2;92

Rev. 5:2

Caesarius A	222,4-6
Primasius	82,490-83,493
Beatus commentary	3,4,94-95

Rev. 5:3

Caesarius A	222,7-11
Bede	145,30-36
Beatus commentary	3,4,98

Rev. 5:4

Caesarius A	222,11-14
Primasius	85,515-84,519
Beatus commentary	3,4,99

Rev. 5:5

Caesarius A	222,14-18
Primasius	84,520-85,536
Bede	145,44-45
Beatus commentary	3,4,100-102

Rev. 5:6

Caesarius A	222,18-25
Primasius	85,536-553
Bede	145,49-50
Beatus commentary	3,4,105-106;112-113

Rev. 5:7

Caesarius A	222,26-30
Primasius	86,573-576
Beatus commentary	3,4,114-115

Rev. 5:8-9

Caesarius A	223,1-4
Primasius	87,590-594;88,615
Bede	146,11-12
Beatus commentary	3,4,116;120

Rev. 5:10

Primasius	89,634-642
Bede	146,16-20
Beatus commentary	3,4,121-122

Rev. 5:11

Caesarius A	223,10-11
Primasius	89,645-647;651
Beatus commentary	3,4,123-124

Rev. 5:12

Caesarius A	223,11-17
Primasius	90,658-670
Beatus commentary	3,4,125-126

Rev. 5:13

Caesarius A	223,17-23
Primasius	91,677-699
Beatus commentary	3,4,127-128

Rev. 6:2

Caesarius A	223,26-224,1
Caesarius B	224,22-25
Primasius	94,62-64;69-70
Ambrosius Autpertus	277,97-100
Beatus preface	4,8
Beatus commentary	4,1,1

Rev. 6:4

Caesarius A	224,15-21
Caesarius B	224,26-225,3
Primasius	95,78-81
Cassiodore	1409,37-40
Pseudo-Jerome	10,26
Cod. Oratorii B6	476,8
Bede	147,6-15
Beatus preface	4,8
Beatus commentary	4,1,6-9

Rev. 6:5

Jerome-Victorinus	71,17
Caesarius B	225,4
Primasius	95,82-83
Cod. Oratorii B6	10,28-29
Bede	147,20-22
Beatus preface	4,8
Beatus commentary	4,1,11-12

Rev. 6:6

Jerome-Victorinus	71,15-17
Caesarius A	226,10-18
Caesarius B	225,5-9
Primasius	95,83-85;91-99
Pseudo-Jerome	11,4
Bede	147,23-25
Beatus commentary	4,1,13-19
Budapest Fragment	recto,A,1-recto,B,14

Rev. 6:7

Beatus commentary	4,1,23-24
Budapest Fragment	verso,B,1-20

Rev. 6:8

Caesarius A	226,18-25;226,26-227,2
Primasius	97,119-99,168
Pseudo-Jerome	11,7
Cod. Oratorii B6	476,7
Bede	146,46-47;147,47-49

Beatus preface	4,8
Beatus commentary	4,1,24-41;42-44;46-47
Liber regularum	75,5-6

Rev. 6:9

Caesarius A	227,2-7
Caesarius B	225,15-16
Primasius	99,167-170
Cassiodore	1409,47-50
Cod. Oratorii B6	476,8
Beatus preface	4,9

Rev. 6:12

Jerome-Victorinus	77,3-9
Caesarius A	227,7-17
Caesarius B	225,16-22
Primasius	100,214-101,233
Bede	148,38-45
Beatus preface	4,9-11
Beatus commentary	4,3,3-7
Liber regularum	55,4-5

Rev. 6:13

Jerome-Victorinus	77,10-13
Caesarius A	227,17-20
Caesarius B	225,22-25
Primasius	101,233-102,249
Beatus preface	4,11
Beatus commentary	4,3,7-11

Rev. 6:14

Jerome-Victorinus	77,14-79,2
Caesarius A	227,20-29
Caesarius B	225,25-27
Primasius	102,249-103,267
Beatus preface	4,12
Beatus commentary	4,3,11-16

Rev. 6:15

Caesarius A	227,29-228,1
Caesarius B	225,27-30
Primasius	103,267-269
Bede	149,2-5
Beatus commentary	4,3,17-18

Rev. 6:16

Caesarius A	228,1-4
Primasius	105,295-297
Beatus commentary	4,3,22

Rev. 6:17

Primasius	105,299-308
Bede	130,52-131,6
Beatus commentary	4,3,42-44

Rev. 7:1 (cf. Rev. 9:13-14)

Primasius	106,8-19
Cod. Oratorii B6	476,9
Beatus preface	4,16-17
Beatus commentary	4,4,4-7

Rev. 7:3

Caesarius A	228,7-15
Beatus preface	4,19
Beatus commentary	4,4,17-18

Rev. 7:4

Caesarius A	228,15-19
Primasius	108,52-58
Beatus commentary	4,5,1

Rev. 7:9

Caesarius A	228,18-26
Cod. Oratorii B6	476,10
Bede	152,41-44
Beatus commentary	4,6,45-48
<u>Liber regularum</u>	60,5-7

Rev. 7:11

Caesarius A	228,27-29
Caesarius B	231,17-29
Beatus commentary	4,6,50

Rev. 7:12

Primasius	127,498-505
Beatus commentary	4,6,66-68

Rev. 7:13

Caesarius A	228,29-32
Caesarius B	231,19-20
Primasius	129,540-541
Beatus commentary	4,6,69

Rev. 7:14

Caesarius A	229,1-5
Caesarius B	231,21-23
Bede	153,30-34
Beatus commentary	4,6,70

Rev. 7:15

Caesarius A	229,5-7
Caesarius B	231,23-25
Primasius	130,570-131,579
Beatus commentary	4,6,71

Rev. 7:16

Caesarius A	229,7-9
Caesarius B	231,25-26
Beatus commentary	4,6,72
Turin Fragment	118

Rev. 7:17

Caesarius A	229,9-13
Caesarius B	231,26-29
Primasius	131,584-589;132,598-602
Beatus preface	4,21
Beatus commentary	4,6,73-79
Turin Fragment	119-123;125-127

Rev. 8:1

Jerome-Victorinus	81,5-9
Caesarius A	229,13-15
Caesarius B	231,29-30
Primasius	132,1-8
Pseudo-Jerome	13,13
Cod. Oratorii B6	476,11
Bede	154,41-45
Beatus preface	4,22
Beatus commentary	4,7,1-2;5,1,1
Turin Fragment	128-130
<u>Liber regularum</u>	56,11-12

Rev. 8:2

Caesarius A	229,15-18
Caesarius B	232,1-2
Primasius	135,1-6
Pseudo-Jerome	13,15-16
Cod. Oratorii B6	476,12
Beatus preface	4,23
Beatus commentary	5,1,1
Turin Fragment	131

Rev. 8:3

Caesarius A	229,18-23
Caesarius B	232,2-5
Primasius	135,6-136,26
Pseudo-Jerome	13,17-18
Bede	155,1-13
Beatus commentary	5,1,2-6
Turin Fragment	132-141
<u>Liber regularum</u>	32,9-12

Rev. 8:5

Caesarius A	229,24-28
Caesarius B	232,5-6
Primasius	137,52-138,71
Beatus commentary	5,1,6-9
Turin Fragment	142-147

Rev. 8:6

Caesarius A	229,28-230,2
Caesarius B	232,6-8
Primasius	138,71-75
Beatus commentary	5,T8,6
Turin Fragment	148

Rev. 8:7

Caesarius A	230,2-8
Caesarius B	232,9-11
Primasius	138,75-139,97
Bede	155,54-56;156,8-16
Ambrosius Autpertus	331,5-6;333,52-62
Beatus preface	4,24
Beatus commentary	5,T8,7;5,2,1-6
Turin Fragment	149-152;153-156
<u>Liber regularum</u>	28,16-22

Rev. 8:8

Caesarius A	230,9-12
Caesarius B	232,11-14
Primasius	139,100-140,105
Beatus preface	4,25
Beatus commentary	5,3,1
Turin Fragment	157-158

Rev. 8:9

Caesarius A	230,12-14
Primasius	140,114-118
Bede	156,31-39
Beatus commentary	5,3,1-5
Turin Fragment	159-162

Rev. 8:10

Caesarius A	230,15-18
Caesarius B	232,15-17
Primasius	140,123-124
Pseudo-Jerome	14,6
Beatus preface	4,26
Beatus commentary	5,4,1
Turin Fragment	164-165
<u>Liber regularum</u>	71,23-72,2

Rev. 8:11

Caesarius A	230,18-22
Caesarius B	232,17-18
Primasius	140,119-123
Ambrosius Autpertus	337,74-76
Beatus commentary	5,4,7-8
Turin Fragment	166;168

Rev. 8:12

Caesarius A	230,23-231,1
Caesarius B	232,19-22
Primasius	141,138-141;143,170-181
Cassiodore	1410,25-28

Bede	156,59-157,5
Beatus preface	4,27
Beatus commentary	5,5,1-7;17
Turin Fragment	170-175

Rev. 8:13

Caesarius A	231,1-5
Caesarius B	232,22-25
Primasius	144,190-191
Bede	157,20-22
Beatus preface	4,28-29
Beatus commentary	5,5,18
Turin Fragment	176-177

Rev. 9:1

Caesarius A	232,32-233,5
Caesarius B	236,6-11
Primasius	144,1-145,11
Bede	157,28-29
Cassiodore	1410,33-35
Pseudo-Jerome	14,12-13
Beatus preface	4,30-31
Beatus commentary	5,6,1;6-7
Turin Fragment	178-182

Rev. 9:2

Caesarius A	233,6-14
Caesarius B	236,10-16
Primasius	146,51-53
Bede	157,32-33
Beatus preface	4,32-33
Beatus commentary	5,6,8-11
Turin Fragment	183-189

Rev. 9:3

Caesarius A	233,16
Caesarius B	236,17-18
Cassiodore	1410,40-44
Pseudo-Jerome	14,17
Bede	157,47-48
Beatus preface	4,34
Beatus commentary	5,6,11
Turin Fragment	190-191

Rev. 9:4

Primasius	147,60-62
Bede	157,51-158,2
Ambrosius Autpertus	335,34-36
Turin Fragment	192-193

Rev. 9:5

Caesarius A	233,18-26
Caesarius B	236,18-24
Primasius	147,85-86
Bede	158,6-10
Beatus commentary	5,6,18-19;19-25
Turin Fragment	194-203
Liber regularum	60,25-26

Rev. 9:6

Caesarius A	233,26-28
Primasius	148,106-149,111

Beatus commentary	5,6,25-26
Turin Fragment	204-210

Rev. 9:7

Caesarius A	233,28-31
Caesarius B	236,24-27
Primasius	149,127-129
Bede	158,24-26;31-35
Beatus preface	4,36-37
Beatus commentary	5,7,1-7
Turin Fragment	211-216

Rev. 9:8

Caesarius A	233,31-234,2
Caesarius B	236,27-29
Primasius	149,136-142
Pseudo-Jerome	14,23
Bede	158,35-36
Beatus preface	4,37-38
Beatus commentary	5,7,11-12
Turin Fragment	217-220

Rev. 9:9

Primasius	150,151-153
Pseudo-Jerome	14,23
Ambrosius Autpertus	352,10-12
Beatus commentary	5,7,12-13
Turin Fragment	221-224

Rev. 9:10

Caesarius A	234,2-5
Caesarius B	236,29-31
Primasius	151,164-171
Pseudo-Jerome	14,26
Ambrosius Autpertus	351,5-8
Beatus preface	4,39
Beatus commentary	5,7,14-16
Turin Fragment	225-228

Rev. 9:11

Caesarius A	234,5-7
Caesarius B	236,31-33
Primasius	152,185-186
Cassiodore	1410,43-44
Beatus preface	4,40
Beatus commentary	5,7,17-18
Turin Fragment	229-232

Rev. 9:13-14 (cf. Rev. 7:1)

Caesarius A	234,10-20
Caesarius B	236,33-237,7

Primasius	152,187-153,206
Bede	159,12-16
Cassiodore	1410,45-46
Beatus preface	4,42-45
Beatus commentary	5,8,1-12
Turin Fragment	234-245

Rev. 9:15-16

Caesarius A	234,20-26
Primasius	153,210-215;154,224;155,246-248
Beatus commentary	5,8,13-16
Turin Fragment	246-255
Liber regularum	60,24-26

Rev. 9:17

Caesarius A	234,26-235,2
Caesarius B	237,8-13
Primasius	156,280-283;157,293-294
Bede	159,54-56;160,3-7
Ambrosius Autpertus	360,5-10
Beatus preface	4,46-47
Beatus commentary	5,9,1-4
Turin Fragment	256-262;264-267

Rev. 9:18

Primasius	157,306-307
Beatus preface	4,48
Beatus commentary	5,9,5
Turin Fragment	268-269

Rev. 9:19

Caesarius A	235,2-5
Caesarius B	237,14-17
Primasius	158,308-311;316-318
Bede	160,9-11;19-21
Beatus preface	4,48
Beatus commentary	5,9,6-8
Turin Fragment	270-274

Rev. 9:20

Bede	160,21-23
Beatus commentary	5,9,9
Turin Fragment	275-277

Rev. 9:21

Primasius	158,326-159,336
Cod. Oratorii B6	476,15
Bede	160,23-25;28-30
Beatus commentary	5,9,16-19

Rev. 10:1 (cf. Rev. 1:15;1:16)

Caesarius A	235,5-18
Caesarius B	237,17-22
Primasius	159,1-13;160,28-30
Beatus preface	4,49-50
Beatus commentary	5,10,1-3
Turin Fragment	283-291
<u>Liber regularum</u>	81,20

Rev. 10:2

Caesarius A	235,18-20
Caesarius B	237,23-25
Primasius	160,23-26;160,30-161,38
Cassiodore	1410,50-54
Bede	160,50-57
Beatus preface	4,50-51
Beatus commentary	5,10,4-5;10
Turin Fragment	292-296

Rev. 10:3

Caesarius A	235,20-22
Caesarius B	237,26-27
Primasius	161,38-43
Bede	161,2-7
Ambrosius Autpertus	391,2-6
Beatus preface	4,52-53
Beatus commentary	5,10,11
Turin Fragment	297-300

Rev. 10:4 (cf. Rev. 22:10;22:11)

Caesarius A	235,22-236,2
Caesarius B	237,27-238,3
Primasius	161,48-57
Bede	161,12-18
Beatus preface	4,53-54
Beatus commentary	5,10,12-18
Turin Fragment	301-307

Rev. 10:7

Caesarius A	236,2-5
Primasius	162,60-71
Beatus preface	4,55-57
Beatus commentary	5,10,23-25
Turin Fragment	308-311

Rev. 10:8

Caesarius A	238,7-8
Primasius	162,73-77

Beatus preface	4,57
Beatus commentary	5,10,25-26
Turin Fragment	312-313

Rev. 10:9

Caesarius A	238,9-15
Primasius	163,85-92
Cassiodore	1411,3-7
Bede	161,49-55
Beatus preface	4,57-58
Beatus commentary	5,10,27;30;34
Turin Fragment	314-319

Rev. 10:11

Primasius	164,105-116
Pseudo-Jerome	15,22-24
Cod. Oratorii B6	476,16
Bede	161,58-162,4
Beatus preface	4,59-61
Beatus commentary	5,10,35-38
Turin Fragment	320-323

Rev. 11:1

Caesarius A	238,21-25
Primasius	165,1-3
Bede	162,11-13
Ambrosius Autpertus	410,144-146
Beatus preface	4,62-63
Beatus commentary	5,10,39
Turin Fragment	324-326

Rev. 11:2

Caesarius A	238,26-239,2
Primasius	166,14-20;23-28
Pseudo-Jerome	15,29-30
Beatus preface	4,67-69
Beatus commentary	5,10,41-42;43
Turin Fragment	327-331

Rev. 11:3

Caesarius A	239,2-9
Primasius	166,28-32;167,49-50
Cassiodore	1411,10-15
Pseudo-Jerome	15,31-16,1
Cod. Oratorii B6	476,17
Bede	162,26-32;36-43;44-46
Beatus preface	4,70-71
Beatus commentary	5,11,1-7
Turin Fragment	332-336;338-341
<u>Liber regularum</u>	60,24-61,4

Rev. 11:4

Caesarius A	239,9-18
Primasius	167,51-168,60
Bede	162,47-53
Ambrosius Autpertus	416,13-20;30-32
Beatus preface	4,72-74
Beatus commentary	5,11,8-13
Turin Fragment	342-348

Rev. 11:5

Caesarius A	239,18-22
Primasius	168,60-66
Pseudo-Jerome	16,3
Bede	162,54-163,2
Beatus preface	4,75
Beatus commentary	5,11,13-14
Turin Fragment	349;351

Rev. 11:6

Caesarius A	239,22-27
Primasius	168,66-76
Pseudo-Jerome	16,6
Bede	163,6-15
Beatus preface	4,77
Beatus commentary	5,11,15-16;17-19
Turin Fragment	352-359;361

Rev. 11:7

Caesarius A	239,27-32
Primasius	169,85-96
Bede	163,20-24;31-36
Beatus preface	4,78
Beatus commentary	5,11,20;5,12,1-2
Turin Fragment	363-369

Rev. 11:8

Caesarius A	239,32-240,4
Primasius	169,96-170,103
Beatus preface	4,79-81
Beatus commentary	5,12,3-5
Turin Fragment	370-373;375-377
Liber regularum	50,5-10

Rev. 11:9

Caesarius A	240,4-13
Primasius	170,103-106;120-122
Cassiodore	1411,27-30
Bede	163,53-164,3
Beatus preface	4,81-86
Beatus commentary	5,12,6-12
Turin Fragment	378-387
Liber regularum	61,5-12

Rev. 11:10

Caesarius A	240,13-22
Primasius	170,110-119
Bede	163,50-52;164,4-11
Beatus preface	4,86-88
Beatus commentary	5,12,13-16
Turin Fragment	388-394

Rev. 11:11-12

Caesarius A	240,22-241,6
Primasius	174,204-206
Bede	164,12-23
Beatus preface	4,89-98
Beatus commentary	5,13,1-11

Turin Fragment	395-405

Rev. 11:13

Caesarius A	241,9-21
Primasius	174,208-175,224
Bede	164,24-36
Beatus preface	4,99-103
Beatus commentary	5,13,12-17
Turin Fragment	406-420
Liber regularum	56,11-12

Rev. 11:14

Primasius	175,225-235
Bede	165,1-7
Beatus preface	4,103-106
Beatus commentary	5,13,17-20
Turin Fragment	420-423

Rev. 11:18

Primasius	175,235-177,264
Cod. Oratorii B6	476,18
Bede	165,14-18;29-32
Beatus preface	4,106;108-111
Beatus commentary	5,14,1-4
Turin Fragment	424-431

Rev. 11:19

Caesarius A	241,21-27
Primasius	177,264-275;178,286-294;302-305
Cod. Oratorii B6	476,19
Bede	165,33-50
Beatus preface	4,112-114
Beatus commentary	6,1,1;3-4;6,inscriptio (p.456)
Turin Fragment	432-439;467

Rev. 12:1

Caesarius A	241,27-242,2
Primasius	179,1-15;180,26-28
Bede	165,52-53;166,8-9
Ambrosius Autpertus	443,9-444,33;445,6-9
Beatus preface	5,1-4
Beatus commentary	6,2,1-3;7-8
Turin Fragment	440-449

Rev. 12:2

Caesarius A	242,13-15
Primasius	180,30-34
Beatus preface	5,5
Turin Fragment	450-451

Rev. 12:3

Caesarius A	242,4-8
Primasius	180,34-38
Cod. Oratorii B6	476,20
Bede	166,28-29
Ambrosius Autpertus	447,12
Beatus preface	5,6-7
Beatus commentary	6,2,9-13
Turin Fragment	452-457

Rev. 12:4

Caesarius A	242,8-13;15-18
Primasius	180,38-40;181,45-51
Bede	166,36-39;41-46
Ambrosius Autpertus	449,15-19
Beatus preface	5,8
Beatus commentary	6,2,17;22-30
Turin Fragment	458-464;466
<u>Liber regularum</u>	65,22-25

Rev. 12:5

Caesarius A	242,18-20
Primasius	181,56-59;182,66-71
Bede	166,47-49;52-56;166,59-167,2
Beatus preface	5,9-10
Beatus commentary	6,2,31-34
Turin Fragment	475-481

Rev. 12:6

Caesarius A	242,20-25
Primasius	182,80-183,89
Bede	167,3-7
Beatus preface	5,11

Beatus commentary	6,2,35-40;49
Turin Fragment	482;484-489
Liber regularum	35,7-11

Rev. 12:7

Caesarius A	242,25-31
Primasius	183,103-107;184,120-122
Beatus preface	5,12-13
Beatus commentary	6,2,41-43

Rev. 12:8

Caesarius A	242,31-243,1
Bede	167,36-39
Beatus preface	5,14
Beatus commentary	6,2,44

Rev. 12:9

Caesarius A	243,1-5
Primasius	185,143-147
Bede	167,42-44
Beatus commentary	6,2,45-47

Rev. 12:10

Caesarius A	243,5-19
Primasius	185,150-153
Beatus commentary	6,2,50-55

Rev. 12:12

Caesarius A	243,19-29
Beatus commentary	6,2,57-58

Rev. 12:13

Caesarius A	243,32-244,2
Bede	168,13-16
Beatus preface	5,15
Beatus commentary	6,2,59

Rev. 12:14

Caesarius A	244,2-11
Primasius	187,197-200;188,215-218
Pseudo-Jerome	17,1-2
Cod. Oratorii B6	476,21
Ambrosius Autpertus	470,6-8
Beatus commentary	6,2,60-62

Rev. 12:15

Caesarius A	244,11-12

Beatus preface	5,16
Beatus commentary	6,2,62-63

Rev. 12:16

Caesarius A	244,13-18
Primasius	189,230-235
Beatus commentary	6,2,64-65

Rev. 12:17

Caesarius A	244,23-27
Primasius	189,241-245
Bede	168,44-47
Beatus commentary	6,2,66-67;72

Rev. 12:18

Caesarius A	244,27-28
Pseudo-Jerome	17,22
Bede	169,1-2
Beatus commentary	6,2,72
Liber regularum	27,10-12

Rev. 13:1

Caesarius A	244,28-245,1
Primasius	193,1-16
Cassiodore	1411,47-51
Cod. Oratorii B6	477,22
Bede	169,21-26
Beatus preface	5,17-18
Beatus commentary	6,3,1-6;15-19

Rev. 13:2

Caesarius A	245,1-6
Primasius	193,16-21
Pseudo-Jerome	17,7
Bede	169,27-30
Beatus commentary	6,3,19-20
Liber regularum	29,2-4

Rev. 13:3-4

Caesarius A	245,9-14
Primasius	194,25-42
Bede	169,44-53
Beatus commentary	6,3,27-34
Liber regularum	31,7-32,12

Rev. 13:5

Caesarius A	245,26-28
Primasius	194,46-195,50
Cassiodore	1411,51-1412,1
Beatus commentary	6,3,37

Rev. 13:6

Caesarius A	245,28-35
Bede	169,58-170,2
Beatus commentary	6,3,38-39;44-45

Rev. 13:7

Caesarius A	245,35-246,5
Primasius	196,82-86
Bede	170,9-10;14-15
Beatus commentary	6,3,46-48
Liber regularum	55,4-5

Rev. 13:8

Caesarius A	246,5-8
Primasius	196,87-89
Bede	170,25-28
Ambrosius Autpertus	501,55-58

Beatus commentary	6,3,49-51
Liber regularum	24,7-11

Rev. 13:9

Primasius	196,94-95
Ambrosius Autpertus	504,5-8
Beatus commentary	6,3,52

Rev. 13:10

Primasius	196,99-197,107
Bede	170,45-48
Beatus commentary	6,3,52-55

Rev. 13:11

Caesarius A	246,11-18
Primasius	197,116-198,122
Bede	170,49-51;170,55-171,3
Beatus preface	5,19
Beatus commentary	6,4,2;11-14

Rev. 13:12-13

Caesarius A	246,19-25
Primasius	198,122-129;198,132-200,176
Bede	171,7-8
Beatus preface	5,20-21
Beatus commentary	6,4,46-62

Rev. 13:14

Bede	171,10-11
Beatus commentary	6,4,65

Rev. 13:15

Caesarius A	246,25-27
Bede	171,49-52;171,56-172,1
Beatus commentary	6,4,70;74-76

Rev. 13:16

Caesarius A	246,27-247,15
Primasius	202,237-239
Bede	172,3-8
Beatus commentary	6,4,77-81

Rev. 13:17-18

Caesarius A	247,15-29
Primasius	203,254-258;209,3-4
Beatus commentary	6,4,89-93;95-96;112

Rev. 14:1

Caesarius A	248,1-5
Primasius	209,17-18
Bede	173,13-16
Beatus preface	5,22
Beatus commentary	6,8,1

Rev. 14:2

Caesarius A	248,5-8
Beatus commentary	6,8,2

Rev. 14:4

Caesarius A	248,8-15
Bede	174,32-33
Beatus commentary	6,8,8-9

Rev. 14:5

Caesarius A	248,15-19
Primasius	214,146-148
Bede	174,22-32
Beatus preface	5,22
Beatus commentary	6,8,10-12;26

Rev. 14:6

Caesarius A	248,20-22
Primasius	215,153-154;166-167
Pseudo-Jerome	17,28-18,1
Bede	174,40
Beatus preface	5,23
Beatus commentary	7,1,1-2

Rev. 14:8

Caesarius A	248,25-249,4
Primasius	215,175-216,187
Beatus preface	5,24-26
Beatus commentary	7,1,3-12
Liber regularum	52,4-12

Rev. 14:9

Bede	175,7-9
Beatus commentary	7,1,14

Rev. 14:10

Caesarius A	249,4-6
Bede	175,13-17
Beatus commentary	7,1,15-16

Rev. 14:12

Cod. Oratorii B6	477,24
Ambrosius Autpertus	547,3-8
Beatus commentary	7,1,19-20

Rev. 14:14

Caesarius A	249,6-11
Primasius	218,239-240;245-248
Cod. Oratorii B6	477,25
Beatus preface	5,29-30
Beatus commentary	7,2,1-4

Rev. 14:15

Bede	178,9-13
Beatus commentary	7,2,9

Rev. 14:18

Bede	178,13-15
Beatus commentary	7,2,13

Rev. 14:19

Caesarius A	249,11-15;17-19
Primasius	219,267-220,280
Bede	176,59-177,4;178,6-9
Beatus preface	5,31-32;38
Beatus commentary	7,2,14-20

Rev. 14:20

Jerome-Victorinus	135,10-137,2
Caesarius A	249,19-27
Primasius	220,280-284;291-294
Cod. Oratorii B6	477,25
Bede	177,15-18;178,3-6
Beatus commentary	7,2,21-22;35-37

Rev. 15:1

Jerome-Victorinus	137,4-8
Caesarius A	250,3-8
Bede	177,27-33
Beatus preface	5,33-34
Beatus commentary	7,3,1-3

Rev. 15:2

Caesarius A	250,8-11
Primasius	221,10;19-20
Pseudo-Jerome	18,18-19
Cod. Oratorii B6	477,26
Bede	177,34-36
Beatus preface	5,35-37
Beatus commentary	7,3,5;12

Rev. 15:3

Caesarius A	250,11-15
Primasius	222,33-34
Bede	177,44-45;49-53
Beatus commentary	7,3,15-16

Rev. 15:5-6

Caesarius A	250,15-23
Ambrosius Autpertus	589,10-17
Beatus preface	5,37
Beatus commentary	7,4,1-10

Rev. 15:7

Caesarius A	250,23-251,2
Primasius	223,70-74
Bede	178,40-43
Beatus preface	5,39-41
Beatus commentary	7,4,11-15

Rev. 15:8

Caesarius A	251,2-4
Bede	179,3-4
Beatus preface	5,42
Beatus commentary	7,4,15-19

Rev. 16:1

Primasius	225,1-6
Pseudo-Jerome	18,26-27
Bede	179,17-20
Beatus preface	5,43
Beatus commentary	8,1,1-2

Rev. 16:2

Caesarius A	251,4-9
Cod. Oratorii B6	477,27
Bede	181,55-182,1
Ambrosius Autpertus	602,99-103
Beatus preface	5,44
Beatus commentary	8,1,27-30

Rev. 16:3

Bede	181,53-55
Beatus commentary	8,2,1

Rev. 16:4-7 ?

Caesarius A	251,9-21
Primasius	231,146-148;228,83-86
Bede	181,50-53;179,53-180,1
Beatus preface	5,46-47
Beatus commentary	8,3,3-6;24;28

Rev. 16:8-9

Caesarius A	251,21-30
Primasius	229,107-111
Bede	180,19-25
Beatus commentary	8,4,1-4;6-8

Rev. 16:10

Caesarius A	251,30-252,4
Bede	180,35-37
Beatus commentary	8,5,1-3

Rev. 16:11

Caesarius A	252,4-5
Beatus commentary	8,5,5

Rev. 16:12

Caesarius A	252,5-10;13-14
Primasius	231,148-150
Cod. Oratorii B6	477,28
Bede	180,46-53

Beatus commentary	8,6,1-3

Rev. 16:13

Caesarius A	252,14-19
Primasius	232,164-168
Beatus preface	5,48-49;61
Beatus commentary	8,7,1-4

Rev. 16:14

Caesarius A	252,20-253,20
Primasius	232,170-234,211
Bede	181,1-5;13-22
Ambrosius Autpertus	620,35-39
Beatus preface	5,62
Beatus commentary	8,7,5-19

Rev. 16:15

Primasius	234,211-219
Beatus commentary	8,7,30-31

Rev. 16:16-17

Caesarius A	253,20-21
Primasius	234,219-227
Cod. Oratorii B6	477,29
Bede	181,48-50;182,1-2
Ambrosius Autpertus	625,5-8
Beatus preface	5,63
Beatus commentary	8,7,32-34;8,8,1-2

Rev. 16:19

Caesarius A	253,21-254,3
Primasius	235,233-239
Beatus preface	5,64-65
Beatus commentary	8,8,3-4

Rev. 16:20

Caesarius A	254,3-10
Primasius	236,253-254
Bede	182,18-22
Beatus preface	5,66-69
Beatus commentary	8,8,5-12

Rev. 16:21

Caesarius A	254,10-14
Primasius	236,266-268
Bede	182,29-40;180,42-43
Beatus preface	5,70-71
Beatus commentary	8,8,13-18

Rev. 17:3

Caesarius A	256,19-24 (cf. 254,24-255,1;256,1-10)
Caesarius B	254,14-23
Primasius	238,24-33
Pseudo-Jerome	19,14
Cod. Oratorii B6	477,30
Bede	183,3-5
Beatus preface	5,72-73
Beatus commentary	9,2,1-5

Rev. 17:4

Caesarius A	256,24-30
Caesarius B	257,22-29
Primasius	241,112-120
Bede	183,11-18
Beatus preface	5,77-78
Beatus commentary	9,2,6-7
Liber regularum	82,24-83,2

Rev. 17:5

Caesarius A	256,31-257,3
Caesarius B	258,1-3
Primasius	241,120-124
Beatus commentary	9,2,8-9

Rev. 17:6

Caesarius A	257,3-12
Caesarius B	258,3-8
Bede	183,26-31
Beatus commentary	9,2,10-13

Rev. 17:8

Caesarius A	257,12-21
Caesarius B	258,8-15
Primasius	242,136-137
Bede	183,37-43
Beatus commentary	9,2,19-21

Rev. 17:9

Primasius	243,164-167
Beatus commentary	9,2,45

Rev. 17:12

Caesarius A	258,24-28
Bede	184,27-29
Beatus commentary	9,2,82-83

Rev. 17:13

Caesarius A	258,28-259,2
Beatus commentary	9,2,85-87

Rev. 17:14

Caesarius A	259,2-10
Primasius	245,214-219
Cod. Oratorii B6	477,31
Bede	184,38-40
Beatus preface	5,79
Beatus commentary	9,3,1-2

Rev. 17:16

Caesarius A	259,10-22
Bede	184,48-52
Beatus commentary	9,3,3-6

Rev. 17:17

Caesarius A	259,22-27
Bede	185,1-6
Beatus commentary	9,3,7-9

Rev. 17:18

Caesarius A	259,27-30
Cod. Oratorii B6	477,32
Bede	185,11-15
Beatus commentary	9,3,10;19-20

Rev. 18:2

Caesarius A	259,30-260,9
Primasius	251,19-252,23
Bede	185,27-30
Beatus preface	5,82
Beatus commentary	10,1,2-4

Rev. 18:3

Caesarius A	260,19-27
Primasius	253,45-46
Bede	185,31-35
Beatus commentary	10,1,4-5

Rev. 18:4

Caesarius A	260,27-261,29
Caesarius B	267,27-32
Primasius	253,54-62
Beatus commentary	10,1,6-16
Liber regularum	50,10-12;63,3-64,6

Rev. 18:7

Caesarius A	261,29-262,8
Bede	185,42-44
Beatus commentary	10,1,17-19

Rev. 18:8

Caesarius A	262,8-20
Beatus commentary	10,1,20

Rev. 18:9

Caesarius A	262,20-27
Bede	186,8-11
Beatus commentary	10,1,21-22

Rev. 18:10

Caesarius A	262,27-263,6
Bede	186,12-19
Beatus commentary	10,1,23-24

Rev. 18:14

Bede	186,27-32
Beatus commentary	10,1,26

Rev. 18:16

Caesarius A	263,6-12
Bede	186,33-35;40-43

Beatus commentary	10,1,30

Rev. 18:18

Caesarius A	263,12-17
Bede	186,44-50
Beatus commentary	10,1,32-33

Rev. 18:20

Caesarius A	265,27-266,3
Beatus commentary	10,1,37-38

Rev. 18:21

Caesarius A	266,3-9
Caesarius B	267,33-268,2
Cod. Oratorii B6	447,33
Ambrosius Autpertus	700,17-701,29
Beatus preface	5,84
Beatus commentary	10,2,1

Rev. 18:22

Caesarius A	266,9-12
Beatus preface	5,83
Beatus commentary	10,2,2

Rev. 18:23

Caesarius A	266,12-14
Primasius	259,201-202
Bede	187,35-36
Beatus commentary	10,2,3

Rev. 18:24

Caesarius A	266,15-31
Caesarius B	268,2-8
Bede	187,37-46
Beatus commentary	10,2,4-10
<u>Liber regularum</u>	81,21-23;42,5-9

Rev. 19:3

Caesarius A	268,14-32
Caesarius B	271,23-29
Primasius	260,15-20
Bede	187,48-51;188,3-7
Beatus preface	5,84
Beatus commentary	10,3,1-2

Rev. 19:8

Caesarius A	268,32-269,7
Caesarius B	271,29-33
Bede	188,41-42
Ambrosius Autpertus	712,45;713,22-27
Beatus commentary	10,3,6-8

Rev. 19:10

Primasius	262,63-263,70
Bede	188,54-58;189,4-9
Ambrosius Autpertus	716,30-32
Beatus commentary	10,3,10;15-16

Rev. 19:11

Caesarius B	266,32-267,1
Primasius	263,86
Pseudo-Jerome	18,22
Beatus preface	5,85

Rev. 19:12

Caesarius A	264,9-14
Caesarius B	267,2-9
Primasius	264,94-96
Cod. Oratorii B6	477,34
Bede	189,30-31

Rev. 19:13

Caesarius A	264,14-15
Primasius	266,145-146
Bede	189,37-39
Ambrosius Autpertus	726,4-6

Rev. 19:14

Caesarius A	264,16-20
Primasius	267,166-167
Bede	189,56-57
Beatus commentary	11,1,5-6

Rev. 19:15

Caesarius A	264,20-26
Caesarius B	267,9-17
Pseudo-Jerome	19,24-25
Bede	190,8-10
Ambrosius Autpertus	728,18-729,26
Beatus commentary	11,1,7-9

Rev. 19:16

Caesarius A	264,26-265,6
Primasius	268,188;269,200-201
Bede	190,11-13;15-19;21-23
Beatus commentary	11,1,12

Rev. 19:17

Caesarius A	265,6-13
Primasius	269,202;206-208
Bede	190,29-30;34-36
Beatus commentary	11,2,1

Rev. 19:18

Caesarius A	265,13-17
Caesarius B	267,17-22
Beatus preface	5,86
Beatus commentary	11,2,2

Rev. 19:19

Caesarius A	263,18-21
Primasius	270,222-224
Ambrosius Autpertus	735,12-15
Beatus preface	5,87
Beatus commentary	11,3,1

Rev. 19:20

Primasius	270,226-229;233-235
Beatus preface	5,88-89
Beatus commentary	11,3,4-6;8

Rev. 19:21

Bede	191,7-9
Beatus preface	5,91
Beatus commentary	11,3,12

Rev. 20:1

Caesarius A	263,21-25
Primasius	271,4-5
Cod. Oratorii B6	477,35
Bede	191,12
Beatus preface	5,91-92
Beatus commentary	11,4,1;4

Rev. 20:2

Caesarius A	263,25-264,2
Beatus preface	5,93
Beatus commentary	11,4,5-6

Rev. 20:3

Caesarius A	265,18-27
Caesarius B	267,22-26
Bede	191,29-31
Beatus preface	5,94
Beatus commentary	11,4,8-9;11;18

Rev. 20:4

Caesarius A	269,8-14
Caesarius B	271,33-272,3
Bede	191,54-192,2
Beatus preface	5,95-96
Beatus commentary	11,5,1;12-14

Rev. 20:5

Caesarius A	269,14-20
Caesarius B	272,3-6
Bede	192,26-33
Beatus commentary	11,5,14-15

Rev. 20:6

Caesarius A	269,20-29
Caesarius B	272,6-12
Bede	192,34-35;44-48
Beatus preface	5,97
Beatus commentary	11,5,15-19
Gennadius, <u>De viris inlustribus,</u> 18	68,18-69,22

Rev. 20:7

Caesarius A	269,29-270,5
Caesarius B	272,12-15
Cassiodore	1415,36-43
Bede	192,49-55
Beatus commentary	11,6,1-2

Rev. 20:8

Caesarius A	270,5-12
Caesarius B	272,15-19
Primasius	279,178-185
Bede	192,60-193,6
Beatus preface	5,98-99
Beatus commentary	11,6,11;14-16

Rev. 20:9

Caesarius A	270,12-16
Caesarius B	272,19-23
Bede	193,19-21
Beatus commentary	11,7,1-3

Rev. 20:10

Caesarius A	270,16-21
Beatus commentary	11,7,5

Rev. 20:12

Caesarius A	270,21-30
Caesarius B	272,23-27
Cod. Oratorii B6	477,36
Bede	193,46-55
Beatus preface	5,104-105
Beatus commentary	12,1,4-7

Rev. 20:13

Caesarius A	270,30-271,2
Caesarius B	272,27-31
Bede	194,11-14
Beatus preface	5,105
Beatus commentary	12,1,11-12

Rev. 20:14

Caesarius A	271,2-3
Caesarius B	272,31-35
Bede	194,16-17

Rev. 20:15

Caesarius A	271,3-5
Bede	194,23-24
Beatus preface	5,106

Rev. 21:4

Caesarius A	271,14-15
Cod. Oratorii B6	477,37
Beatus commentary	12,2,1

Rev. 21:6

Caesarius A	271,18
Caesarius B	272,36
Beatus commentary	12,2,11

Rev. 21:9

Ambrosius Autpertus	794,71-73
Beatus commentary	12,2,22

Rev. 21:10

Caesarius A	273,6-15
Caesarius B	276,19-24
Beatus commentary	12,2,24;28-30

Rev. 21:11

Caesarius A	273,16-17
Caesarius B	276,25-26
Bede	195,59-196,1
Beatus commentary	12,2,31

Rev. 21:12

Caesarius A	273,17-22
Caesarius B	276,26-28
Beatus commentary	12,2,42;46

Rev. 21:13

Caesarius A	273,22-26
Caesarius B	276,29-277,1
Bede	196,23-28
Beatus commentary	12,2,49-50

Rev. 21:14

Caesarius A	273,26-29
Bede	196,29-30

Rev. 21:15

Caesarius A	273,29-274,2
Caesarius B	277,1-3
Beatus commentary	12,2,53

Rev. 21:18

Caesarius B	274,3-7
Bede	197,21-26

Rev. 21:21

Caesarius A	274,16-21
Caesarius B	277,7-9
Ambrosius Autpertus	824,11-16

Rev. 21:22

Caesarius A	274,21-23
Caesarius B	277,10-12
Ambrosius Autpertus	826,15-20

Rev. 21:23

Caesarius A	274,23-275,3
Caesarius B	277,12-15
Bede	203,39-41

Rev. 22:5

Caesarius A	275,24-25
Caesarius B	277,21-23
Cod. Oratorii B6	477,38
Beatus commentary	12,3,15

Rev. 22:11 (cf. Rev. 10:4)

Caesarius A	275,29-30
Beatus commentary	12,5,12

Rev. 22:14

Caesarius A	276,5-7
Beatus commentary	12,5,22

Rev. 22:17

Caesarius A	276,11-12
Primasius	309,248
Bede	206,23-24
Beatus commentary	12,5,29
Liber regularum	3,27-29;71,25-27

Rev. 22:20

Caesarius A	276,18-20
Bede	206,34-36
Beatus commentary	12,5,33-34

Notes

A. The problem

1 Later authors, who had only second hand knowledge of Tyconius' commentary, will not be treated in this work; for a history of the later Tyconian tradition see W. Kamlah, Apokalypse und Geschichtstheologie: Die mittelalterliche Auslegung der Apokalypse vor Joachim von Fiore, HS 235 (Berlin: Emil Ebering, 1935).

2 Victorini epsicopi Petavionensis opera, CSEL 49, ed. J. Haußleiter, pp. 14-154.

3 PL 35, 2417-2452; Sancti Caesarii episcopi Arelatensis opera omnia, vol. 2, ed. G. Morin (Maredsous: n.p., 1942), pp. 209-277.

4 PL 68, 793-936; PLS 4, 1207-1220; Commentarius in Apocalypsin, CChr.SL 92, ed. A. W. Adams.

5 PL 70, 1381-1418.

6 Ein Traktat zur Apokalypse des Ap. Johannes in einer Pergamenthandschrift der K. Bibliothek in Bamberg, ed. K. Hartung (Bamberg: n.p., 1904); Incerti Auctoris Commentarius in Apocalypsin, ed. G. Lo Menzo Rapisarda (Catania: Centro di studi sull'antico Cristianesimo, 1967); rpt. from MSLCA, 16 (1966), page reference not available; PLS 4, 1850-1863.

7 The capitulary has been published in Giuseppe Maria Tommasi (Josephus Maria Thomasius), _Opera omnia; ad mss. codices recensuit notisque auxit Antonius Franciscus Vezzosi,_ vol. 1 (Rome: Typographia Palladis, 1747), pp. 475-479.

8 PL 93, 129-206.

9 _Ambrosii Autperti Opera,_ 2 vols., CChr.CM 27-27A, ed. R. Weber.

10 _Sancti Beati presbyteri Hispani Liebanensis in Apocalypsin ac plurimos in utriusque foederis paginas Commentaria, ex veteribus, nonnullisque desideratis patribus mille retro annis collecta, nunc primum edita,_ ed. H. Florez (Madrid: Joachim Ibarra, 1770); _Beati in Apocalypsin libri duodecim,_ PMAAR 7, ed. H. A. Sanders (Rome: American Academy in Rome, 1930).

11 _Tyconii Afri Fragmenta Commentarii in Apocalypsim,_ Spicilegium casinense 3,1 (Montecassino: Typis archicoenobii Montis Casini, 1897), pp. 261-331.; _The Turin Fragments of Tyconius' Commentary on Revelation,_ TaS NS 7, ed. F. Lo Bue (Cambridge: Cambridge University Press, 1963).

12 L. Mezey, "Egy korai Karoling kódextöredek (Ticonius in Apocalypsin?)," _Magyar Könyvszemle,_ 92 (1976), 15-24.

13 P. Lehmann, _Mittelalterliche Bibliothekskataloge_

Deutschlands und der Schweiz, vol. 1, Mittelalterliche Bibliothekskataloge 1 (Munich: C. H. Beck, 1918), p. 71 mentions Saint Gall 728 and Saint Gall 267 as the original catalogue and copy respectively and cites the significant listing on p. 77: Expositio Tichonii Donatistae in apocalypsim, volumen I vetus. Although I have found no further evidence to indicate the existence of other manuscripts of Tyconius' Apocalypse Commentary, this does not necessarily exclude the possibility that a complete manuscript or another fragment may some day be discovered. An extensive manuscript list of medieval Apocalypse commentaries appears in RBMA 10, pp. 78-88.

B. History of the research

14 "Die Kommentare des Victorinus, Tichonius und Hieronymous zur Apocalypse," ZKWL, 7 (1886), 239-257.

15 Die Offenbarung Johannis, KEK 16 (Göttingen: Vandenhoeck & Ruprecht, 1906; rpt. 1966), pp. 56-63.

16 Bousset, p. 56, n. 5.

17 Bousset, p. 57.

18 Tyconius-Studien: Eine Beitrag zur Kirchen- und Dogmengeschichte des 4. Jahrhundrets, SGTK 6,2 (Leipzig: n.p., 1900; rpt. Aalen: Scientia Verlag, 1971).

19 Hahn, p. 9.

20 Hahn, pp. 14-15.

21 Hahn, p. 10-11.

22 Hahn, p. 11.

23 Hahn, p. 13.

24 Hahn, pp. 14-15.

25 Hahn, p. 18.

26 See below, pp. 141-211.

27 For example see Hahn, p. 35, n. 1.

28 De organisatie van de Christelike Kerk van Noord-Afrika in het licht van de brieven van Augustinus (Groningen: J. B. Wolters, 1927), p. 112, n. 1.

29 H. L. Ramsay, "Le commentaire de l'Apocalypse par Beatus de Liébana," RHLR, 7 (1902), 424-425.

30 See below, p. 171.

31 "Warum wurde Tyconius nicht katholisch?," ZNW, 57 (1966), 260-283.

32 See below, pp. 144-148.

33 "Fuentes literarias de Beato de Liébana," Actas del simposio para el estudio de los codices del "Commentario al Apocalipsis" de Beato de Liébana, vol. 1, (Madrid: Joyas Bibliográfias, 1978), pp. 117-162.

34 Untersuchungen zur Geschichte der lateinischen

<u>Apokalypse-übersetzung</u> (Dusseldorf: L. Schwann, 1920).

35 Vogels, p. 71.

36 Vogels, p. 58.

37 Vogels, p. 63.

38 Vogels, p. 65.

39 Vogels, pp. 66-70.

40 Vogels, p. 91.

41 Vogels, pp. 177-208.

42 <u>Histoire littéraire de l'Afrique chrétienne depuis les origines jusqu'à l'invasion arabe,</u> vol. 5 (Paris: n.p., 1920; rpt. Bruxelles: Culture et Civilisation, 1966), pp. 165-219.

43 Sanders, pp. xi-xxiii.

44 <u>Die Apokalypse des hl. Johannes in der altspanischen und altchristlichen Bibel-Illustration: Das Problem der Beatus-Handschriften,</u> vol. 1, SFGG 2,2-3, (Münster: Aschendorff, 1931).

45 See below, pp. 161-165.

46 "Le commentaire de l'Apocalypse par Beatus de Liébana," RHLR, 7 (1902), 419-447.

47 "The Manuscripts of the Commentary of Beatus of Liébana," Revue des bibliothèques, 12 (1902), 74-103.

48 Ramsay, "Le commentaire," pp. 424-425.

49 Ramsay, "Le commentaire," p. 427.

50 Apringius of Béja plays a secondary role in the reconstruction of Tyconius' commentary. Since he was a major source of Beatus, I will treat his commentary when I investigate Beatus in detail. See below, pp. 153-157.

51 Ramsay, "Le commentaire," p. 436.

52 Ramsay, "Le commentaire," p. 443.

53 "Da Ticonio a sant'Agostino," RicRel, 1 (1925), 443-446.

54 Pincherle, pp. 451-52.

55 Monceaux, p 200.

56 Vogels, p. 63.

57 See below, pp. 31-32.

58 CSEL 49, p. 160.

59 Bousset, p. 57.

60 Pincherle, p. 252, n. 1.

61 Pincherle, pp. 453-456.

62 Pinchele, p. 457.

63 See above, pp. 9-11.

64 See below, pp. 208-211.

65 "Los commentarios de Beato al Apocalypsis y Elipando," Miscellanea Giovanni Mercati, vol. 2, StT 122 (Vatican City: Biblioteca Apostolica Vaticana, 1946) pp. 16-33.

66 PL 96, 859-1030; CChr.CM 59, ed. B. Löfstedt.

67 See below, pp. 146-148.

68 Lo Bue, p. 20.

69 Lo Bue, p. 23.

70 Lo Bue, pp. 24-27.

71 Lo Bue, pp. 29-38.

72 The Book of Rules of Tyconius, TaS 3,1, ed. F. C. Burkitt (Cambridge: Cambridge University Press, 1894; rpt. Nendeln: Kraus Reprint Limited, 1967). This is the only work of Tyconius which has been passed down intact.

73 "El perdido comentario de Ticonio al Apocalipsis: Principos de critica literaria y textual para su reconstruccion," Miscellanea biblica B. Ubach, SDM 1 (Montserrat: n.p., 1953), pp. 387-411.

74 De viris inlustribus 18 (ed. C. A. Bernoulli, SQS 11, 68-69).

75 De doctrina christiana 3,30,42 (ed. Joseph Martin, CChr.SL 32, 102-103).

76 Monceaux, Histoire, vol. 5, p. 201.

77 Apringii Pacensis Episcopi Tractatus in Apocalysin [sic], SEHL 10-11 (Escurial: Typis Augustinianis Monasterii Escurialensis,

1941), p. xi.

78 See above, n. 2.

79 "Drei Editiones principes des Apocalypsekommentars des Primasius," ThLBl, 25 (1904), 1-4.

80 "Le commentaire homilétique de s. Césaire sur Apocalypse," RBen, 45 (1933), 43-61.

81 See above, n. 3.

82 Saint Bede in the Tradition of Western Apocalyptic Commentary, JarL 1966 (Newcastle upon Tyne: n.p., 1966).

83 Die lateinischen Apokalypse der alten afrikanischen Kirche, FGNK 4 (Erlangen: Andr. Deichert [G. Bohme], 1891), pp. 195-196.

84 See below, pp. 91-92.

85 "Le fonti del commento di Ambrogio Autperto sull'Apocalipisse," Miscellanea biblica et orientalia Athanasio Miller, StAns 27-28 (Rome: Herder, 1951), pp. 372-403.

86 "Bermerkungen zum pseudo-hieronymischen Commemoratorium in Apocalypsin, " FZPhTh, 26 (1979), 220-242.

87 See above, n. 12.

C. Toward a solution

88 Lo Bue, p. xiv.

89 Gómez, pp. 388-389.

90 See below, pp. 258-262.

91 Vogels, pp. 63-64.

92 Hahn, pp. 11-12.

93 See below, pp. 123-124.

94 Alvarez Campos, pp. 135-162.

95 "Ticonio y el sermon 'in natali sanctorum innocentium' (Exegesis de Mt. 2)," Gr., 60 (1979), 513-544.

96 See below, p. 239.

97 See above, p. 13.

98 Cf. Vogels, p. 75 and Lo Bue, p. 31.

99 Vogels, pp. 177-208.

(Chapter II, pp. 28-196)

A. Victorinus and Jerome-Victorinus

1 O. Bardenhewer, Geschichte der altkirchlichen Literatur, vol. 2 (Freiburg: Herder, 1914), p. 658; a contrary opinion is held by J. Quasten, Patrology, vol. 2 (Utrecht: Spectrum, 1964), p. 411.

2 De viris inlustribus 74 (ed. Bernoulli, SQS 11, 42,1-7).

3 Translatio homiliarum Origenis in Lucam, praefatio (PL 26, 220,21); Commentariorum in Mattheum libri quattuor, prologus (ed. D. Hurst and M. Adriaen, CChr.SL 77, 5,96); cf. Haußleiter, CSEL 49, pp. xxi-xxii.

4 J. Haußleiter, "Victorinus," RE 20, p. 616; Bardenhewer, vol. 2, p. 660.

5 A. Harnack, Geschichte der altchristlichen Literatur bis Eusebius, vol. 2 (Leipzig: J. C. Hinrichs, 1893), p. 733.

6 G. Mercati,"Anonymi chiliastae in Matthaeum fragmenta" Varia sacra, vol. 1, StT 11 (Rome: Tipografia Vaticana, 1903), p. 9.

7 A. Wilmart, "Un anonyme ancien 'De X virginibus'," BALAC, 1 (1911), 102.

8 J. Wöhrer, "Eine kleine Schrift die vielleicht dem hl. Martyrbischof Victorinus von Pettau angehort," Jahresbericht des

Privatgymnasiums der Zisterzienser in Wilhering, (1927), 3-8; "'Victorini epsicopi Petauionensis (?) ad Iustinum Manichaeum':1-8," Jahresbericht des Privatgymnasiums der Zisterzienser in Wilhering, (1928), 3-7.

9 Epistola, 61,2 (ed. I. Hilberg, CSEL 54, 577,18-573,3); cf. Bardenhewer, vol. 2, p. 658.

10 Institutiones, 1,7,1 (ed. R. A. B. Mynors, 28,6).

11 E. von Dobschütz, Das Decretum Gelasianum de libris recipiendis et non recipiendis in kritischem Text herausgegeben und untersucht, TU 38,4 (Leipzig: J. C. Hinrichs, 1912), p. 56.; cf. Haußleiter, CSEL 49, p. xxvii; Bardenhewer, vol. 2, p. 659.

12 CSEL 49; cf. J. Haußleiter, "Der chiliastische Schlussabschnitt im echten Apocalypsekommentar des Bischofs Victorinus von Pettau," ThLBl, 16 (1895), 193-199; J. R. Harris, "A new patristic Fragment," Exp., (1895), 448-455.

13 G. Grützmacher, Hieronymus: Eine biographische Studie zur alten Kirchengeschichte, vol. 3, SGTK 10,2 (Berlin: n.p., 1906; rpt. Aalen: Scientia Verlag, 1969), pp. 221-222.

14 Grützmacher, vol. 3, pp. 235-240.

15 For a detail description of the extent of Jerome's

revisions see Haußleiter, CSEL 49, pp. xxxvi-xlv.

16 Institutiones, 1,9,2 (ed. Mynors, 33,9-10); cf. Bardenhewer, vol. 2, p. 659.

17 E. B. Allo, Saint Jean: l'Apocalypse, (Paris: J. Gabalda, 1921), p. ccxxi; Bousset, Offenbarung, p. 54.

18 Liber regularum 6 (ed. Burkitt, TaS 3,1, 66-70).

19 Allo, p. ccxxi; my own study of the subject is scheduled to be published in AugSt under the title "Recapitulatio in Tyconius and Augustine."

20 See L. Atzberger, Geschichte der christlichen Eschatologie innerhalb der vornicanischen Zeit (Freiburg: Herder, 1896), pp. 566-573; F. Loofs, Theolphilus von Antiochen: Adversus Marcionem und die anderen theologischen Quellen bei Irenaeus, TU 46,2 (Leipzig: J. C. Hinrichs, 1930), pp. 126-131; J. Fischer, "Die Einheit der beiden Testamente bei Laktanz, Victorin von Pettau und deren Quellen," MThZ, 1 (1950), 97-99.

21 CSEL 49,62, 6-11.

22 CSEL 49,80,2-3; 98,11.

23 CSEL 49,118,1-120,6.

24 CSEL 49,114,3-15.

25 CSEL 49,66,10; 152,4-154,18.

26 G. Bardy, "Victorin de Pettau," DThC 15, p. 2886; W. Machholz, <u>Spuren binitarischer Denkeweise im Abendland seit Tertullian,</u> Diss. Halle 1902 (Jena: Ant. Kampfe, 1902), pp. 16-20; Loofs, pp. 126-129.

27 CSEL 49,106,10-12.

28 CSEL 49,18,3-14.

29 CSEL 49,104,17-106,6.

30 CSEL 49,60,3-62,5.

31 G. Morin, <u>"Hieronymus de monogrammate:</u> Un nouvel inédit hiéronymien sur le chiffre de la bête dans l'Apocalypse," RBen, 20 (1903), 225-236.

32 CSEL 49,145,10.

33 Grützmacher vol. 3, pp. 235-240.

34 CSEL 49, p. 160.

35 Bousset, p. 57.

36 A. Pincherle, "Da Ticonio a sant'Agostino," RicRel, 1 (1925), 452-453.

37 CSEL 49, 139-145; cf. index on p. 158.

38 Beatus 4,1,10-14; Caesarius 226,9-15; 225,4-8; Primasius 836, 50-58; Bede 147, 2-23.

39 Caesarius 250,7; Beatus 7,3,3.

40 Expositionis in Apocalypsin libri, praefatio (ed. Weber, CChr.CM 27, 5,8-13).

41 Bonner, Saint Bede, p. 3.

B. Caesarius

42 For comprehensive biographical information see A. Malnory, _Saint Césaire évêque d'Arles 503-543_, BEHE.H 103 (Paris: Emile Bouillon, 1894) and C. F. Arnold, _Caesarius von Arelate und die gallische Kirche seiner Zeit_ (Leipzig: J. C. Hinrichs, 1894; rpt. Leipzig: Zentralantiquariat der deutschen democratischen Republik, 1972).

43 G. Morin, ed. _Sancti Caesarii episcopi Arelatensis opera omnia nunc primum in unum collecta,_ vol. 1 (Maredsous: n.p., 1937); rpt. CCh 103-104. Although Morin offers the best comprehensive edition, for references to some newly discovered and edited individual sermons see B. Altaner and A. Stuiber, _Patrologie: Leben, Schriften und Lehre der Kirchenväter_ (Freiburg: Herder,1978), pp. 476; 654.

44 For aspects of the literary history and for bibliography see Bardenhewer, vol. 5, pp. 345-356; M. Schanz and C. Hosius, _Geschichte der römischen Literatur bis zum Gesetzgebungswerk des Kaisers Justinian,_ HAW 8,4,2 (Munich: C. H. Beck, 1920; rpt. 1921), pars. 1227-1229; E. Dekkers, _Clavis patrum latinorum,_ SE 3 (Brugge: C. Beyaert; The Hague: M. Nijhoff, 1961), pars. 1008-1017; Altaner-Stuiber, pp. 475-476; 654.

45 G. Morin, ed. _Sancti Caesarii episcopi Arelatensis opera omnia nunc primum in unum collecta,_ vol. 2 (Maredsous: n.p., 1942), pp. 209-277; PL 39, 1735-2354.

46 Cf. Morin, "Le commentaire," 43-61.

47 Bardenhewer, vol. 4, pp. 597-598.

48 _De viris inlustribus_ 97 (ed. Bernoulli, SQS 11,95).

49 Morin, "Le commentaire," 51-53.

50 G. Langgärtner, "Der Apokalypse-Kommentar des Caesarius von Arles," ThGl, 57 (1967), 221-222.

51 _Sicut videmus modo hereticos esse in hoc saeculo potentes, qui habent virtutem diaboli; sicut quondam pagani, ita nunc illi vastant ecclesiam_ (245,7-9).

52 _Utique habent potestatem heretici, sed praecipue Arriani_ (245, 19-20).

53 _Potest hoc loco dies magnus intellegi illa desolatio, quando a Tito et Vespasiano obsessa est Hierusolima, ubi exceptis his qui in captivitatem ducti sunt, undecies centena milia mortua referuntur_ (255,17-20).

54 Arnold, p. 198; K. D. Schmidt, _Die Bekehrung der Ostgermanen zum Christentum: Der ostgermanische Arianismus,_ Die Bekehrung der Germanen zum Christentum 1 (Göttingen: Vandenhoeck &

Ruprecht, 1939), p. 263.

55 Arnold, pp. 240-259.

56 Sermo 127 (ed. Morin 1,1,501-504).

57 Arnold, pp.390-392; Schmidt, pp. 344-348; E. Ewig, "Die Missionsarbeit der lateinischen Kirche," HKG(J), vol. 2,2 (Freiburg: Herder, 1975), pp. 138-140.

58 Arnold, p. 393.

59 Vogels, Untersuchungen, p. 59.

60 E.g., 212,14-15; 212,23-24; 221,9-12.

61 Cf. 220,27.

62 Cf. 244,18.

63 Cf. A. D'Alés, "Impedimenta mundi fecerunt eos miseros chez saint Cesaire d'Arles," RSR, 28 (1938), 290-298.

64 Cf. 228,4; 238,16.

65 E.g., 217,13; 235,13-15.

66 Cf. 248,23-24.

67 Vogels, Untersuchungen, pp. 61-62; I have adopted Vogels' identification of the recensions as A or B.

68 Vogels, Untersuchungen, pp. 62-63.

69 Cf. 211,4-7; 213,19-20; 226,25-26, which are to be found in Victorinus' commentary at 18,9-11; 18,6; 68,6-7 respectively.

70 E.g., 218,27-219,1 and 221,13-15, identified by Vogels with Victorinus at 42,6-11 and 58,9-14, show a far greater similarity to Primasius 812,17-27 and 820,2-7 respectively. The clearest example is 238,13-25, once again identified by Vogels as Victorinian, which is almost a word for word quotation of the Turin Fragment 319.

71 The following articles have proven helpful in determining stylistic characteristics: G. Morin, "Quelques raretes philologiques dans les ecrits de Cesaire d'Arles," ALMA, 11 (1937), 5-14; A. D'Alés, "Les 'sermones' de saint Cesaire d'Arles," RSR, 28 (1938), 315-384; G. Bardy, "La predication de saint Cesaire d'Arles," RHEF, 29 (1943), 201-236; A. Vaccari, "Volgarismi notevoli nel latino di s. Cesario di Arles (+543)," ALMA, 17 (1943), 135-148; I. Bonini, "Lo stile nei sermoni di Cesario di Arles," Aevum, 36 (1962), 240-257; A. Salvatore, "Uso delle similitudini e pedagogia pastorale nei Sermones di Cesario di Arles," RCCM, 9 (1967), 177-225; C. A. Rapisarda, "Lo stile umile nei sermoni di s. Cesario d'Arles: Giustificazione teoriche e

C. Primasius

73 The little information which does exist has been meticulously examined by Haußleiter, Die lateinische Apokalypse, pp. 1-8.

74 H. G. Beck, "Die Frühbyzantinische Kirche," HKG(J), vol. 2,2 (Freiburg: Herder, 1975), pp. 30-37.

75 Victor of Tunnuna, Chronica (ed. T. Mommsen, MGH.AA 11,202,20-22).

76 Hardouin 3, collatio p. 69; Mansi 9,199,39-40.

77 Victor of Tunnuna, Chronica (ed. Mommsen, MGH.AA 11,203,1-7).

78 Bardenhewer, vol. 5, p. 332; Altaner-Stuiber, p. 491.

79 Haußleiter, Die lateinische Apokalypse, p. 8.

80 Die lateinische Apokalypse, pp. 20-23.

81 Institutiones 1,9,4 (ed. R. A. B. Mynors 33,21-27).

82 De viris illustribus 9 (ed. C. Codoñer Merino 139).

posizioni polemiche," Orph., (1970), 115-159.

72 Vogels, Untersuchungen, p. 62.

83 _Commentaria in epistolas sancti Pauli_ (PL 68,415-794).

84 Haußleiter, _Die lateinische Apokalypse,_ pp. 24-35; H. Zimmer, _Pelagius in Irland: Texte und Untersuchungen zur patristischen Literatur_ (Berlin: Weidmann, 1901), pp. 121-137.

85 Haußleiter, _Die lateinische Apokalypse,_ pp. 35-57. I have discovered that Madrid, Acad. Hist. Cortes 12.11.1:3 f. 147, which was erroneously believed to be a Primasius fragment, actually comes from a sermon of Smaragdus and should be stricken from any list of Primasius manuscripts; cf. PLS 4, 1220-1221.

86 _Die lateinische Apokalypse_ , pp. 57-58.

87 Haußleiter, _Die lateinische Apokalypse,_ pp. 35-57; Haußleiter, "Drei editiones principes," 1-4.

88 PL 68, 794-936.

89 PLS 4, 1211-1220.

90 Haußleiter, _Die lateinische Apokalypse_ , pp. 79-175.

91 Vogels, _Untersuchungen,_ pp. 19-36; 153-164.

92 CChr.SL 92.

93 Institutiones 1,9,4 (ed. Mynors 33,22-25): nostris quoque temporibus Apocalypsis praedicta beati episcopi Primasii, antistitis Africani, studio minute ac diligenter quinque libris exposita est.

94 CChr.SL 92, 179,18-20.

95 Bardenhewer, vol. 4, 79-82.

96 Haußleiter, Die lateinische Apokalypse, p. 12, n. 10.

97 CChr.SL 92, 1-4.

98 Epistola 58 (ed. I. Hilberg, CSEL 54, 463,9-11).

99 For example see the anonymous, Commemoratorium in Apocalypsin (ed. Hartung 1,11-13) or Walafried Strabo, Apocalypsis b. Joannis (PL 114,709-710).

100 CChr.SL 92, 312-316.

101 Haußleiter, Die lateinische Apokalypse, pp. 179-183.

102 CChr.SL 92, 312-316.

103 CChr.SL 92, 5,1-7,36.

104 CChr.SL 92, 59,1-61,30.

105 D. de Bruyne, Préfaces de le Bible latine (Namur: Godenne, 1920).

106 CChr.SL 92, 59,1-61,30.

107 Haußleiter, Die lateinische Apokalypse, pp. 193-196.

108 CChr.SL 92, 271,1-284,5; CChr.SL 92, 249,27-46; Augustine, De civitate Dei 20, 7-17 (eds. B. Dombert and A. Kalb, CChr.SL 48, 708-729.

109 Haußleiter, Die lateinische Apokalypse, pp. 184-194 numbered the capitula consecutively from one to 96, omitting the first two headings which refer to Primasius' introduction of Book I.

110 CChr.SL 92, 133,15;134,3;248,5.

111 Cf. CChr.SL 92, p. 365; CSEL 49, p. 160.

112 CChr.SL 92, pp. 353, 363.

113 CChr.SL 92, 1,7-2,36.

114 CChr.SL 92, 155,246

115 Sometimes Primasius writes alia editio or simply alia contrasting it with haec translatio. Twice he used the adverbial expression alibi . However, alibi should not always be interpreted as referring to an alternate biblical text. For example, at Rev. 20:3 Primasius writes: hinc alibi legimus: Qui clausisti abyssum et signasti super eum (CChr.SL 92, 272,13-14). What we read is similar to the biblical text with the third person singular being changed to the second person singular. Since there are no witnesses to any alternate reading in the Apocalypse text, one suspects here not another translation but a liturgical usage.

116 Since the lists of both Haußleiter, Die lateinische Apokalypse, p. xiii and Vogels, Untersuchungen, p. 68 are incomplete, I include a complete listing here.

117 Haußleiter, Die lateinische Apokalypse, pp. xiii; 77.

118 Vogels, Untersuchungen, p. 68.

119 Vogels, Untersuchungen, pp. 68-69.

120 CChr.SL 92, 61,1-82,484.

121 Haußleiter, Die lateinische Apokalypse, pp. 18-19.

122 CChr.CM 27, 230-256.

123 The unusual inversion of words in the quotation from Micah 6:8 is present in both Primasius (CChr.SL 92, 62,37) and Autpertus (CChr.CM 27, 232,42): diligere iudicium et facere misericordiam.

124 CChr.SL 92, 67,133-134; CChr.CM 27, 236,163-183.

125 Liber regularum 3 (ed. Burkitt, TaS 3,1, 13,13-18).

126 Tractatus in Apocalypsim (ed. J. Férotin, PLS 4, 1247,6-13)

127 Contra Judaeos (PL 83,449-450).

128 Beatus 2,4,96.

129 CChr.CM 27, 254,848-877.

130 De septem sigillis , Wolfenbüttel, Herzogliche Bibliothek, Weissenburg 68, ff. 191v-192v, s. x.

131 See below, pp. 137-139.

132 De viris inlustribus 18 (ed. Bernoulli, SQS 11, 68,4).

133 Monceaux, Histoire, vol. 5, pp. 171-178.

134 Liber regularum 3 (ed. Burkitt, TaS 3,1, 28,17-18); trans. D. Anderson, The Book of Rules of Tyconius: An Introduction and Translation with Commentary, Diss. Southern Baptist Theological Seminary, Louisville, 1974 (Ann Arbor: University Microfilms, 1974), p. 89,1-2.

135 Matt. 13:24-30; 36-43.

136 For example, Breviculus collationis cum Donatistis , collatio tertii diei, 9,15 (ed. M. Petschenig, CSEL 53, 64-65); for additional references see Y. M. J. Congar, "Introduction générale," Traités Anti-Donatistes 1, Oeuvres de Saint Augustin 28 (Paris: Desclée de Brouwer, 1963), p. 85, n. 3.

137 Contra epistulam Parmeniani 1,1,1 (ed. M. Petschenig, CSEL 51, 19-20).

138 Liber regularum 2 (ed. Burkitt; TaS 3,1, 8-11).

139 Liber regularum 3 (ed. Burkitt; TaS 2,1, 29,29).

D. Cassiodore

140 There are several good introductions to Cassiodore: Bardenhewer, vol. 5, 264-277; M. Cappuyns, "Cassiodore," DHGE 11, 1349-1408; P. Courcelle, Les lettres grecques en occident de Macrobe à Cassiodore, BAFAR 159 (Paris: E. de Boccard, 1948), pp. 313-341; A. Momigliano, "Cassiodorus and Italian Culture of his Time," PBA, 41 (1955), 207-245; A. Franz, M. Aurelius Cassiodorius [sic] Senator: Ein Beitrag zur Geschichte der theologischen Literatur (Breslau: G. P. Aderholz 1872); J. J. van den Besselaar, Cassiodorus Senator: Leven en Werken van een Staatsman en Monnik uit de zesde Eeuw (Haarlem: J. H. Gottmer, 1950); A. van de Vyver, "Cassiodore et son oeuvre," Spec. 6 (1931), 244-292; H. J. Vogt, "Ausklang der altchristlichen lateinischen Literatur," HKG(J), vol. 2,2 (Freiburg: Herder, 1975), pp. 309-310, 313-317.

141 A. Franz, p. 5; for a thorough discussion of the problem concerning the dates of Cassiodore's birth and death see pp. 3-6; 11-13.

142 Bardenhewer, vol. 5, p. 265 estimates Cassiodore's life span to be approximately from 485 to 580; Altaner-Stuiber, p. 486, gives the same dates; Schanz-Hosius, par. 1044 follows T. Mommsen, Cassiodori senatoris variae, MGH.AA 12 (Berlin: Weidmann, 1894), pp. x-xi, who judges Cassiodore to have lived from 490 to 583.

143 De Orthographia, praefatio (ed. H. Keil, 144,13-14).

144 K. S. Frank, Frühes Mönchtum im Abendland, vol. 1 (Zurich: Artemis Verlag, 1975), p. 198.

145 PL 70, 1319-1418. This title is to be prefered to Complexiones in epistolas apostolorum et acta apostolorum et apocalypsin; cf. Th. Stangl, "Cassiodoriana," Blätter für das Gymnasial-Schulwesen, 34 (1898), 249, n.1.

146 De Orthographia, praefatio (ed. Kiel, 144,13-14).

147 Stangl, "Cassiodoriana," 250.

148 RBMA par. 1918.

149 Stangl, "Cassiodoriana," 250-253.

150 Reifferscheid, "Biblioteca patrum latinorum Italica," SAWW.PH, 49 (1865), 48-52.

151 Stangl, "Cassiodoriana," 249-283; 545-591; Th. Stangl, "Zu Cassiodorius [sic] Senator," SAWW.PH, 114 (1887), 405-413; Th. Stangl, "Cassiodoriana II," Wochenschrift für Klassiche Philologie, 32 (1915), 203-214; 228-240.

152 Expositio Psalmorum, praefatio, 14 (ed. M. Adriaen,

CChr.SL 98,17); Franz, p. 102; Stangl, "Cassiodoriana," 249; Schanz-Hosius, par. 1050.

153 _De Orthographia,_ praefatio (ed. Kiel, 144, 5).

154 _Complexiones in epistolis apostolorum,_ praefatio (PL 70,1321,9-1322,3).

155 Cf. S. Prete, _Il "Commonitorium" nella letteratura cristiana antica,_ Studi e ricerche NS 6 (Bologna: Nicola Zanichelli, 1962).

156 Steinhauser, "Bemerkungen," 223-225

157 _Complexiones in epistolis apostolorum,_ praefatio (PL 70,1321,3-5).

158 _Complexiones actuum apostolorum et apocalypsis Ioannis,_ prologus (PL 70, 1381,19-1382,7).

159 _Institutiones,_ 1,1,8 (ed. Mynors, 14,16-15,6).

160 Stangl, "Cassiodoriana," 562, corrects Minge by adding _nobis_ at this point in the text.

161 Stangl, "Cassiodoriana," 563.

162 Primasius, CChr.SL 92, 175,225; cf. Beatus 5,13,17; Turin Fragment 421.

163 Vogels, Untersuchungen, p. 221.

164 Caesarius 234,8; Beatus praefatio,4,40; 5,T.9,11; 5,7,18.

165 Primasius, CChr.SL 92, 151,178.

166 The word is present in the codex demidovianus; cf. H. Rönsch, Itala und Vulgata: Das Sprachidiom der urchristlichen Itala und der katholischen Vulgata unter Berücksichtigung der römischen Volkssprache (Marburg: Elwert, 1875), p.56.

167 Van de Vyver, 266-271; P. Courcelle, Les lettres grecques, pp. 356-362; Stangl, "Cassiodoriana," 250; J. Chapman, "Cassiodorus and the Echternach Gospels," RBen, 28 (1911), 287-288; Vogels, Untersuchungen, pp. 113-117.

168 Beatus praefatio,4,81; 5,12,6; Caesarius 240,6; Primasius, CChr.SL 92, 170,120-122.

169 Beatus 9,T.17,7; 9,2,14.

170 There are witnesses to sacramentum in the Itala at Rev. 17:7; cf. Rönsch, p. 323.

E. Pseudo-Jerome's Commemoratorium

171 Cf. K. B. Steinhauser, "Bemerkungen zum pseudo-hieronymischen Commemoratorium in apocalypsin," FZPhTh, 26 (1979), 220-242. Since I have already investigated Pseudo-Jerome's Commemoratorium in Apocalypsin at length, I intend here merely to summarize the more salient observations of my previous study and specifically those which pertain to the research at hand. Although in some instances I do present further information about the Commemoratorium, I have altered none of my previous conclusions.

172 K. Hartung, ed., Ein Trakat zur Apokalypse des Ap. Johannes in einer Pergamenthandschrift der K. Bibliothek in Bamberg, (Bamberg: n.p., 1904), p. iv.

173 G. Lo Menzo Rapisarda, ed., Incerti auctoris Commentarius in Apocalypsin (Catania: Centro di studi sull'antico Cristianesimo, 1967); rpt. from MSLCA, 16 (1966), page reference not available; PLS 4, 1850-1863.

174 B. Lambert, Bibliotheca Hieronymiana Manuscripta: La tradition manuscrite des oeuvres de saint Jerome, IP 4 (The Hague: Nijhoff, 1970), par. 491.

175 G. Lo Menzo Rapisarda, "La tradizione manoscritta di un Commentarius in Apocalypsin," MSLCA, 15 (1965), 137-139; cf.

Rapisarda, Incerti auctoris Commentarius in Apocalypsin, 18-50.

176 Rapisarda, Incerti auctoris Commentarius in Apocalypsin, 24.

177 Jerome, Liber interpretationis hebraicorum nominum (ed. P. de Lagarde, CChr.SL 72, 160).

178 Cf. Steinhauser, "Bemerkungen," 222; 232-236.

179 I am using here the Apocalypse translation of Tyconius as reconstructed by Vogels, Untersuchungen, p. 194.

180 Hartung, p. iv.

181 Rapisarda, 9-11.

182 Cf. Steinhauser, "Bemerkungen," 223-225.

183 In some manuscripts we find commemorator or commemoratio. The designation commemoratorium is so rare that it confused later scribes. All three words have the same root -- commemorator refers to a person, commemoratio to an action and commemoratorium to a thing. Although commemorator does make sense -- the word being in apposition with iohannis -- Hartung, p. 3, n. 21, does indicate that it represents a correction in the manuscript by another hand.

184 Ambrose, De officiis ministrorum 1,25,116 (PL 16, 57,35); cf. Forcellini I, 706; DuCange II 441.

185 Hartung 19,13-17.

186 Eugippius, Epistola ad Pascasium 2 (ed. P. Knöll, CSEL 9,2, 2,5); cf. Palladius, Historia Lausiaca, prooemium (ed. C. Butler, TaS 6,2, 3-5).

187 Cf. S. Prete, p. 32. In opposition to Prete, I do not consider commemoratorium a narrative form. Furthermore, Prete does not seem to trust the true significance of his findings. I believe that the commonitorium is a specific literary genre. Both of these expressions are in my opinion quite specific, each referring to two different types of literature.

188 Hartung 1,1-3,10.

189 Cf. Steinhauser, "Bemerkungen," 225-239.

190 Hartung, p. vii; cf. Steinhauser, "Bemerkungen," 236-237.

191 Hartung 1,1-2,17; 3,5-10.

192 Hartung 2,18-3,5.

193 Steinhauser, "Bemerkungen," 225-226.

194 Steinhauser, "Bemerkungen," 239-242.

195 Ambrosius Autpertus, Expositionis in Apocalypsin libri, praefatio (ed. Weber, CChr.CM 27, 13,320-322).

196 Hartung 3,16-18.

197 A complete catalogue of the library at Vivarium may be found in A. Franz, pp. 80-92.

198 Hartung 13,33; 17,28; 19,22; cf. Steinhauser, "Bemerkungen," 230.

199 Primasius, CChr.SL 92, 263,86 corresponds to Hartung 18,22.

200 Corresponding to Hartung 13,13 are Beatus 4,7,2, Turin Fragment 130, and Bede 154,44 while Caesarius 248,31 corresponds to Hartung 17,28.

F. Capitulary of the cod. Oratorii B6

201 Haußleiter, Die lateinische Apokalypse, pp. 184-196.

202 Haußleiter, Die lateinische Apokalypse, pp. 197-199; the manuscripts are Vatican 4221, Munich 17088 and Munich (olim Freising) 6230.

203 For example, see the one sentence heading before every chapter of the letters of Fulgentius of Rupse, Epistolae (ed. J. Fraipont, CCh 91, 189-273).

204 For example, see the Codex Fuldensis (ed. E. Ranke, pp. 433-434).

205 For example, see the discussion of the capitula of Primasius, pp. 76-78, above.

206 Cf. J. Leclercq, "The Exposition and Exegesis of Scripture: From Gregory the Great to Saint Bernard," The Cambridge History of the Bible, vol. 2 (Cambridge: Cambridge University Press, 1976), p. 186.

207 Haußleiter, Die lateinische Apokalypse, p. 196.

208 G. Bianchini, Vindiciae canonicarum scripturarum Vulgatae

latinae editionis (Rome: n.p., 1740), pp. 322-329, cf. B. M. Metzger, The Early Versions of the New Testament: Their Origin, Transmission, and Limitations (Oxford: Clarendon Press, 1977), p. 343; R. Loewe, "The Medieval History of the Latin Vulgate," The Cambridge History of the Bible, vol. 2 (Cambridge: Cambridge University Press, 1976), pp. 138-139; B. Fischer, Die Alcuin-Bibel: Aus der Geschichte der lateinischen Bibel, vol. 1 (Freiburg: Herder, 1957).

209 G. M. Tommasi, Opera omnia; ad mss. codices recensuit notisque auxit antonius Franciscus Vezzosi, vol. 1 (Rome: Typographia Palladis, 1747), pp. 475-479.

210 Beatus 4,1,24-35.

211 PL 93, 129.48-130,45.

212 PL 93, 182,1-2; 185,13-15.

213 PL 93, 146,46-47; 154,44-45; 160,28-30.

214 Cf. K. B. Steinhauser, "The Structure of Tyconius' Apocalypse Commentary: A Correction," VigChr, 35 (1981), 354-357; for a further discussion of the problem see below pp. 118-122; 191-195.

215 See below, pp. 191-195.

216 CChr.SL 92 (ed. Adams).

217 See below, pp. 118-122.

218 My conclusions are below, pp. 263-264.

G. Bede the Venerable

219 Historia ecclesiastica 24 (ed. B. Colgrave and R. A. B. Mynors, 574).

220 De obitu Bedae (ed. Colgrave and Mynors, 580-586).

221 Cf. S. Bonifatii et Lulli epsitolae 91 (ed. E. Dümmler, MGH.Ep 3, 376-377); Alcuini epistolae 19 (ed. E. Dümmler, MGH.Ep 4, 55).

222 PL 93, 129-206; cf. Stegmüller, par. 1640; Dekkers, par. 1363.

223 Cf. M. L. W. Laistner, A Hand-List of Bede Manuscripts, (Ithaca: Cornell University Press, 1943), pp. 25-26.

224 Since the same poem prefaces the commentary of Alcuin on the Apocalypse (PL 100, 1088), one might suspect Alcuinian origin. Furthermore, a literary similarity to another work of Alcuin supports this possibility; cf. PL 101, 734, where the line Exsul ab humano expellitur orbe pius bears more than coincidental resemblance to the opening line of the poem incorporated into Bede's commentary.

225 Laistner, p. 25.

226 Cf. Hahn, pp. 18-19 and Monceaux, _Histoire,_ vol. 5, p. 201.

227 Gennadius, _De viris inlustribus_ 18 (ed. Bernoulli, 68): _Exposuit et apocalypsin Iohannis ex integro._ Of course, _ex integro_ does not mean 'completely' but 'in a new way'; see below, p. 191.

228 _Epistola ad Eusbeium_ (PL 93, 134,2-10): _Cumque opus memoratum in tres libellos..._

229 Beatus 2, inscriptio, p.159: _Hic liber continet quattuor animalia et quattuor equos, animas interfectorum, quattuor ventos et duodena milia;_ cf. Haußleiter, "Die Kommentare," 248.

230 Cf. Steinhauser, "Structure," 354-357.

231 PL 93, 133,10-18.

232 PL 93, 134,2-3.

233 This position is also maintained by C. Jenkins, "Bede as Exegete and Theologian," _Bede his Life Times and Writings: Essays in Commemoration of the Twelfth Centenary of his Death_ (Oxford: Clarendon Press, 1935), p. 155.

234 PL 93, 134,4-6; trans. by Jenkins, p.155.

235 PL 93, 129,45.

236 Gennadius, De viris inlustribus 18 (ed. Bernoulli, 68): Scripsit de bello intestino libros...

237 Liber regularum 3 (ed. Burkitt, 28,6-29,27).

238 See above, p. 112.

239 Cf. De doctrina Christiana 3,30,42-37,56 (ed. J. Martin, CChr.SL 32, 102-116), which is paraphrased by Bede, Epistola ad Eusebium (PL 93, 131-133).

240 For example the novissima pressura mentioned at PL 93, 131,4 could have derived from Rev. 2:22; 7:14; etc.; cf. Vogels, Untersuchungen pp. 124-125.

241 PL 93, 129,46-47.

242 G. Bonner, Saint Bede in the Tradition of Western Apocalyptic Commentary, JarL 1966 (Newcastle-upon-Tyne: n.p., 1966), p. 10.

243 For example Bede PL 93, 139,32-33; 141,59-142,1; and 191,19 correspond to Jerome, Liber interpretationis hebraicorum nominum (ed. De Lagarde, CChr.SL 72, 160,20,23, and 1 respectively).

244 See below, pp. 267-316.

245 A. Willmes, "Bedas Bibelauslegung," AKuG, 44 (1962), 281-314.

246 Bonner, Saint Bede, p. 11.

247 PL 93, 145,49; 155,54; 156,12; 174,22; 178,6; 181,49; 183,37; 191,6; 194,11.

248 PL 93, 172,33.

249 PL 93, 133,14.

250 PL 93 178,3-17; 181,48-182,2; a similar summary, where the influence of Tyconius is not apparent, may be found in the section on the seven trumpets at 153,47-154,53, the beginning of Bede's second book.

251 Cf. Apringius of Béja, Tractatus in Apocalypsin 2 (ed. Férotin, PLS 4, 1247,6-13); Beatus of Liébana Adversus Elipandum 1,113 (ed. B. Löfstedt, CChr.CM 59, 86,3309-3312); Isidore of Seville, Contra Judaeos, epistola dedicatoria (PL 83, 449-450,9-11).

252 Beatus 3,4,96.

253 Cf. anonymous, Inc. _Figura septem sigillorum,_ Vienna, österreichische Nationalbibliothek, 1712, fols. 41r-43v; anonymous, _Sermo de septem sigillis,_ Frankfurt, Universitätsbibliothek, Ms. Praed. 27, fols. 184v-186r; pseudo-Jerome, _De septem sigillis,_ Wolfenbüttel, Herzogliche Bibliothek, Weissenburg 68, fols. 191v-192v.

254 Loewe, p. 117.

255 PL 93, 136,31; 144,43; 147,47; 155,7; 156,35; 156,59; 158,9; 159,41; 170,25; 171,43; 178,31; 181,23; 187,12; 192,33; 193,46.

H. Ambrosius Autpertus

256 Expositionis in Apocalypsin libri decem (ed. R. Weber, CChr.CM 27 and 27A). The autobiographical note is at 872,124-134.

257 Cf. J. Winandy, Ambroise Autpert: moine et théologien (Paris: Libraire Plon, 1953), pp. 13-30; J. Winandy, "Les dates de l'abbatiat et de la mort d'Ambroise Autpert," RBen, 59 (1949), 206-210.

258 Cf. J. Winandy, "L'oeuvre littéraire d'Ambroise Autpert," RBen, 60 (1950), 96-97.

259 Cf. Winandy, Ambroise Autpert, p. 47; H. Weisweiler, "Das frühe Marienbild der Westkirche unter dem Einfluß des Dogmas von Chalcedon: Ambrosius Autpertus und sein Kreis," Schol., 28 (1953), 505-513.

260 Cf. Winandy, "Oeuvre litteraire," 97.

261 Ambrosius Autpertus 465,1-4.

262 Cf. Winandy, "Oeuvre litteraire," 97; R. Weber, "Edition princeps et tradition manuscrite du commentaire d'Ambroise Autpert sur l'Apocalypse," RBen, 70 (1960), 526-539.

263 The first part clearly ends at Ambrosius Autpertus 7,102

while the second part begins with the very next line.

264 Ambrosius Autpertus 6,47-48.

265 Cf. Ambrosius Autpertus 7,93-100; for additional references see S. Bovo, "Le fonti del commento di Ambrogio Autperto sull'Apocalisse," Miscellanea biblica et orientalia R. P. Athanasio Miller, StAns 27-28 (Rome: Herder, 1953), p. 375.

266 Ambrosius Autpertus 13,320-322; cf. Steinhauser, "Bemerkungen," 239.

267 Cf. Winandy, Ambroise Autpert, p. 25.

268 Bovo, 372-403.

269 Ambrosius Autpertus 359,24.

270 Primasius 155,245.

271 Ambrosius Autpertus 589,10.

272 Liber regularum, 2 (ed. Burkitt, 8-11).

273 Beatus 7,4,3.

I. Beatus of Liébana

274 Cf. F. Sainz de Robles, Elipando y San Beato de Liébana (Madrid: M. Aguilar, 1935), pp. 125-146; M. C. Diaz y Diaz, "Beato de Liébana," DHEE 1, 201-202; J. Perez de Urbel, "S. Béat (Beatus)," DHGE 7, 89-90.

275 Epistola 3 (PL 96, 868,19): nefandus presbyter et pseduo-propheta.

276 Adversus Elipandum 2,38 (ed. Löfstedt, CChr.CM 59, 132,1113-1115.

277 Cf. H. L. Ramsay, "Le Commentaire de l'Apocalypse par Beatus de Liébana," RHLR, 7 (1902), 423-425.

278 Cf. Sainz de Robles, p. 131.

279 Cf. J. Bach, Die Dogmengeschichte des Mittelalters vom christologischen Standpunkte oder die mittelalterliche Christologie, vol. 1 (Vienna: Braümiller, 1873), p. 120.

280 Cf. Sainz de Robles, pp. 144-145.

281 PL 96, 890-894.

282 Cf. P. B. Gams, Die Kirchengeschichte von Spanien, vol.2,2 (Regensburg: Manz, 1874), pp. 275-277.

283 On the history of the adoptionist controversy there is sufficient literature: A. Helfferich, Der westgothische Arianismus und die spanische Ketzer-Geschichte (Berlin: Julius Springer, 1860); Gams, pp. 261-298; H. Größler, Die Ausrottung des Adoptionismus im Reiche Karls des Grosse, Jahres-Bericht über das königliche Gymnasium zu Eisleben von Ostern 1878 bis Ostern 1879 (Eisleben: n.p., 1879); A. Hauck, Kirchengeschichte Deutschlands, vol. 2 (Leipzig: Hinrichs, 1890), pp. 250-276; C. J. Hefele and H. Leclercq, Histoire des Conciles d'aprés les documents originaux, vol. 3 (Paris: Letouzey, 1910), pp. 1001-1060; F. Ansprenger, "Untersuchungen zum adoptionischen Streit im 8. Jahrhundert," Diss. Freie Universität Berlin, 1952; W. Heil, "Alkuinstudien I: Zur Chronologie und Bedeutung des Adoptionismusstreites," Diss. Freiburg 1966; W. Heil, "Der Adoptionismus, Alkuin und Spanien," Karl der Grosse: Lebenswerk und Nachleben, vol. 2 (Düsseldorf: L. Schwann, 1967), pp. 95-155; W. Heil, "Adoptionismus," Lexikon des Mittelaltes, vol. 1, 162-163. For the theological aspects of the controversy see: F. C. Bauer, Lehrbuch der christlichen Dogmengeschichte (Leipzig: n.p., 1867), pp. 212-213; Bach, pp. 102-146; A. Harnack, Lehrbuch der Dogmengeschichte, vol. 3 (Tubingen: J. C. B. Mohr, 1910); J. F. Rivera, "La Maternidad divina de Maria, en una cotroversia cristológica española de fines del siglo VIII," Certamen Público en honor de Ntra. Sra. de Belén, de Carrión de los Condes 3 (Lérida: Imprenta Mariana,

1933); E. Amann, "L'adoptionisme espagnol du VIIIe siècle," RevSR, 16 (1936), 281-317.

284 Cf. Elipandus, Epistola, 4,1 (PL 96, 870,6-7).

285 Cf. M. Férotin, Le liber mozarabicus sacramentorum et les manuscrits mozarabes, MELi 6 (Paris: Firmin-Didot, 1912), pp. xxix-xxxii; D. de Bruyne, "De l'origine de quelques texts liturgiques mozarabes," RBen, 30 (1913), 421-436; J. F. Rivera, "La controversia adopcionista del siglo VIII y la ortodoxia de la liturgia mozárabe," EL, 47 NS 7 (1933), 506-536.

286 Adversus Elipandum 1,43 (ed. Löfstedt, CChr.CM 59, 30,1139-1140;1146-1147.

287 Adversus Elipandum 1,43-44 (ed. Löfstedt, CChr.CM 59, 30,1125-31,1173.

288 Cf. Adversus Elipandum 1,1 (ed. Löfstedt, CChr.CM 59, 1,3-13).

289 On the involvement of Beatus in the adoptionist controversy see: Sainz de Robles, pp. 23-35; J. F. Rivera, Elipando de Toledo: Nueva aportacion a los estudios mozarabes (Toledo: Editorial Catolica Toledana, 1940); J. F. Rivera, "Más fórmulas y profesiones de fe hispanovisigoticas," Collectanea theologica al R. P. Joaquin Salaverri, S.I. en el cincuentenario de su vida religiosa,

Misceláneа Comillas 34-35 (Comillas: Universidad Pontificia Comillas, 1960), pp. 343-352; M. del Alamo, "Los comentarios de Beato al Apocalipsis y Elipando," Miscellanea Giovanni Mercati, vol. 2, StT 122 (Vatican City: Biblioteca Apostolica Vaticana, 1946), pp. 16-33.

290 Alamo, p. 18.

291 Rivera, Elipando, pp. 12-17.

292 Alamo, pp. 30-33.

293 Sanders, pp. 1-43.

294 See above, pp. 146-148.

295 Ramsay, "Le commentaire," pp. 424-425.

296 Cf. E. Ranke, ed., Codex Fuldensis: Novum Testamentum latine interprete Hieronymo (Marburg: N. G. Elwert, 1868), p. 432.

297 Cf. J. Chapman, Notes on the Early History of the Vulgate Gospels (Oxford: Clarendon Press, 1908), pp. 256-258.

298 Florez, pp. 4-35; Sanders, pp. 6-43.

299 Praefatio,4,1-3 contains a quotation from Isidore followed by a section on the 24 elders and the sevenfold grace.

300 Sanders, pp. 44-645.

301 Sanders, pp. 102-158.

302 Before the evil horses, there is a short note on the three horses of Zachariah.

303 See for example: _....quia quisquis ab unitate ecclesiae in consilio segregatur...._ (prologus,7,3) _....tamen hereticus appellari potest...._ (prologus,7,5) _....hi sunt sacerdotes, qui desiderant primas cathedras...._ (prologus,10,14); the last two quotations are direct references to Elipando, his heretical opinion, and his role as Primate of Spain.

304 Prologus,9,43-10,3.

305 Beatus 2,8,1-42.

306 _De civitate Dei_ 20,19 (eds. Dombart and Kalb, CChr.SL 48, 730,1-732,89).

307 Vogels, pp. 70-93; E. S. Buchanan, _The Catholic Epistles and Apocalypse from the Codex Laudianus numbered Laud. Lat. 43 in the Bodleian Library together with the Apocalypse Text of Beatus from the tenth Century MS. in the Morgan Library, New York,_ Sacred Latin Texts 4 (London: Heath, Cranton & Ouseley, 1916); A. Souter, "Tyconius's

Text of the Apocalypse: A partial Reconstruction," JThS, 14 (1913), 338-358.

308 Praefatio,1,5.

309 Ramsay, "Le Commentaire," pp. 428-429.

310 Hahn, pp. 10-11; Ramsay, "Le Commentaire," pp. 427 and 433; Alvarez Campos, Sergio. "Fuentes literarias de Beato de Liébana," Actas del simposio para el estudio de los codices del "Commentario al Apocalipsis" de Beato de Liébana, vol. 1 Madrid: Joyas Bibliográfias, 1978, pp. 135-162.

311 See above, pp. 35-44.

312 Ramsay, "Le Commentaire," p. 422.

313 Ramsay, "Le Commentaire," pp. 424-425.

314 Ramsay, "Le Commentaire," p. 426.

315 Isidore, De viris illustribus 30,40 (PL 83, 1098,25-1099,2).

316 Cf. A. C. Vega, ed., Apringii Pacensis Episcopi Tractatus in Apocalysin [sic], SEHL 10-11 (Escurial: Typis Augustinianis Monasterii Escurialensis, 1941), p. vii.

317 Cf. W. Bousset, "Nachrichten über eine Kopenhagener Handschrift (Arnamagnaeanske Legat 1927 A M. 795 4to) des Kommentars des Apringius zur Apocalypse," NGWG.PH (1895), 187-209. On the existence of other manuscripts see M. Férotin, ed., Apringius de Béja: Son commentaire de l'Apocalypse, Bibliothèque Patrologique 1 (Paris: Alphonse Picard, 1900), pp. xi-xii; C. Weyman, "Textkritische Bemerkungen zum Apokalypsekommentar des Apringius," BZ, 1 (1903), 176; Stegmüller, par. 1422.

318 M. Férotin, ed., Apringius de Béja: Son commentaire de l'Apocalypse, Bibliothèque Patrologique 1 (Paris: Alphonse Picard, 1900); rpt. PLS 4, 1222-1248; A. C. Vega, ed., Apringii Pacensis Episcopi Tractatus in Apocalysin [sic], SEHL 10-11 (Escurial: Typis Augustinianis Monasterii Escurialensis, 1941).

319 Vega, pp. xxviii-xl.

320 Cf. F. Fita, "Patrología latina: Apringio, obispo de Béja," BRAH, 41 (1902), 410-416.

321 PL 5.

322 CSEL 49.

323 Vega, pp. xxviii-xxxv; B. Altaner, Rev. of S. Isidori Hispalensis Episcopi Liber de variis questionibus, ed. by A. C. Vega

and A. E. Anspach and Apringii Pacensis Episcopi Tractatus in Apocalypsin, ed. by A. C. Vega. ThRv, 41 (1942), 117-120; M. del Alamo, "Hacia una edición definitiva de Apringio y observaciones a una nueva," CDios, 153 (1941), 399-406; A. C. Vega, "Observation a las observaciones," CDios, 153 (1941), 406-407; M. Cappuyns, Rev. of Apringii Pacensis Episcopi Tractatus in Apocalypsin, ed. by A. C. Vega. BThAM, 5 (1946-1949), 15-16; 300.

324 DS 486.

325 Liturgia Mozarabica (PL 85, 487-614).

326 Alamo, "Hacia una edición," pp. 405-406; Haußleiter, CSEL 49, pp. lv-lix; Haußleiter, "Victorinus," RE 20, 617.

327 See Weyman, "Textkritische Bemerkungen," pp. 175-181; C. Weyman, Rev. of Victorini episcopi Petavionensis opera, ed. by J. Haußleiter, Wochenschrift für klassische Philologie, 34 (1917), 1103-1111.

328 Fita, p. 356.

329 Gómez, p. 407.

330 H. Florez, ed. Sancti Beati presbyteri Hispani Liebanensis in Apocalypsin ac plurimos in utriusque foederis paginas Commentaria, ex veteribus, nonnullisque desideratis patribus mille

retro annis collecta, nunc primum edita (Madrid: Joachim Ibarra, 1770).

331 H. A. Sanders, ed., Beati in Apocalipsin libri duodecim, PMAAR 7. (Rome: American Academy in Rome, 1930).

332 For example see: Alamo, "Los comentarios," p. 19 n. 16; A. E. Brooke, Rev. of Beati in Apocalipsin, by H. A. Sanders. JThS, 32 (1931), 409-410. E. Romero Pose, "Una nueva edición del Comentario al Apocalipsis de S. Beato de Liébana: Su importancia para la reconstrucción del Comentario de Ticonio," Bollettino dei Classici, 1 (1980), 225 goes so far as to state that the older edition of Florez is superior to that of Sanders.

333 This number is based upon A. M. Mundó, "Sobre los Códices de Beato," Actas del simposio para el estudio de los codices del "Commentario al Apocalipsis" de Beato de Liébana, vol. 1 (Madrid: Joyas Bibliográphias, 1978), pp. 107-116.

334 W. Neuss, Die Apokalypse des hl. Johannes in der altspanischen und altchristlichen Bibel-Illustration: Das Problem der Beatus-Handschriften, vol. 1, SFGG 2,2-3 (Münster: Aschendorff, 1931), pp. 81-110.

335 I am simply listing the manuscripts by library and signature as recorded by Neuss, pp. 9-61, whose method of notation I have adopted. For a description of the manuscripts, one may consult

the following works: L. Delisle, Mélanges de paléographie et de bibliographie (Paris: Champion, 1880), pp. 177-148; K. Miller, Mappae Mundi: Die ältesten Weltkarten, vol. 1: Die Weltkarte des Beatus (776 n. Chr.) (Stuttgart: J. Roth, 1895), pp. 10-22; E. Bratke, "Beatus von Libana [sic], Hieronymus und die Visio Hesdrae," ZKG, 23 (1902), 428-430; H. L. Ramsay, "The Manuscripts of 'The Commentary of Beatus of Liébana' on the Apocalypse," Revue des bibliothèques, 12 (1902), 74-103; A. Blazquez, "Los manuscritos de los commentarios al Apocalipsis de S. Juan por San Beato de Liébana," RABM, 14 (1906), 257-273; Sanders, pp. xii-xiv; T. Rojo Oracjo, Estudios de codices visigóticos: El "Beato" de la Biblioteca de Santa Cruz de Valladolid, (Madrid: Tip. de Archivos, 1930); A. Millares-Carlo, Contribución al "corpus" de códices visigóticos, Publicaciones de la Facultad de Filosofia y Letras Universidad de Madrid 1 (Madrid: Maestre, 1931), pp. 108-113; 240-253; Sainz de Robles, pp. 148-159; Stegmüller, par. 1597; A. de Ergy, Um estudo de O Apocalipse do Lorvão: e a sua relação con as ilustraçoes medievais do Apocalipse (Lisbon: Fundação Calouste Gulbenkain, 1972); U. Eco, Beato di Liébana: Miniature del Beato de Fernando I y Sancha (codice B. N. Madrid Vit. 14-2) (Parma: F. M. Ricci, 1973); P. K. Klein, Der ältere Beatus-Kodex Vitr. 14-1 der Biblioteca Nacional zu Madrid: Studien zur Beatus-Illustration und der spanischen Buchmalerei des 10. Jahrhunderts, vol. 1, Studien zur Kunstgeschichte 8, Diss. Bonn 1976 (Hildesheim: Olms, 1976), pp. 83-85; A. M. Mundó and M. Sanchez Mariana, El comentario de Beato al Apocalipsis: catálogo de los códices (Madrid: Biblioteca Nacional, 1976); A. M. Mundó, "Sobre los

Códices de Beato," pp. 107-116; D. S. Raizman, The later Morgan Beatus (M. 249) and late romanesque illumenationn in Spain, Diss. Pittsburgh 1980 (Ann Arbor: University Microfilms, 1980).

336 Delisle, pp. 117-148.

337 Sanders, pp. xii-xviii.

338 Neuss, pp. 101-111.

339 Klein, p. 152.

340 Klein, p. 173.

341 M. C. Díaz y Díaz, "Tradición del texto de los Comentarios al Apocalipsis," Actas del simposio para el estudio de los codices del "Commentario al Apocalipsis" de Beato de Liébana, vol. 1 Madrid: Joyas Bibliográfias, 1978, p. 184.

342 The word "redaction" is more accurate than "edition"; cf. Klein, p. 175.

343 Florez, p. 4.

344 Haußleiter, "Die Kommentare," pp. 253-254.

345 Hahn, pp. 13-14.

346 Ramsay, "Le Commentaire," pp. 440-444.

347 A second large section of Adversus Elipandum, 1,55-56 (ed. Löfstedt, CChr.CM 59, 39,1500-42,1587) has been copied directly from the Apocalypse commentary at 5,6,1-12.

348 Caesarius 252,19-253,8; 255,6-8.

349 Primasius 232,169-233,202.

350 P. Cazier, "Le Livre des règles de Tyconius: Sa transmission du De doctrina christiana aux Sentences d'Isidore de Séville," REAug, 19 (1973), 241-261; cf. Isidore, Sentenciarum libri tres 9,19,1-19 (PL 83, 581-586) and Augustine, De doctrina christiana 3,30,42-3,37,56 (ed. Martin, CChr.SL 32, 102-116).

351 The passages are contained in praefatio,5,51-60 and Prologus libri II,7,108; cf. Isidore, Etymologiae, 8,3,1-6 (eds. J. Oroz Reta and A. Marcos Casquero, BAC 433, 688-691).

352 Haußleiter, "Die Kommentare," p. 250.

353 Ramsay, "Le Commentaire," pp. 339-340.

354 Bousset, Die Offenbarung Johannis, p. 57.

355 Praefatio,5,53-54; 5,56-59; cf. Isidore, Etymologiae, 8,5,53 (eds. Oroz Reta and Marcos Casquero, BAC 433, 698-699); De ecclesiasticis officiis, 2,16,2 (PL 83, 794,31-40); Etymologiae, 10,H,119-121 (eds. Oroz Reta and Marcos Casquero, BAC 433, 822-833). There is one exception to this statement, namely 5,59b does appear also in 4,1,41 but in an entirely different context.

356 Ramsay, "Le Commentaire," p. 442.

357 Haußleiter, "Die Kommentare," p. 250.

358 Hahn, p. 13.

359 Isidore, Etymologiae, 8,5,53 (eds. Oroz Reta and Marcos Casquero, BAC 433, 698-699); cf.Isidore, De ecclesiasticis officis, 2,16,7 (PL 83,796,18-797,3).

360 R. Lorenz, "Circumcelliones - cotopitae - cutzupitani," ZKG, 82 (1971), 54-59.

361 E. Tengström, Donatisten und Katholiken: Soziale, wirtschaftliche und politische Aspekte einer nordafrikanischen Kirchenstpaltung, SGLG 18 (Gothenburg: Acta Universitatis Gothoburgensis, 1964), pp. 24-78.

362 Augustine, Enarrationes in Psalmos 132,3 (ed. E. Dekkers and J. Fraipont, CChr.SL 40, 1927-1928).

363 Isidore, De ecclesiasticis officiis 2,16,7 (PL 83, 796-798).

364 Regula Magistri 1,13-74 (ed. A. de Vogüé, SC 105, 332-346); Regula Benedicti 1,10-11 (ed. R. Hanslik, CSEL 75, 20).

365 Cassiodore, Expositio Psalmorum 132,1 (ed. M. Adriaen, CChr.SL 98, 1206).

366 Praefatio,5,49-50; 51; 52; 55; 59; 60-61.

367 Praefatio,5,59.

368 Praefatio,5,53; 55.

369 Hahn, p. 13.

370 Praefatio,5,53; 55.

371 Praefatio,5,52; 55.

372 Praefatio,5,52.

373 Rivera, Elipando, pp. 21-28.

374 Haußleiter, "Die Kommentare," p. 251.

375 CSEL 49, 131,12-13.

376 Hahn, p. 13.

377 Praefatio,4,58; 71; 72; 74; 75; 78; 79; 80; 89; 97; 105; 5,23.

378 CChr.CM 59, 10,369; 10,386; 12,435; 15,557; 34,1292; 50,1893; 76,2924; 114,432; 114,433; 117,559; 122,725.

379 Haußleiter, "Die Kommentare," pp. 251-252.

380 CChr.CM 59, 15,565-573.

381 CChr.CM 59, 9,349; 15,567; 24,904; 109,225; 128,990; 149,1811; also cf. 8,279; 96,3712.

382 Rivera, Maternidad, pp. 17-25; cf. Z. Garcia Villada, Historia Eclesiástica de España, vol. 2 (Madrid: Compañia ibero-americana de publicaciones, 1933), pp. 274-280.

383 Vogels, Untersuchungen, pp. 59-66.

384 Vogels, Untersuchungen, p. 70.

385 Praefatio,5,91.

386 See above, pp. 118-120.

387 See above, pp. 118-120.

388 Gennadius, De viris inlustribus, 18 (ed. Bernoulli, 68).

389 Monceaux, Histoire, vol. 5, p. 202; Alvarez Campos, "Fuentes literarias de Beato de Liébana," p. 123.

390 Beatus, inscriptio, p. 159.

391 Beatus, inscriptio, p. 159.

392 PLS 4, 1241,38.

393 Beatus, inscriptio, p. 456.

394 Alvarez Campos, pp. 124-125.

395 Beatus 12,2,22-23.

396 For example, quis: Liber regularum praefatio (ed. Burkitt, 1,7).

397 Beatus, prologus libri II, 2,4; see also 2,22; 3,19-20.

398 Beatus, prologus libri II, 10,4.

399 Tyconius, Liber regularum 5 (ed. Burkitt, 55,2-5).

400 Gennadius, De viris inlustribus 18 (ed. Bernoulli, 68).

A. The Turin Fragment

1 F. Lo Bue, ed., The Turin Fragments of Tyconius' Commentary on Revelation, TaS NS 7 (Cambridge: Cambridge University Press, 1953), pp. 3-5.

2 Spicilegium Casinense 3,1 (Montecassino: Typis archicoenobii Montis Casini, 1897), pp. 261-331.

3 Bonner, Saint Bede in the Tradition of Western Apocalyptic Commentary, p. 16 n. 32.

4 Cf. H. Foerster, Abriss der lateinischen Paläographie (Stuttgart: Anton Hiersemann, 1963), pp. 153-159; the plates of the Turin codex could readily be compared to Figure 16 (p. 275) and Figure 28 (p. 289).

5 Cf. Lehmann, p. 71.

6 Hahn, pp. 14-16.

7 Pincherle, "Da Ticonio a sant'Agostino," p. 456.

8 Lo Bue, p. 21.

9 Lo Bue, p. 23.

10 *Liber regularum* 6 (ed. Burkitt 67,11).

11 *Liber regularum* 5 (ed. Burkitt 61,20-24).

12 Lo Bue, p. 32.

13 Bonner, *Saint Bede in the Tradition of Western Apocalyptic Commentary*, p. 6.

14 Cf. Lo Bue, pp. 33-34.

15 Cf. Lo Bue, pp 25-26 and 23 respectively.

16 See above, pp. 205-206; 203-204.

17 *Epistola* 73,21 (ed. W. Hartel, CSEL 3,2, 794. Although Tyconius uses the word *foris* in his *Liber regularum* 2 (ed. Burkitt 11,1), the expression is substantially different because it is not followed by a preposition.

18 *Liber regularum* 2 (ed. Burkitt 11,25-28).

19 Lo Bue, p. 37 n. 1.

20 Cf. H. J. Vogt, "Die Auseinandersetzung der Kirche mit dem Arianismus der Vandalen und Goten," HKG(J), vol. 2,2, pp. 282-297; K. D. Schmidt, *Die Bekehrung der Ostgermannen zum Christentum: Der*

ostgermanische Arianismus, Die Bekehrung der Germanen zum Christentum 1 (Göttingen: Vandenhoeck & Ruprecht, 1939), pp. 387-403. Though rare some Arian sources are extant in Latin, see R. Gryson, ed., Les palimpsestes ariens latins de Bobbio: Contribution à la méthodologie de l'étude des palimpsestes, Armarium codicum insignium 1 (Turnhout: Brepols, 1983) and R. Gryson, ed., Scripta Arriana Latina I, CChr.SL 87, pp. x-xvii.

B. The Budapest Fragment

21 I have given the manuscript this name on the basis of its location. The fragment was discovered and researched initially by L. Mezey, "Egy Korai Karoling Kódextöredek (Ticonius in Apocalypsin?)," Magyar könyvszemle 92 (1976), 15-24, and subsequently investigated by A. Pincherle, "Alla ricerca di Ticonio," Studi storico religiosi, 2 (1978), 362-365.

22 S(eminarium centrale cleri Hungarie Budapestini) Fr(agmentum) l(atinum) m(embranaceum) 1.

23 Mezey, p. 18; Pincherle, "Alla ricerca di Ticonio," p. 363.

24 See above, pp. 199-200.

25 Recto B 2 and 3 have only 13 letters in each line. In recto B 5 there are 20 letters but sanctitas could have very well been abbreviated.

(Chapter IV, pp. 222-253)

A. The non-Tyconian authorship of the sermon In natali

1 E. Romero Pose, "Ticonio y el sermon 'in natali sanctorum innocentim' (Exegesis de Mt. 2)," Gr., 60 (1979), 513-544. Pincherle, "Alla ricerca di Ticonio," p. 358, mentions a dissertation without giving its title written by Romero Pose concerning Tyconius and submitted to the theological faculty of the Gregorian University. I could not obtain a copy.

2 A. Wilmart, "Un Sermon de saint Optat pour la fete de Nöel," RevSR, 2 (1922), 271-302.

3 G. Morin, "Pour une future édition des opuscules de saint Quodvultdeus, évêque de Carthage au Ve siècle," RBen, 31 (1914), 161.

4 L. Delisle, Notice sur plusieurs manuscrits de la biblothèque d'Orleans (Paris: Imp. Nationale, 1883), p. 374.

5 Wilmart, "Un Sermon," pp. 273-280.

6 Cf. E. Amann, "Optat de Mileve," DThC 11, 1083; S. Blomgren, Eine Echtheitsfrage bei Optatus von Mileve, AASU 5 (Stockholm: Almqvist & Wiksell, 1959); H. D. Altendorf, Rev. of Eine Echtheitsfrage bei Optatus von Mileve, by S. Blomgren, ThLZ, 85 (1960), 599-560.

7 P. Courcelle, Histoire littéraire des grandes invasions germaniques (Paris: Etudes Augustiennes, 1964), p. 137 n. 1.

8 A. Pincherle, "Un sermone donatista attribuito a s. Ottato di Milevi," Bil., 22 (1923), 134-148.

9 Cf. W. H. Frend, The Donatist Church: A Movement of Protest in Roman North Africa (Oxford: Clarendon, 1952), p. 337.

10 F. Scorza Barcellona, "L'interpretazione dei doni dei magi nel sermone natalizio di [Pseudo] Ottato di Milevi," Studi storico religiosi, 2 (1978), 129-149.

11 Concerning Optatus of Thamugadi see B. Quinot, "Notes complémentaires," Traités anti-donatistes, vol. 3, Oeuvres de saint Augustine 30 (Paris: Desclée de Brouwer, 1967), pp. 757-760.

12 Romero Pose, "Ticonio y el sermon," pp. 517-541.

13 Romero Pose, "Ticonio y el sermon," p. 525 n. 85.

14 Romero Pose, "Ticonio y el sermon," p. 533 n. 201.

15 Romero Pose, "Ticonio y el sermon," pp. 522-523; see below, pp. 230-232.

16 Cf. Possidius, Sancti Augustini vita a Possidio episcopo

5,3 (ed. H. T. Weiskotten, 48,20-23).

17 Cf. J. Ratzinger,"Ticonius," LThK 10, 180-181.

18 Gennadius, _De viris inlustribus_ 18 (ed. Bernoulli, p. 68).

19 Augustine, _Contra epistulam Parmeniani_ 1,1,1 (ed. Petschenig, CSEL 51, 19-20); _De doctrina christiana_ 3,30,42-37,56 (ed. Martin, 102-116)

20 _Sermo_ 2 (ed. Wilmart, 282,18-23); cf. Scorza Barcellona, p. 130 n. 7; Romero Pose, "Ticonio y el sermon," pp. 522-523.

21 For example: _subdolis tamen subtilitatibus...subtractum._

22 For example: _adoraturum se_ dominum _simulat ut_ hominem _deo mixtem._

23 For example: _insanus...diabulus._

24 For example: _ereptam...coniunctam._

25 Romero Pose, "Ticonio y el sermon," p. 542.

26 Pincherle, "Un sermone donatista," pp. 142-148.

27 Cyprian, _Epistola_ 56 (ed. Hartel, CSEL 3,1, 695-698).

28 Maximinus the Arian, In natale infantum (ed. Gryson, CChr.SL 87, 69-72); B. Capelle, "Un homiliare de l'évêque arien Maximin," RBen, 34 (1922), 81-108; B. Capelle, "Optat et Maximin," RBen, 35 (1923), 24-26; C. H. Turner, "Notes on the Apostolic Constitutions, " JThS, 16 (1915), 54-61; 523-538.

29 F. Kauffmann, Aus der Schule des Wulfila: Auxenti Dorostorensis epistula de fide uita et obitu Wulfilae im Zusammenhang der Dissertatio Maximini contra Ambrosium, Texte und Untersuchungen zur altgermanischen Religionsgeschichte, Texte 1 (Strasbourg: K. J. Trubner, 1899), pp. 65-90.

30 Kauffmann, p. lv; cf. Scorza Barcellona, p. 148.

31 Schanz-Hosius, par. 907; cf. also Altaner-Stuiber p. 372 and Bardenhewer, vol. 3, pp. 595-596, both of whom remain neutral on the question.

32 B. Botte, Les Origines de la Noël et de l'Epiphanie, Textes et études liturgiques 1 (Louvain: Abbaye du Mont César, 1932); H. Frank, "Frühgeschichte und Ursprung des römischen Weihnachtsfests," ALW, 2 (1952), 1-24.

33 Sermo 6 (ed. Wilmart, 284,73); cf. F. J. Dölger, Sol Salutis: Gebet und Gesang im christlichen Altertum mit besonderer Rücksicht auf die Ostung in Gebet und Liturgie (Münster: Aschendorf,

1925); F. J. Dölger, "Das Sonnengleichnis in einer Weihnachtspredigt des Bischofs Zeno von Verona: Christus als wahre und ewige Sonne," AuC, 6 (1950), 1-56; F. J. Dölger, Die Sonne der Gerechtigkeit und der Schwarze: Eine religionsgeschichtliche Studie zum Taufgelöbnis, LWQF 14 (Münster: Aschendorff, 1971), pp. 83-110.

34 Augustine, Sermo 202,2 (PL 38, 1033); cf. Frank, "Frühgeschichte," p. 15; H. Rahner, Griechische Mythen in christlicher Deutung (Basel: Herder, 1984), pp. 89-158

35 Pincherle, "Un sermone donatista," pp 134-148.

36 Sermo de passione Donati et Advocati (PL 8, 752-758).

37 Passio Marculi presbyteri (PL 8, 760-766).

38 Passio Maximiani et Isaac Donatistarum auctore Macrobio (PL 8, 767-774).

B. Characteristics of the Liber regularum

39 Liber regularum 3 (ed. Burkitt, 12,2-4).

40 Liber regularum 3 (ed. Burkitt, 30,17-18).

41 Liber regularum 6 (ed. Burkitt, 68,28-29).

42 Liber regularum 3 (ed. Burkitt, 17,30-18,1).

43 Hahn, p. 40 n. 1.

44 Liber regularum 3 (ed. Burkitt, 31,4-5).

45 P. Fredriksen Landes, "Tyconius and the End of the World," REAug, 28 (1982), 64.

46 For another example see Liber regularum 3 (ed. Burkitt, 16,18).

47 Liber regularum praefatio (ed. Burkitt, 1,1-9); for other examples see Liber regularum 2 (ed. Burkitt, 11,28; 31,10);4 (ed. Burkitt, 62,2);5 (ed. Burkitt, 63,1-2; 70,6).

48 Anderson, p. 24

49 Anderson, p. 23; cf. p. 13.

50 Liber regularum 1 (ed. Burkitt, 3,10-11).

51 Liber regularum 1 (ed. Burkitt, 3,12).

52 Liber regularum 6 (ed. Burkitt, 66,11).

53 Liber regularum 6 (ed. Burkitt, 66,15).

54 Liber regularum 6 (ed. Burkitt, 67,7-8).

55 Liber regularum 6 (ed. Burkitt, 67,29-30).

56 Monceaux, Histoire, vol. 5, p. 188; I. Christe, "Traditions littéraire et iconographiques dans l'interprétation des images apocalyptiques," L'Apocalypse de Jean: Traditions exégétiques et iconographiques IIIe-XIIIe siècles, Etudes et documents publiés par la section d'histoire de la faculté des lettres de l'Université de Genève 11 (Geneva: Librairie Droz, 1979), p. 111.

57 Liber regularum praefatio (ed. Burkitt, 1,7-8); trans. Anderson, p. 24.

58 Anderson, p. 24 n. 6.

59 Liber regularum 6 (ed. Burkitt, 67,10-11); trans. Anderson, p. 183.

60 H. D. Rauh, _Das Bild des Antichrist im Mittelalter: Von Tyconius zum Deutschen Symbolismus,_ BGPhMA NS 9, Diss. Erlangen-Nürnberg 1969 (Münster: Aschendorff, 1979), p. 105.

61 Here I have used the translation of the New American Bible.

62 _Adversus Marcionem_ 3,24 (ed. and trans. E. Evans, 246-247).

63 Fredriksen Landes, p. 63.

64 _Liber regularum_ praefatio (ed. Burkitt, 1,3-9); trans. Anderson, p. 24.

65 Once again I take exception with Anderson p. 23 n. 2.

66 _De doctrina christiana_ 3,30,43 (ed. Martin, CChr.SL 32, 103,39-43); trans. Robertson, p. 105.

67 L. J. van der Lof, "Warum wurde Tyconius nicht katholish?" ZNW, 57 (1966); Y. M. J. Congar, "Notes complémentaires," _Traités Anti-Donatistes,_ vol. 1, Oeuvres de saint Augustin 28 (Paris: Desclée de Brouwer, 1963), p. 718 n. 10.

68 _De doctrina christiana_ 3,30,42 (ed. Martin, CChr.SL 32,

102,1-2).

69 Contra epistulam Parmeniani 1,1 (ed. Petschenig, CSEL 51, 19,4-20,14).

70 Cf. Liber regularum 2 (ed. Burkitt, 10,30; 11,26; 8,9).

71 De doctrina christiana 3,32,45 (ed. Martin, CChr.SL 32, 104,1-105,29).

72 Cf. W. Kamlah, Christentum und Selbstbehauptung: Historische und philisophische Untersuchungen zur Entstehung des Christentums und zu Augustins "Bürgerschaft Gottes" (Frankfurt: Victorio Klostermann, 1940), pp. 224-225; H. Scholz, Glaube und Unglaube in der Weltgeschichte: Ein Kommentar zu Augustins De civitate Dei (Leipzig:J. C. Hinrichs, 1911; rpt. Leipzig: Zentral-Antiquariat der deutschen demokratischen Republik, 1967), pp. 37-54.

73 Scholz, pp. 109-121.

74 Cf. Gennadius, De viris inlustribus 18 (ed. Bernoulli, 68-69).

75 Liber regularum 7 (ed. Burkitt, 81,22-23);3 (ed. Burkitt, 29,7-28).

76 E. S. Morgan, Visible Saints: The History of the Puritan

Idea (Ithaca: Cornell University Press, 1963) describes remarkable parallels between the Puritans of colonial New England and the Donatists of Roman North Africa.

77 Cf. Augustine, De baptismo 7,2,2-3 (ed. Petschenig, CSEL 51, 343-345); for an elaboration of the attitude see A. C. de Veer, "Notes complémentaires," Traités Anti-Donatistes, vol. 4, Oeuvres de saint Augustine 31 (Paris: Desclée de Brouwer, 1968), pp. 839-842 n. 51.

78 De viris inlustribus 18 (ed. Bernoulli, 68-69).

79 Monceaux, Histoire, vol. 5, p. 170.

80 Turin Fragment 183.

81 Turin Fragment 259.

82 Turin Fragment 127, cf. Beatus 4,6,71.

83 Primasius 132,5; cf. Beatus 4,7,1.

84 Primasius 132,5.

85 Steinhauser, "The Structure," pp. 354-356.

86 Beatus 6,3,20.

87 Liber regularum 3 (ed. Burkitt, 29, 2-4); cf. 7 (ed. Burkitt, 72,15).

Bibliography

Sources

1. Individual Authors (including anonymous authors)

Alcuin

Commentariorum in Apocalypsin libri quinque
PL 100, 1085-1156.

Alcvini sivi Albini epistolae
Dümmler, Ernestus, ed. MGH.Ep 4, 1-493.

Alcuini (Albini) carmina
PL 101, 723-848
Dümmler, Ernestus, ed. MGH.PL 1, 160-351.

Ambrose

De officis ministrorum libri tres
PL 16, 23-184.

Ambrosius Autpertus

Expositionis in Apocalypsin libri decem
Weber, Robert, ed. CChr.CM 27-27A.

anonymous

Barnabae epistola
Wengst, Klaus, ed. and trans. *Didache (Apostellehre), Barnabasbrief, zweiter Klemensbrief, Schrift an Diognet,* SUC 2. Darmstadt: Wissenschaftliche Buchgesellschaft, 1984, pp. 138-195.

anonymous

Capitula libri Apocalypsis Joannis apostoli
Haußleiter, Johannes, ed. *Die lateinische Apokalypse der alten afrikanischen Kirche,* FGNK 4. Erlangen: A Deichert (G. Böhme), 1891, pp. 197-199.

anonymous

Codex Oratorii B 6
Tommasi, Giuseppe Maria (Thomasius, Josephus Maria), ed. *Opera omnia; ad mss. codices recensuit notisque auxit Antonius Franciscus Vezzosi,* vol. 1. Rome: Typographia Palladis, 1747, pp. 475-479.

anonymous

De decem virginibus
Wilmart, André. "Un anonyme ancien 'De X virginibus'," BALAC, 1 (1911), 35-38; rpt. PLS 1, 172-174.

anonymous

Inc. *Figura septem sigillorum*
Vienna, österreichische Nationalbibliothek, 1712, fols. 41r-43v.

anonymous

In Matthaeum XXIV
Mercati, G. "Anonymi chiliastae in Matthaeum XXIV fragmenta," *Varia sacra,* vol. 1, StT 11. Rome: Tipograpfia Vaticana, 1903, pp. 23-49.
Turner, C. H. "An exegetical Fragment of the third Century," JThS 5 (1904), 227-241; rpt. PLS 1, 655-668.

anonymous

Passio Marculi sacerdotis donatistae
PL 8, 760-766.

anonymous

Passio sanctarum Perpetuae et Felicitatis
Musurillo, Herbert, ed. and trans. *The Acts of the Christian Martyrs.* Oxford: Clarendon, 1972, pp. 106-131.

anonymous

Regula Magistri

De Vogüé, Adalbert, ed. and trans. La règle du maître, 3 vols., SC 105, 106, 107.

anonymous

Sermo in natali sanctorum innocentium
Lemarié, Joseph, ed. "Sermon africain inédit pour la fête des innocents," AnBoll, 96 (1978), 114-116.

anonymous

Sermo de passione sanctorum Donati et Advocati
PL 8, 752-758.

anonymous

Sermo de septem sigillis
Frankfurt, Universitätsbibliothek, Ms. Praed. 27, fols. 184v-186r.

anonymous

Vita sancti Beati
PL 96, 890-894.

Apringius of Béja

Tractatus in Apocalypsin
Férotin, Marius, ed. Apringius de Béja: Son Commentaire de l'Apocalypse, Bibliothèque Patrologique 1, Paris: Alphonse Picard, 1900; rpt. PLS 4, 1222-1248.
Vega, A. C., ed. Apringii Pacensis Episcopi Tractatus in Apocalysin [sic], SEHL 10-11, Escurial: Typis Augustinianis Monasterii Escurialensis, 1941.

Augustine

Breviculus collationis cum Donatistis
Petschenig, M., ed. CSEL 53,37-92.
Lancel, S., ed. CCh.SL 149A, 259-306.

Contra epistulam Parmeniani libri tres
Petschenig, M., ed. CSEL 51, 17-141.

Contra Gaudentium Donatistarum episcopum libri duo
Petschenig, M., ed. CSEL 53, 199-274.

Contra litteras Petiliani libri tres
Petschenig, M., ed. CChr.SL 52, 1-227

De baptismo contra Donatistas libri septem
Petschenig, M., ed. CSEL 51, 143-375

De civitate Dei libri viginti duo
Dombart, B. and A. Kalb, eds. CChr.SL 47-48.

De doctrina christiana libri quattuor
Martin, Joseph, ed. CChr.SL 32, 1-167.
(English translation: Robertson, D. W. On Christian Doctrine. Indianapolis: Bobbs-Merrill, 1958.)

De haeresibus ad Quodvultdeum liber unum
Vander Plaeste, R. and C. Beukers, eds. CChr.SL 46, 273-345.

De sancta virginitate
Zycha, J., ed. CSEL 41, 233-302.

De unico baptismo contra Petilianum (epistula 120)
Petschenig, M., ed. CSEL 53, 1-34.

De vera religione
Daur, K. D., ed. CChr.SL 32, 187-260.

De videndo Deo ad Paulinum (epistula 147)
Goldbacher, A., ed. CSEL 44, 274-331.

Enarrationes in Psalmos
Dekkers, E. and J. Fraipont, eds. CCh.SL 38; 39; 40.

Epistula ad catholicos de secta Donatistarum
Petschenig, M., ed. CSEL 52, 229-322.

Gesta cum Emerito Donatistarum episcopo
Petschenig, M., ed. CSEL 53, 179-196.

Psalmus contra partem Donati
Lambot, C., ed. "Texte complété et amendé du 'Psalmus contra partem Donati' de Saint Augustin," RBen, 47 (1935), 318-328.

Retractionum libri duo
Knöll, P., ed. CSEL 36.

Sermo ad Caesariensis ecclesiae plebem
Petschenig, M., ed. CSEL 53, 165-178.

Sermones
PL 38-39.
Lambot, C., ed. CChr.SL 41.
Morin, G., ed. Miscellanea Agostiniana, vol. 1. Rome: Typis Polyglottis Vaticanis, 1930.

Barnabas
See anonymous, Barnabae epistola.

Beatus of Liébana

Commentaria in Apocalipsin libri duodecim
Florez, Henricus, ed. Sancti Beati presbyteri Hispani Liebanensis in Apocalypsin ac plurimos in utriusque foederis paginas Commentaria, ex veteribus, nonnullisque desideratis patribus mille retro annis collecta, nunc primum edita, Madrid: Joachim Ibarra, 1770.
Sanders, Henry A., ed. PMAAR 7. Rome: American Academy in Rome, 1930.

Beatus of Liébana and Etherius of Osma

Beati Liebanensis et Eterii Oxomensis adversus Elipandum libri duo
PL 96, 893-1030.
Löfstedt, Bengt, ed. CChr.CM 59 (Lexicological indices: Instrumenta lexicologica latina, Series A - Formae 19).

Bede the Venerable

Explanatio Apocalypsis
PL 93, 129-206.

Historia ecclesiastica gentis Anglorum
Colgrave, Bertram and R. A. B. Mynors, eds. Bede's Ecclesiastical History of the English People. Oxford: Clarendon, 1969, pp. 1-576.

Benedict of Nursia

Regula Benedicti
Hanslik, R., ed. CSEL 75.

Boniface

S. Bonifatii et Lulli epistolae

Dümmler, Ernestus, ed. MGH.Ep 3, 215-433.

Caesarius of Arles

Expositio de Apocalypsi sancti Iohannis
PL 35, 2417-2452.
Morin, Germain, ed. *Sancti Caesarii episcopi Arelatensis opera omnia,* vol. 2, Mardesous: n.p., 1942, pp. 209-277.

Sermones
Morin, Germain, ed. *Sancti Caesarii episcopi Arelatensis opera omnia,* vol. 1, Mardesous: n.p., 1937; rpt. CChr.SL 103-104.

Cassiodore

Complexiones actuum apostolorum et apocalypsis Joannis
PL 70, 1381-1418.

Complexiones in epistolis apostolorum
PL 70, 1321-1380.

Complexiones in epistulis sancti Pauli
Donelin, Paul F., ed. *Cassiodori Senatoris Complexiones in epistolis sancti Pauli: A Critical Text with Introduction and Commentary,* Diss. Catholic University of America, Washington, 1971. Ann Arbor: University Microfilms, 1971.

De orthographia
Keil, Heinrich, ed. *Grammatici latini,* vol. 7. Leipzig: B. G. Teubner, 1880; rpt. Hildesheim: George Olms, 1961.

Expositio Psalmorum
Adriaen, M., ed. CChr.SL 97-98.

Institutionum divinarum et humanarum lectionum libri duo
Mynors, R. A. B, ed. *Cassiodori Senatoris Institutiones.* Oxford: Clarendon, 1937.

Variarum libri duodecim
Mommsen, Theodorus, ed. MGH.AA 12.
Fridh, Å. J., ed. CChr.SL 96, 1-499.

Cuthbert

De obitu Bedae
Colgrave, Bertram and R. A. B. Mynors, eds. *Bede's Ecclesiastical History pf the English People.* Oxford: Clarendon, 1969, pp. 580-586.

Cyprian of Carthage

De lapsis
Bevenot, M., ed. CChr.SL 3, 221-242.
Hartel, W., ed. CSEL 3,1, 235-264.

Epistolae

Hartel, W., ed. CSEL 3,2

Cyprian of Toulon, Firminus, and Viventius

Vita sancti Caesarii episcopi
PL 67, 1001-1042.

Dionysius Bar Salibi

In Apocalypsim, Actus et Epistulas Catholicas
Sedlacek, I., ed. and trans. CSCO 53; 60.

Elipando of Toledo

Epistolae
PL 96, 859-882.

Etherius of Osma
See Beatus and Etherius

Eugippius

Epistola Eugippii presbyteri ad Pascasium diaconum
Knöll, Pius, ed. CSEL 9,2, 1-6.

Vita sancti Severini
Knöll, Pius, ed. CSEL 9,2, 7-67.

Fulgentius of Rupse

Epistolae asceticae et morales septem
Fraipont, J., ed. CChr.SL 91, 189-273.

Gelasius I

Decretum Gelasianum de libris recipiendis et non recipiendis
Dobschutz, Ernst von, ed. TU 38,4

Gennadius of Marseilles
See Jerome and Gennadius.

Hegesippus

Hegesippi qui dicitur historiae libri quinque
Vssani, Vicentius, ed., CSEL 66.

Isidore of Seville

De fide catholica contra Judaeos libri duo
PL 83, 449-538.

De ecclesiasticis officis libri duo
PL 83, 737-826.

De viris illustribus liber

PL 83, 1081-1106.
Codoñer Merino, Carmen, ed. El "De viris illustribus" de Isidoro de Sevilla: Estudio y edicion critica. Theses et studia philologica salmanticensia 12. Salamanca: Consejo Superior de Investigaciones Cientificas, 1964.

Etymologiarum sive originum libri viginti
Oroz Reta, Jose and Manuel A. Marcos Casquero, eds. and trans. BAC 433-434.

Mysticorum expositiones sacramentorum seu questiones in vetus testamentum
PL 83, 207-424.

Sentenciarum libri tres
PL 83, 537-738.
Roca Melia, Ismael, ed. and trans. BAC 321, pp. 213-525.

Jerome

Commentariorum in epistolam ad Titum liber
PL 26, 555-600.

Commentariorum in Mattheum libri quattuor
Hurst, D. and M. Adriaen, eds. CChr.SL 77.

De monogrammate
Morin, Germain, ed. "Hieronymus de monogrammate: Un nouvel inédit hiéronymien sur le chiffre de la bête dans l'Apocalypse," RBen, 20 (1903), 232-236.

Epistolae
Hilberg, I., ed. CSEL 54.

Liber interpretationis hebraicorum nominum
De Lagarde, P., ed. CChr.SL 72.

Translatio homiliarum Origenis in Lucam
PL 26, 229-332.
Rauer, Max., ed. Die Homilien zu Lukas in der übersetzung des Hieronymus und die griechischen Reste der Homilien und des Lukas-Kommentars. GCS 35.

Jerome and Gennadius

De viris inlustribus
Bernoulli, Carl Albrecht, ed. SQS 11, Freiburg: J. C. B. Mohr, 1895; rpt. Frankfurt: Minerva, 1968.

Macrobius

Passio Maximiani et Isaac Donatistarum
PL 8, 767-774.

Maximinus (episcopus Gothorum)

Dissertatio contra Ambrosium
Kauffmann, F., ed. *Aus der Schule des Wulfila: Auxenti Dorostarensis epistula de fide uita et obitu Wulfilae im Zusammenhang der Dissertatio Maximini contra Ambrosium,* Texte und Untersuchungen zur altgermanischen Religionsgeschichte, Texte 1. Strasbourg: K. J. Trubner, 1899, pp. 65-90; rpt. PLS 1, 693-728.
Gryson, Roger, ed. CChr.SL 87, 149-171.

In natale infantum
Spagnolo, A. and C. H. Turner, "An ancient homilary," JThS 16 (1915), 314; rpt. PLS 1, 747-748.
Gryson, Roger, ed. CChr.SL 87, 69-72.

Origen

Scholia Origenis in Apocalypsin Johannis
Diobouniotis, Constantin and Adolf Harnack, eds. *Der Scholien-Kommentar des Origenes zur Apokalypse Johannis,* TU 38,3. Leipzig: n.p., 1911.

Homiliae Origenis in Lucam
See Jerome, *Translatio homiliarum Origenis in Lucam*

Palladius

Historia Lausiaca
Butler, Cuthbert, ed. *The Lausiac History of Palladius,* TaS 6,1-2. Cambridge: Cambridge University Press, 1898; rpt. Hildesheim: Georg Olms, 1967.

Possidius

Sancti Augustini vita a Possidio episcopo
Weiskotten, Herbert T., ed. and trans. *Sancti Augustini vita scripta a Possidio epsicopo: Edited with revised text, introduction, notes, and an English version,* Diss. Princeton 1918. Princeton: Princeton University Press; London: Oxford University Press, 1919.

Primasius of Hadrumetum

Commentaria in epistolas sancti Pauli (spurious)
PL 68,415-794.

Commentariorum super Apocalypsim libri quinque
Winter, Robertus, ed. *Primasii Uticensis in Africa Iustinopoli civitate episcopi, Commentariorum libri quinque in Apocalypsim Ioannis Evangelistae, ante mille annos ab auctore conscripti nunc et primum aediti.* Basel: n.p., 1544.
PL 68, 793-936; PLS 4,3,1207-1220.
Adams, A. W., ed., CChr.SL 92 (Lexicological indices: Instrumenta lexicologica latina, Series A - Formae 26).

Pseudo-Augustine
See Caesarius of Arles, *Expositio de Apocalypsi sancti Iohannis.*

Pseudo-Jerome

Commemoratorium in Apocalypsin
Hartung, K., ed. *Ein Traktat zur Apokalypse des Ap. Johannes in einer Pergamenthandschrift der K. Bibliothek in Bamberg.* Bamberg: n.p., 1904.
Rapisarda, Grazia Lo Menzo, ed. *Incerti auctoris commentarius in Apocalypsin.* Catania: Centro di studi sull'antico Cristianesimo, 1967; rpt. from MSLCA, 16 (1966), page reference not available; rpt. PLS 4, 1850-1863.

De septem sigillis
Wolfenbüttel, Herzogliche Bibliothek, Weissenburg 68, fols. 191v-192v.

Pseudo-Optatus

In natali sanctorum innocentium
Wilmart, André, ed. "Un sermon de saint Optat pour la fête de Noël," RSR, 2 (1922), 282-288; rpt. PLS 1, 289-294.

Smaragdus

Collectiones in epistolas et evangelia
PL 102, 13-552.

Tertullian

Adversus Marcionem
Evans, E., ed. and trans. *Adversus Marcionem,* 2 vols. Oxford: Clarendon, 1972.

Tyconius

Liber regularum
Burkitt, F. C., ed. *The Book of Rules of Tyconius,* TaS 3,1, Cambridge: Cambridge University Press, 1894; rpt. Nendeln: Kraus Reprint Limited, 1967.
(English translation: Anderson, Douglas Leslie. *The Book of Rules of Tyconius: An Introduction and Translation with Commentary,* Diss. Southern Baptist Theological Seminary 1974. Ann Arbor: University Microfilms, 1974, pp. 23-234.)

Commentarius in Apocalypsin, fragment from Codex Taurensis F. IV. 1. 18 (olim Bobbiensis 62)
Spicilegium casinense 3,1. Montecassino: Typis archicoenobii Montis Casini, 1897, pp. 261-331.
Lo Bue, Francesco, ed. *The Turin Fragments of Tyconius' Commentary on Revelation,* TaS NS 7. Cambridge: Cambridge University Press, 1963; rpt. PLS 1, 621-652.

Commentarius in Apocalypsin, fragment from Codex Budapestiensis S. Fr. l. m. 1.
Mezey, László, ed. "Egy korai karoling kódextöredek (Ticonius in Apocalypsin?)," *Magyar Könyvszemle* 92 (1976), p. 19.

See above, pp. 217-220.

Victor of Tunnuna

Chronica
Mommsen, Theodor, ed. MGH.AA 11, 178-206.

Victorinus of Pettau

De fabrica mundi
Haußleiter, Johannes, ed. CSEL 49, 1-9.

Commentarii in Apocalypsin
Haußleiter, Johannes, ed. CSEL 49, pp. 14-154; rpt. PLS 1, 103-172.

Walafried Strabo

Apocalypsis beati Joannis
PL 114, 709-752.

2. Latin Translations of the Bible

Colunga, Alberto and Laurentio Turrado, eds. Biblia Sacra iuxta Vulgatam Clementinam, BAC 14. Madrid: Biblioteca de autores cristianos, 1965.

Jülicher, Adolf and others, eds. Itala: Das Neue Testament in altlateinischer überlieferung, 4 vols. Berlin: Walter de Gruyter, 1963-1976.

Ranke, Ernestus, ed. Codex Fuldensis: Novum Testamentum latine interprete Hieronymo, Marburg: N. G. Elwert, 1868.

Tischendorf, Constantius ed. Novum Testamentum latine interprete Hieronymo: Ex celeberrimo codice Amiatino omnium et antiquissimo et praestantissimo nunc primum edidit. Leipzig: Avenarius & Mendelssohn, 1850.

Wordsworth, Johannes and Henricus Julianus White, eds. Novum Testamentum domini nostri Jesu Christi latine secundum editionem sancti Hieronymi ad codicum manuscriptorum fidem. Oxford: Clarendon, 1889-1954.

3. Ecclesiastical Documents

Denzinger, Henricus and Adolfus Schönmetzer, eds. Enchiridon symbolorum definitionum et declarationum de rebus fidei et morum.

Freiburg: Herder, 1967.

Hardouin, Ioannis, ed. Acta conciliorum et epistolae decretales, ac constitutiones summorum pontificum. Paris: Typographia regia, 1714-1715.

Lancel, Serge, ed. Acts de la Conférence de Carthage en 411, 3 vols., SC 194; 195; 224.

Liturgia Mozarabica, PL 85.

Mansi, Joannes Dominicus, ed. Sacrorum conciliorum nova et amplissima collectio. Florence and Venice: n.p., 1759-1798; rpt. and continuation by Ludovicus Petit and Joannes Baptista Martin, eds. Paris: Arnhem; Leipzig: H. Welter, 1899-1927.

Munier, C. ed. Concilia Africae A. 345 - A. 525, CChr.SL 149.

Literature

Adam, Alfred. "Der manichäische Ursprung der Lehre von den zwei Reichen bei Augustin." ThLZ, 77 (1952), 385-390; rpt. _Sprache und Dogma._ Gütersloh: Gerd Mohn, 1969, pp. 133-140.

Adam, Karl. _Die geistige Entwicklung des heiligen Augustinus._ Darmstadt: Wissenschaftliche Buchgesellschaft, 1954; rpt. 1958.

Alamo, Mateo del. "Los comentarios de Beato al Apocalipsis y Elipando," _Miscellanea Giovanni Mercati,_ vol. 2. StT 122. Vatican City: Biblioteca Apostolica Vaticana, 1946, pp. 16-33.

---. "Hacia una edición definitiva de Apringio y observaciones a una nueva," CDios, 153 (1941), 399-406.

Allo, E. B. _Saint Jean: l'Apocalypse._ Paris: Librairie Victor Lecoffre, 1921.

Altaner, Berthold. Review of _S. Isidori Hispalensis Episcopi Liber de variis questionibus,_ ed. by A. C. Vega and A. E. Anspach and _Apringii Pacensis Episcopi Tractatus in Apocalypsin,_ ed. by A. C. Vega. ThRv, 41 (1942), 117-120.

Altaner, Berthold and Alfred Stuiber. _Patrologie: Leben, Scriften und Lehre der Kirchenväter._ Freiburg: Herder, 1978.

Altendorf, Hans-Dietrich. Review of _Eine Echtheitsfrage bei Optatus von Mileve,_ by S. Blomgren. ThLZ, 85 (1960), 598-600.

---. Review of _Donatisten und Katholiken: Soziale, wirtschaftliche und politische Aspekte einer nordafrikanischen Kirchenspaltung,_ by E. Tengström. ZKG, 77 (1966), 133-140.

Alvarez Campos, Sergio. "Fuentes literarias de Beato de Liébana," _Actas del simposio para el estudio de los codices del "Commentario al Apocalipsis" de Beato de Liébana,_ vol. 1. Madrid: Joyas Bibliográfias, 1978, pp. 117-162.

Amann, E. "L'adoptianisme espagnol du VIIIe siècle," RevSR, 16 (1936), 281-317.

---. "Optat de Mileve," DThC 11, 1083.

---. "Primasius," DThC 13, 245-247.

Anderson, Douglas. _The Book of Rules of Tyconius: An Introduction and Translation with Commentary,_ Diss. Southern Baptist Theological Seminary, Louisville, 1974. Ann Arbor: University Microfilms, 1974.

Andresen, Carl, ed. _Bibliographia Augustiniana._ Darmstadt: Wissenschaftliche Buchgesellschaft, 1973.

Ansprenger, Franz. "Untersuchungen zum adoptianischen Streit im 8.

Jahrhundert." Diss. Freie Universität Berlin, 1952.

Arnold, Carl Franklin. Caesarius von Arelate und die gallische Kirche seiner Zeit. Leipzig: J. C. Hinrichs, 1984; rpt. Leipzig: Zentralantiquariat der deutschen demokratischen Republik, 1972.

Atzberger, Leonhard. Geschichte der christlichen Eschatologie innerhalb der vornicänischen Zeit. Freiburg: Herder, 1896.

Aubert, R. "Donatisme," DHGE 14, 654-655.

Bach, Josef. Die Dogmengeschichte des Mittelalters vom christologischen Standpunkte oder die mittelalterliche Christologie, 2 vols. Vienna: Braümuller, 1873.

Bakel, H. A. van. "Tyconius, Augustinus ante Augustinum," NThT, 19 (1930), 36-57.

Bardenhewer, Otto. Geschichte der altkirchlichen Literatur, 5 vols. Freiburg: Herder, 1913-1932.

Bardy, Gustave. "La prédication de saint Césaire d'Arles," RHEF, 29 (1943), 201-236.

---. "Tyconius," DThC 15, 1932-1934.

---. "Victorin de Pettau," DThC 15, 2882-2887.

Bareille, G. "Donatisme," DThC 4, 1701-1728.

Bauer, Ferdinand Christian. Lehrbuch der christlichen Dogmengeschichte. Leipzig: n.p., 1867; rpt. Darmstadt: Wissenschaftliche Buchgesellschaft, 1974.

Beck, Hans-Georg. "Die Frühbyzantinische Kirche," HKG(J) 2,2. Freiburg: Herder, 1975, pp. 1-92.

Beeson, Charles H. "The Manuscripts of Bede," CP, 42 (1947), 73-87.

Bellissima, Giuseppina. "Sant' Agostino grammatico," Augustinus Magister: Congrès international Augustinien, Paris, 21-24 septembre 1954, vol. 1. Paris: Etudes Augustiniennes, n.d., pp. 35-42

Berger, Samuel. "Le palimpseste de Fleury: Fragments du Nouveau Testament en latin," RThPh, 21 (1889), 545-582.

Besselaar, J. J. van den. Cassiodorus Senator: Leven en Werken van een Staatsman en Monnik uit de zesde Eeuw. Haarlem: J. H. Gottmer, 1950.

Beumer, Johannes. "Das Kirchenbild in den Schriftkommentaren Bedas des Ehrwürdigen," Schol., 28 (1953), 40-56.

Bianchini, Giuseppe. Vindiciae canonicarum scripturarum Vulgatae latinae editionis. Rome: n.p., 1740.

Bieler, Ludwig. "The 'Creeds' of St. Victorinus and of St. Patrick," TS, 9 (1948), 121-124.

Bischoff, Bernhard. "Wendepunkte in der Geschichte der lateinischen Exegese im Frühmittelalter," SE, 6 (1954), 189-281.

Blanchini, Josephus. See Bianchini, Giuseppe.

Blazquez, Antonio. "Los manuscritos de los comentarios al Apocalipsis de S. Juan por San Beato de Liébana," RABM, 14 (1906), 257-273.

Blomgren, Sven. *Eine Echtheitsfrage bei Optatus von Mileve,* AASU 5. Stockholm: Almqvist & Wiksell, 1959.

Bolton, W. F. "A Bede Bibliography: 1935-1960," Tr., 18 (1962), 436-445.

Bonini, Irma. "Lo stile nei sermoni di Cesario di Arles," Aevum, 36 (1962), 240-257.

Bonner, Gerald. *Saint Bede in the Tradition of Western Apocalyptic Commentary,* JarL 1966. Newcastle-upon-Tyne: n.p., 1966.

---. "The Christian Life in the Thought of the Venerable Bede," DUJ, 63 (NS 32) (1970-1971), 39-55.

---. "Towards a Text of Tyconius," *Studia Patristica,* vol. 10, TU, 107. Berlin: Akademie Verlag, 1970, pp. 9-13.

Bonwetsch, R. "Donatismus," RE 4, 788-798.

Botte, Bernard. *Les Origines de la Noël et de l'Epiphanie*, Textes et études liturgiques 1. Louvain: Abbaye du Mont César, 1932.

Bousset, Wilhelm. *Die Offenbarung Johannis,* KEK 16. Göttingen: Vandenhoeck & Ruprecht, 1906; rpt. 1966.

---. "Nachrichten über eine Kopenhagener Handschrift (Arnamagnaeanske Legat 1927 A M. 795 4to) des Kommentars des Apringius zur Apocalypse," NGWG.PH (1895), 187-209.

---. Review of *The Book of Rules of Tyconius,* ed. by F. C. Burkitt. ThLZ, 20 (1895), 396-399; 476.

Bovo, Sebastiano. "Le fonti del commento di Ambrogio Autperto sull'Apocalisse," *Miscellanea biblica et orientalia R. P. Athanasio Miller,* StAns 27-28. Rome: Herder, 1951, pp. 372-403.

Boysson, A. de. "Avons-nous un Commentaire d'Origén sur Apocalypse?," RBI, NS 10 (1913), 555-567.

Bratke, E. "Beatus von Libana [sic], Hieronymus und die Visio Hesdrae," ZKG 23 (1902), 428-430.

Brisson, Jean-Paul. *Autonomisme et Christianisme dans l'Afrique* romaine de Septime Sévère à l'invasion vandale. Paris: E. de Boccard, 1958.

Brooke, A. E. Review of Beati in Apocalipsin, ed. by Henry A. Sanders. JThS, 32 (1931), 409-410.

Bruyne, Donatien de. "De l'origine de quelques texts liturgiques mozarabes," RBen, 30 (1913), 421-436.

---."La préface du Diatessaron latin avant Victor de Capoue," RBen, 39 (1927), 5-11.

---. Préfaces de le Bible latine. Namur: Godenne, 1920.

Buchanan, E. S. The Catholic Epistles and Apocalypse from the Codex Laudianus numbered Laud. Lat. 43 in the Bodleian Library together with the Apocalypse Text of Beatus from the tenth Century MS. in the Morgan Library, New York. Sacred Latin Texts 4. London: Heath, Cranton & Ouseley, 1916.

Bürgi, Emil. "Prolegomena quaedam ad S. Ambrosii episcopi Mediolanensis libros de officiis tres," 75 Jahre Stella Matutina Festschrift, vol. 1. Feldkirch: n.p., 1931, pp. 43-68.

Burkitt, F. C. The Old Latin and the Itala, TaS 4,3. Cambridge: Cambridge University Press, 1896; rpt. Nendeln/Liechtenstein: Kraus Reprint Limited, 1967.

---. "Tatian's Diatessaron and the Dutch Harmonies," JThS, 25 (1924), 113-130.

Cabrol, F. "Les écrits liturgiques d'Alcuin," RHE, 19 (1923), 507-521.

Capelle, B. "Optat et Maximin," RBen, 35 (1923), 24-26.

---. "Un homiliaire de l'évêque arien Maximin," RBen, 34 (1922), 81-108.

Capelli, Adriano. Dizionario di abbreviature latine ed italiane. Milan: Editore Ulrico Hoepli, 1973.

Cappuyns, M. "Cassiodore," DHGE 11, 1349-1408.

---. Review of Apringii Pacensis Episcopi Tractatus in Apocalypsin, ed. by A. C. Vega. BThAM, 5 (1946-1949), 15-16; 300.

Cazier, Pierre. "Le Livre des règles de Tyconius: Sa transmission du De doctrina christiana aux Sentences d'Isidore de Séville," REAug, 19 (1973), 241-261.

Chapman, John. "Cassiodorus and the Echternach Gospels," RBen, 28 (1911), 283-295.

---. Notes on the Early History of the Vulgate Gospels. Oxford: Clarendon Press, 1908.

Christe, Ives. "Apocalypse et 'Traditio legis'," Römische Quartalschrift, 71 (1976), 42-55.

---. "Beatus et la tradition latine des Commentaires sur l'Apocalypse," Actas del simposio para el estudio de los codices del "Commentario al Apocalipsis" de Beato de Liébana, vol. 1. Madrid: Joyas Bibliográfias, 1978, pp. 53-67.

---. "Traditions littéraire et iconographiques dans l'interprétation des images apocalyptiques," L'Apocalypse de Jean: Traditions exégétiques et iconographiques IIIe-XIIIe siècles, Etudes et documents publiés par la section d'histoire de la faculté des lettres de l'Université de Genève 11. Geneva: Librairie Droz, 1979, pp. 109-134.

Congar, Yves M. J. "Introduction générale et notes complémentaires," Traités anti-donatistes, vol. 1, Oeuvres de saint Augustin 28. Paris: Desclée de Brouwer, 1963.

Courcelle, Pierre. "Fragments non identifiés de Fleury-sur-Loire (II)," REL, 32 (1954), 92-97.

---. Histoire littéraire des grandes invasions germaniques. Paris: Etudes Augustiennes, 1964.

---. Les lettres grecques en occident de Macrobe à Cassiodore, BEFAR 159. Paris: E. de Boccard, 1948.

---. Recherches sur les confessions de saint Augustin. Paris: Editions E. de Boccard, 1968.

---."Le site du monastere de Cassiodore," MAH, 55 (1938), 239-307.

Courtois, Christian. Les Vandales et l'Afrique. Paris: n.p., 1955; rpt. Aalen: Scientia Verlag, 1964.

Crespin, Rémi. Ministère et Sainteté: pastorale du clergé et solution de la crise Donatiste dans la vie et la doctrine de saint Augustin. Paris: Etudes Augustiniennes, 1965.

D'Alès, Adhemar. "Impedimenta mundi fecerunt eos miseros chez saint Césaire d'Arles," RSR, 28 (1938), 290-298.

---. "Les 'sermones' de saint Césaire d'Arles," RSR, 28 (1938), 315-384.

Dekkers, Eligius. Clavis patrum latinorum, SE 3. Brugge: C. Beyaert; The Hague: M. Nijhoff, 1961.

Delisle, Léopold. Mélanges de paléographie et de bibliographie. Paris: Champion, 1880.

---. Notice sur plusieurs manuscrits de la bibliothèque d'Orleans. Paris: Imp. Nationale, 1883.

De Lubac, Henri. *Exégèse medievale: Les quatre sens de l'écriture,* 4 vols, Théologie 41; 42; 59. n.p.: Aubier, 1959, 1961, 1964.

Dempf, Alois. *Sacrum Imperium: Geschichts- und Staatsphilosophie des Mittelalters und der politischen Renaissance.* Munich: R. Oldenbourg, 1929.

De Veer, A. C. "Introductions et notes complémentaires," *Traités anti-donatistes,* vol. 4, Oeuvres de saint Augustine 31. Paris: Desclée de Brouwer, 1968.

Devereesse, Robert. "L'église d'Afrique durant l'occupation byzantine," MAH, 57 (1940), 143-166.

Díaz y Díaz, M. C. "Beato de Liébana," DHEE 1, 201-202.

---. *Index scriptorum latinorum medii aevi hispanorum.* Madrid: Consejo superior de investigaciones cientificas, 1959.

---. "Tradición del texto de los Comentarios al Apocalipsis," *Actas del simposio para el estudio de los codices del "Commentario al Apocalipsis" de Beato de Liébana,* vol. 1. Madrid: Joyas Bibliográfias, 1978, pp. 163-184.

Diesner, Hans Joachim. *Isidor von Sevilla und das westgotische Spanien,* Occidens 2. Trier: Spee Verlag, 1978.

Dinkler, E. "Ticonius," PRE 6A1, 849-856.

Doignon, Jean. "'Nos bons hommes de foi': Cyprien, Lactance, Victorin, Optat, Hilaire (Augustine, *De doctrina Christiana,* IV, 40, 61)," Latomus, 22 (1963), 795-805.

Dölger, F. J. *Sol Salutis: Gebet und Gesang im christlichen Altertum mit besonderer Rücksicht auf die Ostung in Gebet und Liturgie.* Münster: Aschendorf, 1925.

---. *Die Sonne der Gerechtigkeit und der Schwarze: Eine religionsgeschichtliche Studie zum Taufgelöbnis,* LWQF 14. Münster: Aschendorff, 1971.

---. "Das Sonnengleichnis in einer Weihnachtspredigt des Bischofs Zeno von Verona: Christus als wahre und ewige Sonne," AuC, 6 (1950), 1-56.

Du Change, C. and others. *Glossarium mediae et infirmae latinitatis,* 8 vols. Graz: Akademische Druck und Verlagsanstalt, 1954; rpt. of the edition of 1883-1887 originally in 10 vols.

Durchrow, Ulrich. *Christenheit und Weltverantwortung: Traditionsgeschichte und systematische Struktur der Zweireichlehre,* FBESG 25. Stuttgart: Ernst Klett, 1970.

---. *Sprachverständnis und biblisches Hören bei Augustin.* HUTh 5. Diss. Heidelberg 1963. Tübingen: J. C. B. Mohr (Paul Siebeck), 1965.

Eco, Umberto. Beato di Liébana: Miniature del Beato de Fernando I y Sancha (codice B.N. Madrid Vit. 14-2). Parma: F. M. Ricci, 1973.

Elze, M. "Schriftauslegung: Alte Kirche und Mittelalter," RGG 5, 1520-1528.

Eno, Robert B. "The work of Optatus as a Turing Point in the African Ecclesiology," Thom., 37 (1973), 668-685.

Enßlin, W. "Primasius," PRE 22,2, 1971-1972.

Ergy, Anne de. Um estudo de O Apocalipse do Lorvão: E a sua relação com as ilustraçoes medievais do Apocalipse. Lisbon: Fundação Calouste Gulbenkain, 1972.

Ewig, Eugen. "Die Abwendung des Papsttums vom Imperium und seine Hinwendung zu den Franken," HKG(J), vol. 3,1, pp. 3-30.

---. "Die Missionsarbeit der lateinischen Kirche," HKG(J), vol. 2,2. Freiburg: Herder, 1975, pp. 95-179.

Fahey, Michael Andrew. Cyprian and the Bible: A Study in Third-Century Exegesis, BGBH 9. Diss. Tübingen 1970. Tübingen: J. C. B Mohr (Paul Siebeck), 1971.

Férotin, Marius. Le liber mozarabicus sacramentorum et les manuscrits mozarabe, MELi 6. Paris: Firmin-Didot, 1912.

Fischer, Bonifatius. Die Alkuin-Bibel: Aus der Geschichte der lateinischen Bibel, vol. 1. Freiburg: Herder, 1957.

Fischer, Joseph. "Die Einheit der beiden Testamente bei Laktanz, Viktorin von Petau und deren Quellen," MThZ, 1 (1950), 96-101.

Fita, Fidel. "Patrología latina: Apringio, obispo de Béja," BRAH, 41 (1902), 353-416.

---. "Patrología latina: Renallo gramático de Barcelona," BRAH, 41 (1902), 253-255.

Foerster, Hans. Abriss der lateinischen Paläographie. Stuttgart: Anton Hiersemann, 1963.

Fontaine, Jacques. "La célébration scientifique du millénaire des 'Béatus': du Colloque de Madrid (décembre, 1976) à quelques publications récentes," REAug, 23 (1977), 413-421.

---. "Fuentes y tradiciones paleocristianas en el método espiritual de Beato," Actas del simposio para el estudio de los codices del "Commentario al Apocalipsis" de Beato de Liébana, vol. 1. Madrid: Joyas Bibliográfias, 1976, pp. 75-101.

Forcellini, A. and others. Lexicon totius latinitatis, 6 vols. Padua: Typis Seminarii, 1940.

Forster, Karl. "Die ekklesiologische Bedeutung des corpus-Begriffes im Liber Relularum des Tyconius," MThZ, 7 (1956), 173-183.

Frank, Hieronymus. "Frühgeschichte und Ursprung des römischen Weihnachtsfests im Lichte neurer Forschung," ALW, 2 (1952), 1-24.

Frank, Karl Suso. Frühes Mönchtum im Abendland, 2 vols. Zurich: Artemis Verlag, 1975.

---. Gründzuge der Geschicte des christlichen Mönchtums, Grundzüge 25. Darmstadt: Wissenschaftliche Buchgesellschaft, 1975.

Franz, Adolph. M. Aurelius Cassiodorius [sic] Senator: Ein Beitrag zur Geschichte der theologischen Literatur. Breslau: G. P. Aderholz, 1872.

Franz, Egon. Totus Christus: Studien über Christus und die Kirche bei Augustin. Diss. Bonn 1956. Bonn: n.p., 1956.

Frede, Hermann Josef. Kirchenschriftsteller: Verzeichnis und Siegel, Vetus latina 1,1. Freiburg: Herder, 1981

---. Kirchenschriftsteller: Aktualisierungsheft, Vetus latina 1,1A. Freiburg: Herder, 1984.

Fredriksen Landes, Paula. "Tyconius and the End of the World," REAug, 28 (1982), 59-75.

Frend, W. H. C. The Donatist Church: A Movement of Protest in Roman North Africa. Oxford: Clarendon Press, 1952.

---. "Nomads and Christianity in the Middle Ages," JEH, 26 (1975), 209-221.

---. "The cellae of the African circumcelliones," JThS, NS 3 (1952), 87-89.

---. "Donatismus," RAC 4, 128-147.

Gams, Pius Bonifacius. Die Kirchengeschichte von Spanien, 3 vols. Regensburg: Manz, 1862-1879; rpt. Graz: Akademische Druck und Verlagsanstalt, 1956.

Garcia Soriano, Justo. "Un códice visigótico del siglo IX," BRAH, 106 (1935), 479-484.

Garcia Villada, Zacarias. Historia Eclesiástica de España, 5 vols. Madrid: Compañia ibero-americana de publicaciones, 1929-1936.

Gómez, Ildefonso M. "El perdido comentario de Ticonio al Apocalipsis: Principos de crítica literaria y textual para su reconstrucción," Miscellanea biblica B. Ubach, SDM 1. Montserrat: n.p., 1953, pp. 387-411.

Grasmück, Ernst Ludwig. Coercitio: Staat und Kirche im Donatistenstreit, BHF 22. Diss. Bonn 1959. Bonn: Ludwig Röhrscheid,

1964.

Grierson, P. "Les livres de l'abbé Seiwold de Bath," RBen, 52 (1940), 96-116.

---. "La bibliothèque de St-Vaast d'Arras au XIIe siècle," RBen, 52 (1940), 117-140.

Größler, Hermann. Die Ausrottung des Adoptionismus im Reiche Karls des Grossen, Jahres-Bericht über das Königliche Gymnasium zu Eisleben von Ostern 1878 bis Ostern 1879. Eisleben: n.p., 1879.

Großmann, Ursula. "Studien zur Zahlensymbolik des Frühmittelalters," ZKTh, 76 (1954), 19-54.

Grützmacher, Georg. Hieronymus: Eine biographische Studie zur alten Kirchengeschichte, 3 vols., SGTK 6,3; 10,1; 10,2. Leipzig: n.p., 1901; Berlin: n.p., 1906, 1908; rpt. Aalen: Scientia Verlag, 1969.

Gry, Léon. Le millénarisme dans ses origines et son développement. Diss. Angers 1904. Paris: Alphonse Picard et Fils, 1904.

Gryson, Roger. Les palimpsestes ariens latins de Bobbio: Contribution à la méthodologie de l'étude des palimpsestes, Amarium codicum insignium 2. Turnhout: Brepols, 1983.

Habel, E. Mittellateinisches Glossar. Paderborn: Ferdinand Schùningh, 1959.

Hahn, Traugott. Tyconius Studien: Ein Beitrag zur Kirchen- und Dogmengeschichte des 4. Jahrhunderts, SGTK 6,2. Leipzig: n.p., 1900; rpt. Aalen: Scientia Verlag, 1971.

Halliburton, R. J. "Some Reflections on St. Cyprian's Doctrine of the Church," Studia Patristica, 11,2, TU 108. Berlin: Akademie Verlag, 1972, pp. 192-198.

Harnack, Adolph von. Geschichte der altchristlichen Literatur bis Eusebius, 2 vols. Leipzig: J. C. Hinrichs, 1893.

---. Lehrbuch der Dogmengeschichte, 3 vols. Tübingen: J. C. B. Mohr, 1909-1910; rpt. Darmstadt: Wissenschaftliche Buchgesellschaft, 1964.

Harris, J. R. "A new Patristic Fragment," Exp., (1895), 448-455.

Hauck, Albert. Kirchengeschichte Deutschlands, 5 vols. Leipzig: Hinrichs, 1890-1920; rpt. Berlin: Akademie Verlag, 1952-1953.

Haußleiter, Johannes. "Autpert," RE 2, 308-309.

---. Beiträge zur Würdigung der Offenbarung des Johannes und ihres ältesten lateinischen Auslegers, Festrede der Universität Greifswald 9. Greifswald: n.p., 1900.

---. "Der chiliastische Schlussabschnitt im echten Apokalypsekommentar des Bischofs Victorinus von Pettau," ThLBl, 16 (1895), 193-199.

---. "Drei Editiones principes des Apokalypsekommentars des Primasius," ThLBl, 25 (1904), 1-4.

---. "Die Kommentare des Victorinus, Tichonius und Hieronymus zur Apokalypse," ZKWL, 7 (1886), 239-257.

---. Die lateinische Apokalypse der alten afrikanischen Kirche, FGNK 4. Erlangen: Andr. Deichert (G. Böhme), 1891.

---. Leben und Werke des Bischofs Primasius von Hadrumetum: Eine Untersuchung, Programm der kgl. bayer. Studienanstaldt zu Erlangen zum Schlusse des Schuljahres 1886/87. Erlangen: n.p., 1887.

---. "Primasius," RE 16, 55-57.

---. "Victorinus," RE 20, 614-619.

---. "Ticonius," RE 20, 851-855.

Hefele, Charles Joseph and Henri Leclercq. Histoire des conciles d'après les documents originaux, 11 vols. Paris: Letouzey, 1907-1952.

Heil, Wilhelm. "Adoptionismus," Lexikon des Mittelalters, vol. 1. Munich: Artemis, 1977ff., pp. 162-163.

---. "Alkuinstudien I: Zur Chronologie und Bedeutung des Adoptionismusstreites," Diss. Freiburg 1966.

---. "Der Adoptionismus, Alkuin und Spanien," Karl der Grosse: Lebenswerk und Nachleben, vol. 2. Düsseldorf: L. Schwann, 1965, pp. 95-155.

Helfferich, Adolf. Der westgothische Arianismus und die spanische Ketzer-Geschichte. Berlin: Julius Springer, 1860.

Hill, E. "De doctrina Christiana: A Suggestion," Studia Patristica, 6,4, TU 81. Berlin: Akademie Verlag, 1962, pp. 443-446.

Jackson, B. Darrell. "The Theory of Signs in St. Augustine's De doctrina Christiana," REAug, 15 (1969), 9-49.

James, Montague Rhodes. "'Pseudo-Augustine' on the Apocalypse," ClR, 3 (1889), 222.

Jedin, Hubert and others, eds. Atlas zur Kirchengeschichte. Freiburg: Herder, 1970.

Jenkins, Claude. "Bede as Exegete and Theologian," Bede, his Life, Times, and Writings: Essays in Commemoration of the Twelfth Centenary of his Death. Oxford: Clarendon Press, 1935, pp. 152-200.

Jones, A. H. M. "Were ancient heresies national or social movements in disguise?," JThS, NS 10 (1959), 280-298.

Jülicher, A. "Donatismus," PRE 2, 1540-1542.

---. Review of Victorini episcopi Petavionensis opera ed. by Johannes Haussleiter. GGA, 181 (1919), 44-50.

Kamlah, Wilhelm. Apokalypse und Geschichtstheologie: Die mittelalterliche Auslegung der Apokalypse vor Joachim von Fiore, HS 285. Berlin: Emil Ebering, 1935.

---. Christentum und Selbstbehauptung: Historische und philosophische Untersuchungen zur Entstehung des Christentums und zu Augustins "Bürgerschaft Gottes." Frankfurt: Victorio Klostermann, 1940.

Karpp, H. "Donatismus," RGG 2, 239-241.

---. "Ticonius," RGG 6, 884-885.

Kauffmann, F. Aus der Schule des Wulfila: Auxenti Dorostorensis epistula de fide uita et obitu Wulfilae im Zusammenhang der Dissertatio Maximini contra Ambrosium, Texte und Untersuchungen zur altgermanischen Religionsgeschichte, Texte 1. Strasbourg: K. J. Trubner, 1899.

Keleher, James P. "St. Augustine's Notion of Schism in the Donatist Controversy." Diss. Mundelein, 1961.

Kelly, J. N. D. Early Christian Creeds. London: Longmans, 1960.

---. Jerome: His Life, Writings, and Controversies. New York: Harper and Row, 1975.

Kelly, Joseph F. T. "Bede and the Irish Exegetical Tradition of the Apocalypse," RBen 92, (1982), 393-406.

---. "Early Medieval Evidence for Twelve Homilies by Origen on the Apocalypse," VigChr, 39 (1985), 273-279.

Kihn, Heinrich. Theodor von Mopsuetia und Junilius Africanus als Exegeten. Freiburg: Herder, 1880.

Klausner, Theodor. Das römische Capitulare Evangelorum: Texte und Untersuchungen zu seiner altesten Geschichte: I Typen, Liturgiegeschichtliche Quellen und Forschungen 28. Munster: Aschendorff, 1935.

Klein, Peter K. Der ältere Beatus-Kodex Vitr. 14-1 der Biblioteca Nacional zu Madrid: Studien zur Beatus-Illustration und der spanischen Buchmalerei des 10. Jahrhunderts, 2 vols., Studien zur Kunstgeschichte 8, Diss. Bonn 1976. Hildesheim: Olms, 1976.

---. "Der Apokalypse-Zyklus der Roda-Bibel und seine Stellung in der ikonographischen Tradition," AEAr, 45-47 (1972-1974), 267-333.

---. "La tradición pictórica de los Beatos," Actas del simposio para el estudio de los codices del "Commentario al Apocalipsis" de Beato de Liäbana, vol. 2. Madrid: Joyas Bibliográfias, 1980, pp. 83-106; illustrative material is contained in vol. 3, pp. 51-85.

Koch, Hugo. Cyprianische Untersuchungen, AKG 4. Bonn: A. Marcus und E. Weber, 1926.

Kornyljak, Plato V. "S. Augustini de efficacitate sacramentorum doctrina contra Donatistas." Diss. Propaganda Fidei, Rome, 1953.

Laistner, M. L. W. A Hand-List of Bede Manuscripts. Ithaca: Cornell University Press, 1943.

---. "The Library of the Venerable Bede," Bede, His Life, Times, and Writings: Essays in Commemoration of the Twelfth Centenary of his Death. Oxford: Clarendon, 1935, pp. 237-266.

Lambert, Bernard. Bibliotheca Hieronymiana Manuscripta: La tradition manuscrite des oeuvres de saint Jerome, IP 4. The Hague: Nijhoff, 1970.

Lambot, C. "Texte complété et amendé du 'Psalmus contra partem Donatii' de Saint Augustin," RBen, 47 (1935), 312-330.

Lamirande, Emilien. La Situation ecclésiologique des Donatistes d'après saint Augustin: Contribution à l'histoire doctrinale de l'oecuménisme. Ottawa: Editions de l'Université d'Ottawa, 1972.

Langgärtner, G. "Der Apokalypse-Kommentar des Caesarius von Arles," ThGl, 57 (1967), 210-225.

Leclercq, H. "Donatisme," DACL 4,2, 1457-1505.

Leclercq, Jean. "The Exposition and Exegesis of Scripture: From Gregory the Great to Saint Bernard," The Cambridge History of the Bible, vol. 2, Cambridge: Cambridge University Press, 1976, pp. 183-197.

Lehmann, Paul. Mittelalterliche Bibliothekskataloge Deutschlands und der Schweiz, vol. 1, Mittelalterliche Bibliothekskataloge 1. Munich: C. H. Beck, 1918.

Lemarié, Joseph. "Sermon africain inédit pour la fête des Innocents," AnBoll, 96 (1978), 108-116.

Lo Bue, Francesco. "Old Latin Readings of the Apocalypse in the 'Wordsworth-White' Edition of the Vulgate," VigChr, 9 (1955), 21-24.

Loewe, Raphael. "The Medieval History of the Latin Vulgate," The Cambridge History of the Bible, vol. 2, Cambridge: Cambridge University Press, 1976, pp. 102-154.

Lo Menzo Rapisarda, Grazia. "La tradizione manoscritta di un Commentarius in Apocalypsin," MSLCA 15 (1965), 119-140.

Loofs, Friedrich. Theophilus von Antiochien adversus Marcionem und die anderen theologischen Quellen bei Irenaeus, TU 46,2. Leipzig: J. C. Hinrichs, 1930.

Lorenz, Rudolf. "Circumcelliones - cotopitae - cutzupitani," ZKG, 82 (1971), 54-59.

Lof, L. J. van der. "Warum wurde Tyconius nicht katholisch?," ZNW 57 (1966), 260-283.

Ludwig, Josef. Der heilige Märtyrbischof Cyprian von Karthago: Ein kulturgeschichtliches und theologisches Zeitbild aus der afrikanischen Kirche des 3. Jahrhunderts. Munich: Karl Zink, 1951.

Macholz, Waldemar. Spuren binitarischen Denkweise im Abendlande seit Tertullian, Diss. Halle 1902. Jena: Ant. Kämpfe, 1902.

Malnory, A. Saint Césaire évêque d'Arles 503-543, BEHE.H 103. Paris: Librairie Emile Bouillon, 1894.

Manitius, Max. Geschichte der lateinischen Literatur des Mittelalters, 3 vols., HAW 9,2,1-3. Munich: C. H. Beck, 1911-1931.

Marrou, Henri-Irénée. Saint Augustin et la fin de la culture antique. Paris: Editions E. de Boccard, 1958.

McNally, Robert E. "Isidoriana," TS, 20 (1959), 432-442.

Meer, Frits van der. Augustinus der Seelsorger: Leben und Wirken eines Kirchenvaters., Cologne: J. P. Bachem, 1951.

Mengis, Karl. Ein donatistisches Corpus cyprianischer Briefe, Diss. Freiburg 1916. Freiburg: Caritas-Druckerei, 1916.

Mercati, G. "Anonymi chiliastae in Matthaeum XXIV fragmenta," Varia sacra, vol. 1, StT 11. Rome: Tipograpfia Vaticana, 1903, pp. 3-49.

Metzger, Bruce M. The early Versions of the New Testament: Their Origin, Transmission, and Limitations. Oxford: Clarendon, 1977.

Meyvaert, P. "Colophons dans des manuscrits de Bède," RBen, 69 (1959), 100-101.

Mezey, László. "Egy korai karoling kódextöredek (Ticonius in Apocalypsin?)," Magyar Könyvszemle 92 (1976), 15-24.

Millares Carlo, Agustin. Contribución al "corpus" de códices visigóticos, Publicaciones de la Facultad de Filosofia y Letras Universidad de Madrid 1. Madrid: Maestre, 1931.

---. "Problemas que suscita la escritura de los 'Beatos,'" Actas del simposio para el estudio de los codices del "Commentario al Apocalipsis" de Beato de Liébana, vol. 1. Madrid: Joyas Bibliográfias, 1973, 193-209.

Miller, Konrad. Mappae Mundi: Die ältesten Weltkarten, vol. 1: Die Weltkarte des Beatus (776 n. Chr.). Stuttgart: J. Roth, 1895.

Mohrmann, Christine. Die altchristliche Sondersprache in den Sermones des hl. Augustin, vol. 1, LCP 3. Nijmegen: n.p., 1932; rpt. Amsterdam: Adolf M. Hakkert, 1965.

---. Etudes sur le Latin des Chrétiens, vol. 1. Rome: Edizioni di storia e letteratura, 1961.

Momigliano, Arnaldo. "Cassiodorus and Italian Culture of his Time," PBA, 41 (1955), 207-245.

Monceaux, Paul. Histoire littéraire de l'Afrique chrétienne depuis les origines jusqu'à l'invasion arabe, 7 vols. Paris: n.p., 1901-1933; rpt. Bruxelles: Culture et civilisation, 1966.

---. "Parmenius, primat donatiste de Carthage," Journal des savants, NS 7 (1909), 19-26; 157-169.

Moreau, Madeleine. Le dossier Marcellinus dans la Correspondance de saint Augustin. Paris: Etudes Augustiniennes, 1973

Morgan, Edmund S. Visible Saints: The History of the Puritan Idea. Ithaca: Cornell University Press, 1963.

Morin, Germain. "Le commentaire homilétique de s. Césaire sur l'Apocalypse," RBen, 45 (1933), 43-61.

---. " Hieronymus de Monogrammate: Un nouvel inédit hiéronymien sur le chiffre de la bête dans l'Apocalypse," RBen, 20 (1903), 225-236.

---. "Hilarius l'Ambrosiaster," RBen, 20 (1903), 113-131.

---. "Mes principes et ma méthode pour la future édition de s. Césaire," RBen, 10 (1893), 62-77.

---. "Notes sur Victorin de Pattau," JThS, 7 (1906), 456-459.

---. "L'origine du symbole d'Athanase: Témoignage inédit de s. Césaire d'Arles," RBen, 44 (1932), 207-219.

---. "Pro instantio: contre l'attribution a Priscillien des opuscules du manuscrit de Würzburg," RBen, 30 (1913), 153-173.

---. "Pour une future édition des opuscules de saint Quodvultdeus, évêque de Carthage au Ve siècle," RBen, 31 (1914), 156-162.

---. "Quelques raretés philologiques dans les écrits de Césaire d'Arles," ALMA, 11 (1937), 5-14.

Morrees, F. D. De organisatie von de Christlijke kerk van Noord-Afrika in het licht van de brieven van Augustinus. Groningen: J. B. Wolters, 1927.

Moricca, Umberto. Storia della letteratura latina Cristiana, 3 vols. Turin: Società Editrice Internazionale, 1924-1934.

Mundó, Anscari M. "Sobre los Códices de Beato," Actas del simposio para el estudio de los codices del "Commentario al Apocalipsis" de Beato de Liàbana, vol. 1. Madrid: Joyas Bibliográphias, 1978, pp. 107-116.

Mundó, Anscari M. and Manuel Sanchez Mariana. El comentario de Beato al Apocalipsis: catálogo de los códices. Madrid: Biblioteca Nacional, 1976.

Munier, Charles. Les "Statuta ecclesiae antiqua:" Edition-études critiques, BIDC 5. Paris: Presses Universaires de France, 1960.

Musurillo, Herbert. "History and Symbol: A Study in the Form of early Christian Literature," TS, 18 (1957), 357-386.

Neuss, Wilhelm. Die Apokalypse des hl. Johannes in der altspanischen und altchristlichen Bibel-Illustration: Das Problem der Beatus-Handschriften, vol. 1, SFGG 2,2-3. Münster: Aschendorff, 1931.

Perez de Urbel, Justo. "Origin de los himnos mozarabes," BHisp, 28 (1926), 5-21; 113-139; 209-254; 305-320.

---. "S. Béat (Beatus)," DHGE 7, 89-90.

Pincherle, Alberto. "Alla ricerca di Ticonio," Studi storico religiosi, 2 (1978), 355-365.

---. "Da Ticonio a sant'Agostino," RicRel, 1 (1925), 443-466.

---. "Donatismo," EC 4, 1851-1856.

---. "L'ecclesiologia nella controversia donatista," RicRel, 1 (1925), 35-55.

---. "Nuovi frammenti di Ticonio," RSLR, 3 (1969), 756-757.

---. "Un sermone donatista attributo a s. Ottato di Milevi," Bil., 22 (1923), 134-148.

Pontet, Maurice. L'exégèse de s. Augustin prédicateur, Theologie 7. n.p.: Aubier, 1945.

Prete, B. "I principi esegetici di s. Agostino," SapDom, 8 (1955), 552-594.

Prete, Serafino. Il "Commonitorium" nella letteratura cristiana antica, Studi e ricerche, NS 6. Bologna: Nicola Zanichelli, 1962.

Prigent, Pierre. Apocalypse 12: Histoire de l'exégèse, BGBE 2. Tübingen: Mohr, 1959.

Quacquarelli, Antonio. La concezione della storia nei padri prina di s. Agostino. Rome: ESR, 1955.

---. "La concezione della storia in Ticonio," Studi di storia medievale e moderna in onore di Ettore Rota, Biblioteca storica 3. Rome: Edizioni del Lavoro, 1958.

Quasten, Johannes. Patrology, 3 vols. Utrecht: Spectrum, 1966, 1964, 1966.

---. "Victorinus," LThK 10, 775-776.

Quinot, B. "Introduction générale et notes complémentaires," Traités anti-donatistes, vol. 3, Oeuvres de saint Augustine 30. Paris: Desclée de Brouwer, 1967.

Rahner, Hugo. Griechische Mythen in christlicher Deutung. Basel: Herder, 1984.

Raizman, David Seth. The later Morgan Beatus (M. 249) and late romanesque illumenationn in Spain, Diss. Pittsburgh 1980. Ann Arbor: University Microfilms, 1980.

Ramsay, H. L. "Le commentaire de l'Apocalypse par Beatus de Liébana," RHLR, 7 (1902), 419-447.

---. "The Manuscripts of 'The Commentary of Beatus of Liébana' on the Apocalypse," Revue des bibliothèques, 12 (1902), 74-103.

Rapisarda, Carmelo A. "Lo stile umile nei sermoni di s. Cesario d'Arles: Giustificazioni teoriche e posizioni polemiche," Orph., (1970), 115-159.

Ratzinger, Joseph. "Beobachtungen zum Kirchenbegriff des Tyconius im 'Liber regularum'," REAug, 2 (1956), 173-185.

---. "Ticonius," LThK 10, 179-180.

---. Volk und Haus Gottes in Augustins Lehre von der Kirche, MThS.S 2, 7. Diss. Munich 1951. Munich: Karl Zink, 1954.

Rauh, Horst Dieter. Das Bild des Antichrist im Mittelalter: Von Tyconius zum deutschen Symbolismus, BGPhMA NS 9. Diss. Erlangen-Nürnberg 1969. Münster: Aschendorff, 1973.

Ray, Roger D. "Bede, the Exegete, as Historian," Famulus Christi: Essays in Commemoration of the Thirteenth Centenary of the Birth of the Venerable Bede. London: S.P.C.K., 1976, pp. 125-140.

Reardon, Barnabas. "The Function of Tyconius's Third Hermeneutic Rule." Lic. Thesis Pontifical Biblical Institute, Rome, 1968.

Reifferscheid, August. "Bibliotheca patrum Latinorum Italica," SAWW.PH, 49 (1865), 48-52.

Reitzenstein, R. "Ein donatistisches Corpus cyprianischer Schriften," NGWG.PH (1914), 85-92.

Reuter, Hermann. Augustinische Studien. Gotha: n.p., 1887; rpt. Aalen: Scientia, 1967.

Riedlinger, Helmut. "Apokalypse: Apokalypsekommentare," Lexikon des Mittelalters, vol. 1. Munich: Artemis, 1977ff., pp. 748-750.

Riggenbach, D. Eduard. Die ältesten lateinischen Kommentare zum Hebräerbrief: Ein Beitrag zur Geschichte der Exegese und zur Literaturgeschichte des Mittelalters, FGNK 8,1. Leipzig: A. Deichert (Georg Böhme), 1907.

Rivera, Juan Francisco. "La controversia adopcionista del siglo VIII y la orthodoxia de la liturgia mozárabe," EL, 47 NS 7 (1933), 506-536.

---. Elipando de Toledo: Neuva aportación a los estudios mozárabes. Toledo: Editorial Catolica Toledana, 1940.

---. "Más fórmulas y profesiones de fe hispanovisigoticas," Collectanea Theologica al R. P. Joaquin Salaverri, S. I. en el cincuentenario de su vida religiosa, Miscelánea Comillas 34-35. Comillas: Universidad Pontificia Comillas, 1960, pp. 343-352.

---. "La maternidad divina de Maria, en una controversia cristológica española de fines del siglo VIII," Certamen Público en honor de Ntra. Sra. de Belén, de Carrión de los Condes 3. Lérida: Imprenta Mariana, 1933.

Robinson, J. Armitage. "Origen's Comments on the Apocalypse," JThS, 13 (1912), 295-297.

Rojo Oracjo, Timoteo. Estudios de códices visigóticos: El "Beato" de la Biblioteca de Santa Cruz de Valladolid. Madrid: Tip. de Archivos, 1930.

Romero Pose, Eugenio. "Una nueva edición del Comentario al Apocalipsis de S. Beato de Liébana: Su importancia para la reconstrucción del Comentario de Ticonio," Bollettino dei Classici, 1 (1980), 221-231.

---. "Ticonio y el sermon 'in natali sanctorum innocentium' (Exegesis de Mt. 2)," Gr., 60 (1979), 513-544.

Rönsch, Hermann. Itala und Vulgata: Das Sprachidiom der urchristlichen Itala un der katholischen Vulgata unter Berücksichtigung der römischen Volkssprache. Marburg: Elwert, 1875; rpt. Munich: Max Hueber, 1965.

Rose, Valentin. Verzeichniss der lateinischen Handschriften der Königlichen Bibliothek zu Berlin, 3 vols. Berlin: Asher, 1893.

Sainz de Robles, Federico. Elipando y san Beato de Liébana. Madrid: M. Aguilar, 1935.

Salvatore, Antonio. "Uso delle similitudini e pedagogia pastorale nei Sermones di Cesario di Arles," RCCM, 9 (1967), 177-225.

Sánchez Albornoz, Claudio. "El 'Asturorum Regnum' en los días de Beato de Liébana," Actas del simposio para el estudio de los codices del "Commentario al Apocalipsis" de Beato de Liébana, vol. 1. Madrid: Joyas Bibliográficas, 1978, pp. 19-32.

Schanz, Martin and Carl Hosius. Geschichte der römischen Literatur bis zum Gesetzgebungswerk des Kaisers Justinian, 4 vols., HAW 8,1-4. Munich: C. H. Beck, 1896-1920.

Schmid, J. "Primasius," RGG 5, 583.

Schmidt, Kurt Dietrich. Die Bekehrung der Ostgermanen zum Christentum: Der ostgermanische Arianismus, Die Bekehrung der Germanen zum Christentum 1. Göttingen: Vandenhoeck & Ruprecht, 1939.

Scholz, Heinrich. Glaube und Unglaube in der Weltgeschichte: Ein Kommentar zu Augustins De civitate Dei. Leipzig: J. C. Hinrichs, 1911; rpt. Leipzig: Zentral-Antiquariat der deutschen demokratischen Republik, 1967.

Schuster, I. "Come finì la biblioteca di Cassiodoro?," ScC, 70 (1942), 409-414.

Schuster, Mauriz. "Victorinus," PRE 8A2, 2081-2085.

Scorza Barcellona, Francesco. "L'interpretazione dei doni dei Magi nel sermone natalizio di [Pseudo] Ottato di Milevi," Studi storico religiosi, 2 (1978), 129-149.

Sieben, H. J. "Die 'res' der Bibel: Eine Analyse von 'De doctrina Christiana I-III'," REAug, 21 (1975), 72-90.

Skard, Eiliv. "Zum Scholien-Kommentar des Origenes zur Apokalypse Johannis," SO, 15-16 (1936), 204-208.

Smulders, P. "Een nieuwe vue op het Donatisme," Bijdr., 14 (1953), 307-310.

Soden, Hans von, ed. Das lateinische neue Testament in Afrika zur Zeit Cyprians nach Bibelhandschriften und Väterzeugnissen, TU 33. Leipzig: J. C. Hinrichs, 1909.

---. Urkunden zur Entstehungsgeschichte des Donatismus. KIT 122. Berlin: Walter de Gruyter, 1950.

Soden, Hans von. Die cyprianische Briefsammlung: Geschichte ihrer Entstehung und Überlieferung, TU 25,2. Leipzig: J. C. Hinrichs, 1904.

Souter, A. "Cassiodorus' Library at Vivarium: Some Additions," JThS, 41 (1940), 46-47.

---. "Contributions to the Criticism of Zmaragdus's Expositio libri Comitis, " JThS, 9 (1908), 584-597.

---. "A further Contribution to the Criticism of Zmaragdus's Expositio libri Comitis, " JThS, 34 (1933), 46-47.

---. "Further Contributions to the Criticism of Zmaragdus's Expositio libri Comitis, " JThS, 23 (1922), 73-76.

---. "Tyconius's Text of the Apocalypse: A partial Reconstruction," JThS, 14 (1913), 338-358.

---. "An unrecorded Reference to the Rules of Tyconius," JThS, 11 (1910), 562-563.

Sparks, H. F. D. "A Celtic Text of the Latin Apocalypse preserved in two Durham Manuscripts of Bede's Commentary on the Apocalypse," JThS, NS 5 (1954), 227-231.

Stangl, Th. "Cassiodoriana," Blätter fur das Gymnasial-Schulwesen, 34 (1898), 249-283; 545-591.

---. "Cassiodoriana II," Wochenschrift für klassische Philologie, 32 (1915), 203-214; 228-240.

---. "Zu Cassiodorius [sic] Senator," SAWW.PH, 114 (1887), 405-413.

Stegmüller, Frederich. "Beatus von Liébana," LTK 2, 86-87.

Stegmüller, Frederich and Nicolaus Reinhardt, eds. Repertorium biblicum medii aevi, 11 vols. Madrid: Consejo Superior de Investigaciones Cientificas, 1950-1980.

Steinhauser, Kenneth B. "Bermerkungen zum pseudo-hieronymischen Commemoratorium in Apocalypsin, " FZPhTh, 26 (1979), 220-242.

---. "The Structure of Tyconius' Apocalypse Commentary: A Correction," VigChr, 35 (1981), 354-357.

Stonehouse, Ned Bernard. The Apocalypse in the Ancient Church: A Study in the History of the New Testament Canon. Diss. Free Reformed University of Amsterdam, 1929. Goes: Oosterbaan & le Cointre, 1929.

Strathmann, D. "Origenes und dei Johannesoffenbarung," NKZ, 34 (1923), 228-236.

Strauss, Gerhard. Schriftgebrauch, Schriftauslegung und Schriftbeweis bei Augustin, BGBH 1. Diss. Göttingen 1952. Tübingen: J. C. B. Mohr (Paul Siebeck), 1959.

Tengström, Emin. Donatisten und Katholiken: Soziale, wirtschaftliche und politische Aspekte einer nordafrikanischen Kirchenstpaltung, SGLG 18. Gothenburg: Acta Universitatis Gothoburgensis, 1964.

Treu, K. "Viktorin von Pettau," RGG 6, 1400.

Turner, C. H. "An exegetical Fragment of the third Century," JThS, 5 (1904), 218-241.

---. "Notes on the Apostolic Constitutions: I. The Compiler an Arian," JThS, 16 (1915), 54-61.

---. "Notes on the Apostolic Constitutions: II. The Apostolic Canons," JThS, 16 (1915), 523-538.

---. "Origen Scholia in Apocalypsin, " JThS, 25 (1924), 1-16.

---. "The Text of the newly discovered Scholia of Origen on the Apocalypse," JThS, 13 (1912), 386-397.

Vaccari, A. "S. Caesarius Arelatensis de lectione s. scripturae," VD, 23 (1943), 193-198.

---. "Victorini in Apocalypsim editio princips," Bib. 3 (1922), 340-342.

---. "Volgarismi notevoli nel latino di s. Cesario di Arles (+543)," ALMA, 17 (1943), 135-148.

Vázquez de Parga, Luis. "Beato y el ambiente cultural de su epoca," Actas del simposio para el estudio de los codices del "Commentario al Apocalipsis" de Beato de Liébana, vol. 1. Madrid: Joyas Bibliográficas, 1978, pp. 3-45.

Vega, A. C. "Observation a las observaciones," CDios, 153 (1941), 406-407.

Vogels, Heinrich Joseph. Beiträge zur Geschichte des Diatessaron im Abendland, NTA 8,1. Münster: Aschendorff, 1919.

---. Untersuchungen zur Geschichte der lateinischen Apokalypse-übersetzungen. Düsseldorf: L. Schwann, 1920.

Vogt, Hermann Josef. "Die Auseinandersetzung der Kirche mit dem Arianismus der Vandalen und Goten," HKG(J), vol. 2,2. Freiburg: Herder, 1975, pp. 282-297.

---. "Ausklang der altchristlichen lateinischen Literatur," HKG(J), vol. 2,2. Freiburg: Herder, 1975, pp. 309-329.

Vyver, A. van de. "Cassiodore et son oeuvre," Spec. 6 (1931), 244-292.

Warmington, Brian Herbert. The North African Provinces from Diocletian to the Vandal Conquest. Cambridge: Cambridge University Press, 1954.

Weber, Robert. "Edition princeps et tradition manuscrite du commentaire d'Ambroise Autpert sur l'Apocalypse," RBen, 70 (1960), 526-237.

Weijland, Hendrik Bernard. Augustinus en de kerkelijke tucht: Een *onderzoek naar de grenzen van de kerk bij Augustinus tegen de achtergrond van het donatistisch schisma,* Diss. Kampen 1965. Kampen: J. H. Kok, 1965.

Weisweiler, Heinrich. "Das frühe Marienbild der Westkirche unter dem Einfluß des Dogmas von Chalcedon," Schol., 28 (1953), 321-360; 505-525

Weyman, Carl. Review of *Victorini episcopi Petavionensis opera,* ed. by Johannes Haußleiter, *Wochenschrift für klassische Philologie,* 34 (1917), 1103-1111.

---. "Textkritische Bemerkungen zum Apokalypsekommentar des Apringius," BZ, 1 (1903), 175-181.

Williams, J. "The Beatus Commentaries and Spanish Bible Illustration," *Actas del simposio para el estudio de los codices del "Commentario al Apocalipsis" de Beato de Liébana,* vol. 2. Madrid: Joyas Bibliográfias, 1980, pp. 201-219; illustrative material is contained in vol. 3, pp. 131-146.

Willis, Geoffrey Grimshaw. *Saint Augustine and the Donatist Controversy.* London: S.P.C.K., 1950.

Willmes, Ansgar. "Bedas Bibelauslegung," AKuG, 44 (1962), 281-314.

Wilmart, André. "Un anonyme ancien 'De X virginibus'," BALAC, 1 (1911), 35-49; 88-102.

---. "Un Sermon de saint Optat pour la fête de Noël," RevSR, 2 (1922), 271-302.

---. "La collection tripartite des sermons de Saint Augustin," *Miscellanea Augustiniana: Gedenkboek samengesteld uit verhandelingen over S. Augustinus bij viering van zijn zalig overlijden voor 15 eeuwen.* n.p.: Uitgegeven door de P.P. Augustijnen der Nederlandsche Provincie, 1930, pp. 418-449.

Winandy, Jacques. *Ambroise Autpert: moine et théologien.* Paris: Librairie Plon, 1953.

---. "Les dates de l'abbatiat et de la mort d'Ambroise Autpert," RBen, 59 (1949), 206-210.

---. "L'oeuvre littéraire d'Ambroise Autpert," RBen, 60 (1950), 93-119.

Wischmeyer, Wolfgang. "Die Bedeutung des Sukzessionsgedankens fur eine theologische Interpretation des donatistischen Streites," ZNW, 70 (1979), 68-85.

Wöhrer, Justinus. "Eine kleine Schrift, die vielleicht dem hl. Martyrerbischoff Victorinus von Pettau angehört," *Jahresbericht des Privatgymnasiums der Zisterzienser in Wilhering,* (1927), 3-8.

---. "'Victorini episcopi Petauionensis (?) ad Iustinum

Manichaeum':1-8," Jahresbericht des Privatgymnasiums der Zisterzienser in Wilhering, (1928), 3-7.

Zahn, Theodor. Geschichte des neutestamentlichen Kanons, 2 vols. Erlangen: A. Deichert (Georg Böhme), 1888-1892.

---. "Neue Funde aus der alten Kirche (Schluss)," NKZ, 16 (1905), 415-427.

Zarco Cuevas, Julian. "El nuevo Códice visigótico de la Academia de la Historia," BRAH, 106 (1935), 389-442.

Zeller, Jacques. Les origines chrétiennes dans les provinces danubiennes de l'empire romain, BEFAR 112. Paris: E. de Boccard, 1918.

Zellinger, Johannes. Augustin und die Volksfrömigkeit: Blicke in den frühchristlichen Alltag. Munich: Max Hueber, 1933.

Zimmer, Heinrich. Pelagius in Irland: Texte und Untersuchungen zur patristischen Literatur. Berlin: Weidmann, 1901.